Women and Power

This book is a product of the CODESRIA
Advanced Research Fellowship Programme

Women and Power

Education, Religion and Identity

Olutoyin Mejiuni

CODESRIA

Council for the Development of Social Science Research in Africa

DAKAR

CODESRIA
Council for the Development of Social Science Research in Africa
Avenue Cheikh Anta Diop, Angle Canal IV — P. O. Box 3304 Dakar, CP 18524, Senegal
Website: www.codesria.org

© Olutoyin Mejiuni 2013

ISBN: 978-2-86978-493-2

Layout: Hadijatou Sy
Cover Design: Ibrahima Fofana

Distributed in Africa by CODESRIA
Distributed elsewhere by the African Books Collective, Oxford, UK.
Website: www.africanbookscollective.com

The Council for the Development of Social Science Research in Africa (CODESRIA) is an independent organisation whose principal objectives are to facilitate research, promote research-based publishing and create multiple forums geared towards the exchange of views and information among African researchers. All these are aimed at reducing the fragmentation of research in the continent through the creation of thematic research networks that cut across linguistic and regional boundaries.

CODESRIA publishes a quarterly journal, *Africa Development*, the longest standing Africa-based social science journal; *Afrika Zamani*, a journal of history; the *African Sociological Review*, the *African Journal of International Affairs*; *Africa Review of Books* and the *Journal of Higher Education in Africa*. The Council also co-publishes the *Africa Media Review*; *Identity, Culture and Politics: An Afro-Asian Dialogue*; *The African Anthropologist* and the *Afro-Arab Selections for Social Sciences*. The results of its research and other activities are also disseminated through its Working Paper Series, Green Book Series, Monograph Series, Book Series, Policy Briefs and the *CODESRIA Bulletin*. Select CODESRIA publications are also accessible online at www.codesria.org.

CODESRIA would like to express its gratitude to the Swedish International Development Cooperation Agency (SIDA/SAREC), the International Development Research Centre (IDRC), the Ford Foundation, the MacArthur Foundation, the Carnegie Corporation, the Norwegian Agency for Development Cooperation (NORAD), the Danish Agency for International Development (DANIDA), the French Ministry of Cooperation, the United Nations Development Programme (UNDP), the Netherlands Ministry of Foreign Affairs, the Rockefeller Foundation, FINIDA, the Canadian International Development Agency (CIDA), the Open Society Foundations (OSFs), TrustAfrica, UN/UNICEF, the African Capacity Building Foundation (ACBF) and the Government of Senegal for supporting its research, training and publication programmes.

To all women and children, literate and illiterate, who have resisted
and are resisting oppression quietly and loudly, individually and collectively
and to all men who have supported them in the process

Content

List of Abbreviations

AIDS   Acquired Immune Deficiency Syndrome
ABA-CEELI American Bar Association Central and European Law Initiative
CEDAW   Convention on the Elimination of All Forms of Discrimination Against
                Women
CODESRIA Council for the Development of Social Science Research in Africa
DG   Director General
FGD   Focus Group Discussion
FLF   Female Leadership Forum
FNWS   Federation of Nigerian Women Societies
FOMWAN   Federation of Muslim Women's Associations in Nigeria
HIV   Human Immuno Deficiency Syndrome
HND   Higher National Diploma
I-IDEA   International Institute for Democracy and Electoral Assistance
JSS   Junior Secondary School
NAFDAC   National Directorate for Food and Drugs Administration and Control
NCE   National Certificate in Education
NGO   Non-Governmental Organization
NEPU   Northern Elements Progressive Union
PDP   People's Democratic Party
UNDP   United Nations Development Programme
UNHCHR   United Nations High Commissioner for Human Rights
WARSHE   Women Against Rape, Sexual Harassment and Sexual Exploitation
WIN   Women in Nigeria

List of Tables

List of Boxes

Acknowledgements

I thank the Scientific Committee of the 2003 Advanced Research Fellowship Programme of the Council for the Development of Social Science Research in Africa (CODESRIA), and the Executive Committee of CODESRIA for their approval of, and support for the research reported in this book. I also thank Virginie Niang, who did not fail to respond to my endless inquiries and pestering, and the editorial team and members of staff of the CODESRIA Publications Unit.

I am grateful to Grace Itanyin (then of the Kogi State University, Ayangba), Jumoke Odeyemi (then of the University of Ibadan), Bukola Akinwale (formerly of the Ogun State University, Ago Iwoye), and Bola Olorunyomi (of Information Aid Network, Ibadan) who were my research assistants at different times in the course of the research. They were all enthusiastic about the research. Grace and Jumoke were adept at retrieving information from semi-literate women, and Grace also displayed expertise in the way she coordinated the focus group discussions that were held in Lokoja.

To all the women and men who availed time to supply the data needed for this work, I say thank-you. Many of the respondents I met did not just provide data about themselves, their work and their world; they also provided leads to other sources of data because they were very much interested in the study and, ultimately, we developed friendship. Even some of the religious leaders in Lokoja who had initially viewed my mission with suspicion eventually became friendly and were extremely helpful.

I thank the authority of the Kogi State Polytechnic in Lokoja, and the top hierarchy of the Kogi State Civil Service and the Oyo State Ministry of Establishments and Training for making data collection in their establishments easy. I am grateful to the authority of the Development Resource Centre at the Old Market in Lokoja and the leaders of the Tailors' Association in Bodija Market in Ibadan for allowing the use of their offices for some of the focus group discussions and interviews.

From the bottom of my heart, I thank my friends and colleagues, whom I also regard as my sisters and brothers, for their critical comments and suggestions in respect of the research reported on here, for their moral support, and for connecting me with some of the respondents in this study. They are: Bose Shaba, Olufemi Taiwo, Oluyemisi and Titilola Obilade, Adeolu Ademoyo, Thomas Fasokun, Dorothy Lander, Patricia Cranton and John Aderinto. The others are: Dele and Peju Layiwola,

Sola Olorunyomi, Olutoyin Oyetunji, Sola Owonibi and M.O. Akintayo. I should not fail to thank Abubakar Momoh who 'provoked' me into writing about the women's question. I give a big thumbs up to those scholar-activist sisters whose works I have read in the course of writing, and or whose works I have cited in this book. Their writing, analyses, theorizing, and experiences have been inspiring, transformative and supportive.

I appreciate the enthusiasm and critical questions and comments of participants at the 2005 Conference of the International Association of Feminist Economics (IAFFE). It was under the conference's broad theme of, 'Education and Empowerment in a Global Economy', that I presented a section of this report in the middle of June 2005.

My sincere gratitude goes to my employer, the Obafemi Awolowo University, Ile-Ife, for granting the sabbatical leave that allowed me time to carry out fieldwork and finally put the report of the research together.

I must thank my unofficial research assistants, my young friend, Ireti Jabarr, who was a postgraduate student at the University of Ibadan; my niece, Opeoluwa Oyetunji, who was a student of the Federal University of Technology, Akure; and my daughter, Ifeolutembi Fashina. They came to my rescue several times during the course of this study by typing and proofreading manuscripts (especially in the context of incessant power outages), and by helping me to sort out percentile scores. Ope and Tembi were at their best whenever I was under great pressure, for they were helpful, quiet and loving.

I thank the anonymous reviewer for his/her comprehensive and constructive suggestions, and sometimes sharp comments. I could not have envied anyone who got the task of reviewing the research report that I submitted to CODESRIA to be considered for publication in the CODESRIA book series.

I am always so happy that my mother, Mrs Victoria Olufunmilayo Mejiuni, and my father, Mr Emmanuel Jimoh Mejiuni, are alive and well. Throughout the period that this work lasted, they called regularly to ask how I was doing, how far I had gone with the work, and they urged me to eat well and take adequate rest, in spite of my desire to meet deadlines. Lest I forget, they took Tembi away from me, or rather, Tembi spent part of her long vacation in 2004 with them, while I was gathering data in Lokoja.

Finally, I acknowledge the support of my husband, Olufemi Ojo, who was very helpful while I collected the data for the study reported on here. However, when analyses of data and the report writing started running into months, he began to wonder aloud about when my seclusion with the study would end.

Preface

One day, in my early teens, I asked my mother how possible it was for a woman to have a baby regularly when her husband beat her regularly. Now, I cannot remember my mother's response, but I do remember that she looked at me quizzically, and tried to conceal her amusement at the question. She knew why I had asked that question. I had asked because I had observed the phenomenon in the interaction of a male neighbour, a government worker, who was clearly literate, with his wife. I do not remember whether his wife was also literate. Perhaps I found the phenomenon odd because my father did not hit my mother and, as a matter of fact, my parents had a child after I had asked that question. I do remember that they argued a lot, and my mother challenged my father often; and that included arguments about the decisions he had taken at work, which he discussed with her at lunchtime at home. My father would usually get angry and raise his voice; and whenever he raised his voice on any matter, my mother would remind him that she was not one of his subordinates at work, so he should not shout at her.

On one issue though, my father never raised his voice against my mother, and that was, other women. Whenever she accused him of philandering, she would be the one to raise her voice, and he would actually be pleading with her to lower her voice. My mother was, and still is strong-willed, very practical, and brooks no nonsense. Although she trained in secretarial practice at the Institute of Administration, Kongo, Zaria in Northern Nigeria in the late 1950s, she could not hold a job for a long time as she changed jobs each time her husband, a civil servant, moved to another station on transfer in the then Northern Nigeria. She was not employed by the Northern Nigerian Government because she was not an indigene, even though she was brought up in Kano and had her education in Kano and Zaria. She was brought up by two women, her maternal grandmother and her mother's older sister. Her maternal grandmother was a Muslim Nigerien who first married a Kano man. Something happened (my mother does not know whether it was death or divorce) and then she married a Christian Yoruba man from Apomu in the western part of Nigeria. The Yoruba man, who worked with the Railway Corporation in Kano, converted his wife to Christianity. Before the Christian Yoruba man died in 1954, his wife reverted to the Islamic religion. Fifteen years after his death, she performed the holy pilgrimage to Mecca when her children and grandchildren were able to pool funds for the purpose. My mother's maternal grandmother, who was unlettered in the Western sense, took my mother away from her father, also a Yoruba man from Apomu, because she feared he might marry her off at a young age instead of sending her to school. My mother and my father, who is an Okun, specifically from Mopa in the then Kabba Province of the then Northern Nigeria, met in Kano.

I am the second child in a line of six children, the first of two female children. As children and as teenagers, we all did housework. There were no specific duties assigned to boys and girls. If there were restrictions as to the type of housework a child could do, it was by age. For instance, when we were in the range of ages fourteen and fifteen, we pounded yam, the staple food of the Okun, with pestle and mortar. Even when we had a household help, we all still had duties assigned to us within the household. Of course, within this set-up, some of us were quite lazy, laid back or just unwilling to perform some tasks.

After my mid-teens, my father regularly asked me to go shopping with him at the few supermarkets that were available in Ilorin, in Kwara State, at the time. I later discovered he wanted time alone with me. In his white Peugeot 404 salon car, he told me how wonderful it would be if I let the sky be the limit of my educational attainments, and well, then, think about men later. He would usually also promise to help me reach the sky. When some of us became young adults, my father would tell us, behind our mother's back, that our mother was a very intelligent and intuitive person, and that she was usually right about how to proceed on many issues; but it was just that, well, he had proved stubborn. I used to wonder why? Now, I believe it was a combination of patriarchy and his very nature. I do not know whether he would read this book; but the truth is that even in his mid-seventies, he is still stubborn in his relationship with his wife.

I got on the PhD (Adult Education) programme a year after I began work at the University of Ife (now Obafemi Awolowo University), in Ile-Ife in 1987. I knew my parents were happy. However, occasionally, when I went to visit with them in Ilorin, Central Nigeria, my mother would come home feeling unhappy about a comment a woman had passed about when I would stop acquiring degrees and get married. On such occasions, my father would get angry and tell my mother to keep such talk out of our home, and instead learn to tell those women to mind their business. He would again tell me pointedly that he wanted me to go as far as I pleased educationally, and get married when I wanted to. Men paid attention to me, for whatever reasons, but one was particularly dismayed at my penchant for sitting in the library for hours every day, when he had made it clear that he wanted to marry me, and wanted to see me often. One afternoon, he gave me a piece of his mind on the phone. He chided me for not thinking of my future when my age-mates were already married, and had children. Apparently, my countenance changed as I listened to the 'harangue'. My office-mate, who was my teacher, and had become a close friend, entreated me to stay calm. That was the last time I had a conversation with the fellow.

Up until that time, I believed that being humane was the most important principle that one should hold on to. Gender discrimination was not an issue for me, and the concept did not mean much to me. Our parents did not bring us up in accordance with prevailing sex-role socialization, and they did not make us girls feel that we were inferior to the four boys. Having taken the subject 'Government' at 'A' Levels, from 1978 to 1980, I loved to take part in the analysis of political developments in Nigeria, and I was highly conscious of issues of bad governance, corruption, and how this interfaced with the politics of identity. I blamed the North/South politics of identity for my mother's inability to keep her jobs, and I did not have the framework to explain some of my father's stubbornness in his relationship with my mother, even though he knew her assets and strengths. With the benefit of hindsight, apparently, my father knew we were going to come under societal pressure; that was why he took off time to talk to me about reaching for the sky, first, before thinking about men and marriage. Even then, persons who held the view that women could only become persons when they married attempted to undo the specific kind of nurturing or socialization that my parents gave us.

As a young university lecturer, I took interest in the political dimensions of adult education, and felt at home with them. After my encounter with that suitor, I became slightly conscious of my position as a woman. About that time, a former lecturer of mine in my first year at the University of Ife returned to Ife with a PhD, and I took interest in some feminist literature that I found in his study. One of them was *Women: A Feminist Perspective*, edited by Jo Freeman. That literature and a few others set me thinking. Finally, I got married, had a baby, and there were issues. I began to see my marriage and the marriages of other women through a new lens. I heard whispers about violence against highly educated women and remembered the couple who had babies as frequently as the man hit the wife. I began to put complaints of sexual harassment that were whispered by students in perspective. Finally, I came to the realization that commitment to all human persons will not eliminate discrimination against certain segments of society, especially women, given the prevailing attitudes, beliefs and institutionalized practices. I discovered feminism. In 1998, I finally moved from critical self-reflection, contemplation and one-on-one dialogue about women's rights and the women's question to full political activism in favour of women. And so, in addition to focusing on the political dimensions of adult education, I took interest in exploring the concerns of women in the teaching-learning interaction and context; and have since approached my teaching, research and community development/activist work from the emancipatory perspective.

My background, my experiences, the experiences of women that I am privy to, a paper I wrote in the mid-1990s, and a research I undertook in the year 2000, set the stage for me to undertake the research reported on in this book. Sometime in 1997, a colleague who was active in the Academic Staff Union of his university in Nigeria asked me to present a paper on Democracy and the Working Woman at a seminar.

He requested that I prepare the paper because I was active in the Obafemi Awolowo University Branch of the Academic Staff Union of Universities, in my own right, and also by marriage. The key issue that I raised in the paper entitled, 'Democracy, Popular Participation and Sustainable Development: The Challenge for Working Women' (unpublished) was that 'confessed' democrats, intellectuals, journalists, and observers of electoral politics in Nigeria paid little attention to the impact of gender inequalities and patriarchy, especially in the domestic sphere, on (competitive) democracy, elections being one of the features of democracy. In the paper, I tried to show that patriarchy worked to disadvantage women in the areas of fair distribution of rights and resources in the workplace, in the domestic sphere, and in the entire socio-political and cultural environment in Nigeria. I made the point that women who were disadvantaged in all spheres of life could not participate in the democratic process as equals with men; and if they participated, they could not do so successfully. I called for the democratization of the workplace, the domestic sphere and the entire socio-political and cultural environment in Nigeria. To achieve this, I thought there was an urgent need for an independent, broad-based women's organization that would undertake so many tasks, among which would be to force all issues in gender relations to the open arena, politicize them, and undertake the conscientization of women together with the sensitization of men.

The impact of this paper on me was profound. It was actually after I worked on this paper that I became politically active on the side of women. In the year 2000, the same colleague who had invited me to present the paper on democracy and the working woman, invited me to take part in a research entitled, 'Politics of Ethnicity, Nationality and Identity: Restructuring of State-Society Relations'. I was the only woman on the project, and I worked on the chapter entitled, 'Engendering Political Power: Women and the Struggle for Empowerment'. The key issue for my chapter was that Nigerian women had participated alongside men in many struggles, and they must have expected that they would reap enhanced social, economic, cultural, legal and political status as a result. In terms of aggregates, however, the quality of life of Nigerian women was low when compared with that of men. The key question for the research was: why had the status of Nigerian women not improved markedly, with the aggregate of struggles they had participated in, when their status was compared with that of men? This was a qualitative research study that used the case study research design. The framework for the study was an eclecticism of the strengths of essentialist, social constructionist, and deconstructionist notions of female identity. Data were obtained from primary sources (documents from the legislative and executive arms of government and interviews held with some key actors in, and a few observers of, the struggles in which Nigerian women had been involved) and secondary sources, mainly books. I focused on four cases of identity politics in Nigeria's recent history. I adopted the descriptive, interpretive/explanatory, and evaluative case study models, and also cross-case analyses. I examined the demands that women made as part of groups of men and women, or as women. I considered whose interests those demands would serve, and I considered whether they would serve women's strategic gender interests. I examined the contexts in which those demands were made, and studied the language of the demands. I interrogated the point at which women got into the struggles to actualize the demands made, the strategies employed in those struggles, and the immediate result of the struggles. From my analysis, I reached the conclusion that as long as women did not make gender-specific claims within other struggles (ethnic/racial, religious, economic, etc), and as long as they did not pursue their strategic gender interests actively, their social status would not improve markedly, and their quality of life would continue to be low.

Immediately after I turned in the report of that research in the first quarter of 2001, my reflections on the research reverted on the relevance of the entire research, and the implications of the results for my work as an adult education teacher and researcher. The connection to my activist work was clear to me immediately. In the last quarter of 2003, I got an invitation from colleagues in Canada, some of whom had read the report of my 2001 research, to contribute the entry, 'Identity', to the *International Encyclopedia of Adult Education*. That invitation helped me to focus my attention completely on the connections between adult education and questions of identity and identity politics. About this time, the link that I had tried to establish between the issues I had raised in the seminar paper on democracy and working women, and education, and women's identity politics, started taking shape. I knew I had to undertake a research that would help me to understand and gain new insights into the relationship between the identities of women and our low social status, and what formal and informal education had to do with it. I therefore initiated the research project, entitled 'The Dialectics of "Magic Consciousness", the "Hidden Curriculum" and Formal Education in the Construction of the Identity of Nigerian Women'. I carried out the project under the 2003 Advanced Research Fellowship Programme of the Council for the Development of Social Science Research in Africa (CODESRIA). The research, which began in the second half of 2004, was concluded in July 2005.

From the premise that all educational provisions are value-laden, and from the post-structuralist feminist pedagogy framework, the study challenged the position, often taken for granted, that women's acquisition of formal education is the key to their socio-cultural and political empowerment. The argument presented in the research and in this book is that although colonialism met unequal relations of power between women and men in many Nigerian communities, its legacies, in formal education, remain, and the processes that it created have fused with the omnipresent Christian and Islamic religious ethos within and outside classrooms and schools (as the hidden curriculum, socialization, or informal learning) to construct women's identity, an identity that is essentially disempowering.

The approach that was adopted for the study was a phenomenological reading of the lived experiences of women. Through open-ended questionnaires, interviews, focus group discussions and observations, data were retrieved from female and male religious leaders and lecturers; literate women and men in the formal sector of the economy; illiterate/semi-literate women in the informal economy; and female and male students in two locations in Nigeria. The locations are Ibadan in the south-western part of the country, and Lokoja in the middle belt (central) Nigeria.

One of the conclusions reached was that the identities of women (that is, the character of women), or more precisely, the identities that women favour, and or that many men and religious leaders would rather see women favour, represent a major factor in determining whether women have political power and whether women experience violence; and the actions that they are able to take when they have experienced violence. This is irrespective of the educational attainment of women. I also reached the conclusion that men would rather see women favour identities that disempower and disable them because they have a need to preserve power that dominates.

I know that my upbringing and experiences, the experiences of other women, especially the experiences and identities of the mothers before me, the observations I made and the conclusions I reached in my earlier works, resonate with the experiences of women and the reactions of men towards women in this book. I am sure that women and men who read this book can relate to these experiences and analyses, and the voices of resistance and possibilities contained herein will echo even in hearts and places where they would ordinarily not be tolerated.

Introduction

Justifiably, education has always received wide acclaim as an important engine for the development of human potential. Today, persons and organizations that are interested in developing human capabilities consider knowledge, skills and attitudes, whether obtained through formal, non-formal and incidental learning, as assets. However, it is not just what people know or learn that matters. How they learn, whether or not they are able to learn, and who teaches what, to whom, matters too. Clearly, then, no education(al activity) can be politically neutral, because there is no value-free education (Hooks 1984; Blackburn 1996; Ferrero 2005). The goals and purpose of education, the content, the entire process of education and the procedures chosen for evaluation in education are value-laden. The traditional or indigenous education systems in Nigeria, which covered (and still cover) physical training, development of character, respect for elders and peers, development of intellectual skills, specific vocational trainings, developing a sense of belonging and participation in community affairs, and understanding, appreciating and promoting the cultural heritage of the community (Fafunwa 1974) were, and are, not value-free.

When the Muslim missionaries came with the skills of reading and writing in the Arabic script through the northern part of Nigeria in the 14th century, and the Christian missionaries came with literacy skills, first, in the Portuguese language in the 15th century, and then in the English language in the middle of the 19th century through the southern parts of Nigeria, the goal was to spread the two religions (Fafunwa 1974). When the British colonialists came to Nigeria, they discovered that they could better exploit the colony if they built schools and provided out-of-school education. Their education, they reasoned, would make the task of governing Africans easy. This goal of formal and non-formal education during colonial rule was clear in Frederick Lugard's mind, because at some point during his indirect rule, he was exasperated by what he perceived to be the 'evils' that western education had sown in the southern part of Nigeria, where men were bold enough to challenge the colonial administration (Odi 1983, cited in Fasokun and Mejiuni 1991).

At the point that Lugard was showing frustration with how to deal with those he called the 'educated natives', it was clear that education was becoming somewhat mutually beneficial to both the governor and the governed. Nigerians (men at first) craved for and sought education for many reasons, which included, but were not limited to, having access to the white man's job, which was a badge of superior status, and a means of putting an end to colonialism.

For the colonial era, and for now, Berggren and Berggren's view that 'education was, and still is, a badge of superior status; literacy and schooling served, and still serves, the powerful classes; it is a symbol and justification of privilege and a safeguard for authority and self-interest' (1975:6), is true. Given the exploitative and patriarchal (read exploitative again) character of colonialism, Nigerian women were largely deprived of access to education because, according to Denzer (cited in Mama 1996), 'Nigerian and British attitudes concerning female roles had much in common' (p. 14), and when women started formal schooling, their incorporation into very restricted areas of government service was slow. In this respect, Afonja and Aina (1995) observed that 'the constraints to women's education in the country since the colonial era have cumulatively affected the development of women' (p. 23). They indicated that socio-cultural factors such as child marriage, female seclusion and social prejudices against the education of the female child have consistently caused differentials in male/female education. The 2002 and 2004 UNDP Human Development Reports attest to this. The combined primary, secondary and tertiary institutions gross enrolment ratio for Nigeria in 1999 was 41 per cent of the total number for females and 49 per cent for males; while the adult literacy rate (age 15 and above) was 55.7 per cent for women, and 72.4 per cent for men in year 2000, and 59.4 per cent for women and 74.4 per cent for men in year 2002 (UNDP 2002:22, 2004:219).

An important point that Aina (1995) made was that there is a correlation between educational qualification and competence, and employment in the labour market, and so 'gender disparity in education implies unequal job opportunities' (p. 101). The correlation between wage employment and educational qualification is, in the circumstance, both logical and understandable. The fact on ground in Nigeria today is that while a large number of Nigerian women work in the informal sector of the economy, increasingly, many women are visible in the formal sector, especially in the service sector. Eighty-seven per cent (87%) of employed women are in the service sector. This, to my mind, is a reflection of an increase in the number of women who have access to education. I take a cue from the university. Although a Federal Government of Nigeria publication showed that the average ratio of female to male students in universities was 1:3 between 1980 and 1992 (Federal Government of Nigeria 1997), it is thought that the ratio of female to male students in universities is higher now. If we were to go by equitable distribution of access to resources, and take on board the distribution of the population of Nigeria by sex, there ought to be more girls and women than boys and men enrolled in formal education and adult literacy training. Even then, I still think that we should keep in view that there appears to be more women now, than in the past, in formal education.

No doubt, a lot of benefits accrue to women from education, especially formal schooling. It is clear, however, that women are yet to benefit from investment in formal education the way men have benefited. Afonja and Aina (1995) citing Rosenzweig and Schultz, indicated that women's education is not only a determinant of labour force participation, but that it directly influences the age of marriage, fertility, improved health and better nutrition for women and their families. These appear to be the areas where education has been most beneficial to women, and there seems to be a connection between these observed benefits (salaried employment/better-paying jobs and healthier households) and the social position of Nigerian women. The inference that I am drawing from this is that education has helped women to meet their practical gender needs, and has therefore improved women's condition, but not their social status. We should not forget that women's practical gender needs are derived from their identity – the natural (relating to the entire reproductive system that is present at birth, and which matures as the woman matures) and the constructed (acquired through nurturing). Apart from salaried employment and healthier households (these are important too), there are no indications of benefits to women in the area of political participation. I-IDEA (2000) notes that:

> ... despite a comparatively large pool of well trained and able women, their absence in major institutions of power and decision making processes is particularly striking (p. 3).

I-IDEA further observed that there were only twelve women in the 360-member House of Representatives and three in the Senate of 109 members after the 1999 general elections, while there were proportionately even fewer women in executive positions in the public and private sectors. The 2003 general elections produced two female deputy governors (out of thirty-six) as against one that the 1999 general elections produced. Women thus constituted: 2.7 per cent (3) of the total membership (109) of the senate; 5.83 per cent (21) of the 360-member House of Representatives; and 3.84 per cent of the state Houses of Assembly (Akiyode-Afolabi and Arogundade 2003). Violence against women, both in private and public, persists; and there are no indications that more illiterate than literate girls and women are victims of violence and overt sexism and discrimination. Equally important is the fact that many men (and women), boys and girls (even in educational institutions) are still uncomfortable with the campaigns around a fair share of rights and resources between men and women. For instance, during a workshop that deliberated on human rights in tertiary institutions, a male respondent who was a leader of a students' organization, in response to the presentation on women's human rights said: 'in African tradition, women are expected to be submissive. It is not right for women to be claiming that they have equal rights with men. It is not done' (Fashina 2001:112).

Yet, the consensus among opinion moulders (at public talks and in newspapers) and discussants in non-formal education settings (workshops and seminars) is that access to formal education and literacy training for girls and women will ensure more active involvement of women in politics. This suggestion, and the suggestion that economic power will help women's active involvement in party politics, usually tops the list of recommendations from such forums.

Concerned about the contradiction inherent in what those who have education have not been able to achieve, in spite of their education, and the continued suggestion that education is the key to ensuring that more women are active in politics; reducing violence against women and improving the position of women in society, the question that keeps coming to mind is: why has the social, political and cultural status of highly literate Nigerian women not improved in spite of their education when their status is compared with that of men? This is the key question that I tried to answer in this book. To answer this question, I raised an issue, in form of a proposition, and it is that:

> Contrary to the position, often taken for granted, that formal education sufficiently empowers Nigerian women, the combined pull of the teaching-learning process in schools, 'magic consciousness' (in schools and the larger society) and the 'hidden curriculum' (in schools), which constructs the identities of Nigerian women and so disempowers many educated Nigerian women, challenges this claim.

Concerning the teaching-learning process in schools, Freire (1993) in his objection to what he called the banking concept of education, said 'in the banking concept of education, knowledge is a gift bestowed by those who consider themselves knowledgeable upon those whom they consider to know nothing. Projecting an absolute ignorance unto others, a characteristic of the ideology of oppression, negates education and knowledge as processes of inquiry' (p. 72). In the Nigerian higher education system, memorization of facts as presented by the lecturer, a form of non-reflective learning (Jarvis 1995), epitomizes the banking system of education that Freire describes above. Freire (1973) also considered magic consciousness to be non-rational consciousness, which 'simply apprehends facts and attributes to them a superior power by which it is controlled and to which it must therefore submit' (p. 44). This consciousness appears to be the dominant mode in the practice of the major religions in Nigeria today. According to Freire, magic consciousness is characterized by fatalism, which leads persons to fold their arms and resign themselves to the impossibility of resisting the power of facts. Concerning the hidden curriculum, Byrne (cited in Garret 1987) apprehended it as values, attitudes, and behaviours that are not part of the official curriculum, but which are nevertheless communicated to pupils and students in educational institutions as informal education/socialization in classrooms.

The objectives of the research were: first, to explore the influence of religion, socialization (within and outside the classroom) and formal teaching-learning interactions on women's understanding of who they are and what they believe (their identity); second, to interrogate women's understanding of who they are, and what they believe affect their view of: (a) their roles in the public and private spheres of life, (b) all forms of violence against women and what they advise that women do when they experience such, and (c) the participation of women in political and community life; and third, to examine, in the light of the above, whether formal education has empowered women who have it.

The Nigerian Tertiary Education Context

In an earlier work, I took the position that in the context of the poor funding of university education and the long history of military rule in Nigeria, the poor and degrading conditions under which teachers and students teach and learn, respectively, do not motivate them to challenge one another to take a wider, more liberal and serious view of knowledge dissemination and knowledge acquisition. I reasoned that the growing intolerance of others' views and actions, which political, religious and social groups on campuses exhibit, is symptomatic of the poor school environment. I also stated that faculty and students on campuses exhibit parochial notions of their own and others' status as human beings, the rights of individuals and groups, and the limits of freedom (Fashina 2001). Those observations are still relevant here. In that work, I explored the role of the 'hidden curriculum' in the violation of, and disrespect for, women's human rights in tertiary institutions.

What I did not explore is the lethargy (or the seeming lethargy) that women display concerning the violation of their rights. I approach this from my experience as a volunteer for a non-governmental organization that helps girls and women to prevent sexual violence and abuse, and also to cope with sexual violence and abuse, through education programmes. What our experiences of working with women in tertiary institutions have shown is that: (a) if an education programme (symposium or intensive training workshop) has the backing of the authority of the institution (and the school more or less compels the students to attend), there is high attendance and, usually, we hold lively discussions, after which many try to become volunteers for the NGO; (b) where attendance is totally voluntary, attendance is usually low, and (wait for it), more men than women attend such education programmes; and, (c) for every education programme that we hold, there will be at least two women, who will meet with us after, and express support for our efforts, and also express a wish to work with us. Many explanations can be advanced for a, b and c above, but the explanation that I think is relevant here is that female students have internalized oppression, and are therefore making little or no efforts to seek knowledge outside the classroom.

I need to state that while symposia, seminars and workshops on campuses do not attract many students and faculty, the religious gatherings – prayer meetings, fellowships and revivalist gatherings – attract hundreds.

Also important is the hierarchical structure of relationships in schools, including tertiary education which ensures that faculty are thought to be all-knowing, and so they are to bestow knowledge to those who are considered to know nothing (Freire 1993). Faculty identifies the subject matter that will be taught, and how it is going to be taught. They also set the criteria for assessing how well students have learned the subject matter. Unfortunately, it appears students are used to being told what to learn, how to learn and how they will be assessed. This is because when they had the opportunity to suggest what to learn in a course, bring in resource persons who are not faculty, and indicate how they want to be assessed, they did not seize the opportunity. In fact, the suggestion that they should partake in the decision-making process of teaching and learning was particularly strange to the group of students in question. The students were used to the relations of power that allow lecturers to go to class with particular beliefs/values which they pass across to the students in the process of teaching or omitting to teach particular subject matters, whether knowingly or otherwise. Given that a lecturers occupy a position of power relative to the persons that they teach, the beliefs/values that they pass on by teaching, omitting to teach or teaching subject matters in particular ways, usually go unchallenged. This is more so with respect to issues that border on and have implications for questions of dominance, oppression, equity and justice. Usually, also, most of the lecturers in tertiary institutions are men.

Some studies by Nigerian women are relevant here. In a study titled, 'Stooping to Conquer? Women Bargaining with Religion and Patriarchy in Ile-Ife, Nigeria', Dipo-Salami (2002) went to the field with the assumption that the possession of assets such as education, salaried employment and productive and social capital would help women to resist patriarchal control. She, however, found out that, while the possession of the assets 'improves women's fall-back position and increases their bargaining power to some extent, a wide range of other factors operate to restrict their active agency'. It is instructive that most of Dipo-Salami's respondents had some education. Actually, half of them had higher education. She concluded that given the influence of religion (Christianity and Islam), 'economic independence and possession of other assets are not sufficient for the improvement of women's citizenship status and their functioning within and beyond the household'. Dipo-Salami's study somewhat confirms the position I had earlier taken that the benefits that accrue to highly literate women from education are low.

In another study that investigated the extent to which university education and salaried employment serve as predictors for women empowerment in the public and private sectors, Ogunrin (2004) found out that salaried employment had more influence on the level of women's participation in decision-making processes than university education. Ogunrin also went to the field with the assumption that education is a means to the social and political empowerment of human beings.

In a study carried out by the Female Leadership Forum, the view that tertiary institutions perpetuate a culture of female subordination was highlighted. Some of the interesting responses given by male participants during focus group discussions as reasons why women cannot take up leadership positions in tertiary institutions include: the factor of religion, domestic work, women's flexibility, and women's belief that they are subordinate to men. The report identified, amongst others, the following as being responsible for the failure of female students to take up leadership positions: women's lack of interest in leadership culture, and women's fear, timidity and lack of confidence. Others are violence, corruption, and high financial demands (Irinoye and Idika-Ogunye 2003).

My current study was therefore informed by the observations and conclusions of four previous studies discussed above. First, was my observation that female students seemed lethargic about the violation of their rights; that they would rather attend prayer meetings, fellowships and revivalist gatherings on campuses than attend non-formal education programmes that focused on women's rights; and my other observation about the hierarchical structure of relationships in higher institutions, its implications for power (what is taught, how, by whom and to whom?). Second, was Dipo-Salami's conclusions that religion was a factor that limited women's (including highly literate women's) citizenship status. Third, was the study carried out by the Female Leadership Forum in higher institutions, which indicated that male participants identified religion as one of the reasons why women could not take up leadership positions. Fourth, was Ogunrin's study that found out that salaried employment had more influence on the level of women's participation in decision-making processes than university education. Given these observations and conclusions, I decided to explore how religion (present in formal institutions as formal, non-formal and informal education/learning) interfaces with the processes of teaching-learning in formal education contexts, and socialization/informal learning inside and outside formal schools, to shape the kinds of persons that women become in formal schools, and when they have finished formal schooling, especially higher education. I also decided to interrogate the (limits of) power of women who have emerged from these processes.

Clearly, an awareness of what religious leaders actually teach women and how they teach women about who they are, their interests and their expected roles in society, would throw some light on the processes that shape women's identities in the school environment and in the teaching-learning transaction. We do not want to presume, for instance, that all religious leaders preach (read teach) the subordination of women all the time and in all contexts. And if they do, we ought not to assume that women (and also men) will take their messages to heart, internalize them, and then behave according to their precepts. We note that Stacey (1998) found that evangelical Christians among white working people in the Silicon Valley, California, are not monolithically antifeminist, nor are their family relationships uniformly patriarchal. Similarly, Dipo-Salami (2002), quoting Saadallah, also said that Muslim feminists, 'being aware of the level of oppression directed against women, resort to Islamic sources such as the Qur'an and positive aspects of the Hadiths to validate their discourse on equality between the sexes in attempting to reconcile Islam with the universal principles of human rights' (p. 19).

Locating the Study

The research study reported in this book took place in two locations in Nigeria – Lokoja, the administrative capital of Kogi State, located in the geo-political zone now referred to as the North-Central; and Ibadan, capital of Oyo State, located in the South-West of Nigeria. There are similarities and differences in the character of the two locations. They are both the administrative capitals of their states, although Ibadan is a huge city in comparison with Lokoja. They both have large numbers of adherents of the two major religions in Nigeria (Christianity and Islam), and adherents of traditional religion; although not many people (both literates and illiterates) admit to being adherents of the latter. However, while the majority of the people who inhabit Ibadan are Yoruba, the people in Lokoja are not homogeneous. Kogi State indigenes insist that there are at least twenty-one distinct ethnic groups in the state. And given that Lokoja is the administrative capital, it is thought that all the groups are represented there. Some of the ethnic groups that have been identified include: Egbira Koto/ Musum, Kakanda, Nupe, Oworo, Egbira Okene, Ogori, and the Okun. The Okun are of Yoruba descent, and they speak a variation of the Yoruba language. Within the Okun too, at least three variations of the Okun language are spoken. Others are: Bassa-Nge, Bassa-Komo, Igala and Hausa. It also appears that in Lokoja, the languages of three groups (Igala, Okun and Egbira Okene) are widely spoken, and they are thought to be the three largest ethnic groups in the state. Understandably also, in Lokoja, many of the inhabitants, whether literate or illiterate, speak Pidgin English. The suggestion here therefore is that not all the respondents in Ibadan (Oyo State) and Lokoja (Kogi State) are indigenes of the two states. There were some respondents, especially among women in the informal economy, female apprentices and among students, who came from other parts of Nigeria, but were resident in Ibadan and Lokoja at the time of the study.

The majority of the respondents in this study were within the age range of 20 to 39 at the time of collection of data in 2004. A few were between ages 40 and 49, while a few were between 16 and 20. Only five were above 50. By the criteria of chronological age and the prescription of the Nigerian constitution, the majority of the respondents in the study were adults. While adulthood, in the minds of many people, is biologically determined, and represents the process of ageing, Hunt (2005a), citing Tenant and Pogson, indicated that additional factors such as psychological, social, and cultural factors and their dynamic interplay, coupled with the physical process of ageing, define adulthood. We note that at least half of the respondents in this study were earning a living and married, and possibly acting responsibly towards significant persons around them and members of their communities. The other half were not earning a living and married; apparently because they were still in school and in non-formal education programmes, preparing for a career, a vocation or profession. Although the point has been made that chronological age is not a good determinant of age; by the criteria of social responsibility and age, most of the respondents in this study were adults. As we had earlier indicated, the 'age of majority' in our country is 18, and so when we asked whether respondents had voted and or stood as candidates in elections: we must have assumed that most of the respondents had had the opportunity to vote, and perhaps also, to be voted for.

However, if we assumed the mid-ages of 25 and 35 respectively for the majority of respondents who were in the age brackets 21 to 30 and 31 to 40 in 2004, those in the age bracket of 21 to 30 had had the opportunity to vote during only two general elections in Nigeria, while those within 31 to 40 had had the opportunities thrice. If persons in this age group had voted during the 1993 elections, then their votes were discountenanced by the then military head of state, General Ibrahim Babangida, who annulled the results of the election. The point that is being made here is that although we asked the respondents in this study about their participation in civic-political matters, in terms of participating in the political process, except for union elections, which they may have had the opportunity to participate in while in school (for those who stayed long enough in the formal school system), there were not many opportunities to participate in electoral processes and the process of governance during significant years of their adult lives. This is because Nigeria was ruled by military dictators for much of the adult lives of participants who were in the age bracket of 30 to 39. But for military dictatorship, if they were in the mid-age for that group, they would have been ready to begin participation in elections by 1987 when they turned 18. So, depending on their age, the 1993, 1999 and 2003 elections and the elections that they had taken part in, in the different groups to which they belonged, would probably be for them the reference point as they responded to the questions that they were asked about their civic-political participation.

There were other significant developments during the period of the transition from the military to civilian administration in 1999 and during the transition from civilian to another civilian administration in 2004. After the end of military rule and a long period of 'femocracy' (Mama 1997), when wives of heads of state put themselves forward as the voice of women and helped their husbands to appropriate feminist demands, voices of other women and women's groups began to be heard loud once again all over the country. There was a wave of demands around women's rights to: participate in the political processes in the country; stop all forms of violence against women; grant women rights that they were hitherto denied, *de facto* and *de jure*; and grant women access to power resources, especially formal education and literacy training. Many new not-for-profit organizations worked around these issues, while the existing ones which had hitherto been concerned about democracy started focusing on women's rights. The media picked and published more stories about the abuse of women than they ever did.

Individual women and women's organizations remembered and tried to draw lessons from: women's traditional method of protest in the Eastern part of Nigeria which pre-dated colonialism, which was called 'sitting-on-a man'; Queen Amina of Zazzau's exploits in wars; the Aba women's riots which began in 1929; the activism of Abeokuta Women's Forum in the 1940s and the Federation of Nigerian Women's Societies (FNWS) in the 1940s and 1950s; the writings of Nigerian female scholar/activists, and the activism of Women in Nigeria (WIN) in the 1980s, among others (Mba 1982; WIN 1985; Perreira 2005). Women also drew inspiration from, appealed to, and keyed into international processes, recommendations and conventions that seek to improve women's status in all spheres of life. They include: the United Nations Decade for Women: Equality, Development and Peace (1976–1985); the Convention on the Elimination of all Forms of Discrimination Against Women (CEDAW), adopted by the United Nations General Assembly in 1979; the Vienna Declaration and Programme of Action adopted by the World Conference on Human Rights in 1993 – the section on the equal status and human rights of women; the World Conference to review and appraise the achievements of the UN Decade for Women, held in Nairobi in 1985, and the adoption of the Nairobi Forward-looking Strategies for the Advancement of Women; the Beijing Declaration and Platform for Action adopted at the Fourth World Conference on Women in 1995; and the preparations towards the ten-year review and appraisal of the Beijing Declaration and Platform for Action – Beijing + 10 (UNHCHR 1996; Odah 2001; ABA-CEELI 2002). Within this context, there was some overt and covert backlash, against activism around women's rights issues, especially in some sections of the media and religious institutions (Mejiuni 2005; Obilade and Mejiuni 2006).

Meanwhile, given the economic hardships that Nigerians experienced as a result of the Structural Adjustment Programmes that the military dictators who ruled Nigeria enforced in the 1980s, many more Nigerians moved to religion for succour. Although Nigerians practice a variety of religions, Christianity and Islam predominate. Traditional religions trail these two, and others follow. In many parts of Nigeria, Christianity and Islam have fused with traditional cultures, obliterating traditional religions in such places, with most adherents and custodians of traditional religions being openly Christian and/or Muslim. Religion pervades the private and public lives of Nigerians and scholars have drawn attention to the increasing phenomenon of Christian and Islamic fundamentalism (I-IDEA 2001), and increased politicization of religious differences. Apart from the spiritual benefits that people get from being religious, the practice of religion is one of the processes of socialization, and religions are cultural systems; they are therefore powerful educational agents. Religious leaders usually prescribe the ecclesiastical model of meaning-making (Hunt 2005), and would like adherents to understand their World through the sacred texts, the teachings of religious leaders, and the practices of the religions. The lessons from religious teachings and practices carry rewards and punishment for disobedience, rules are laid down according to the 'will and voice of God', and those rules are normalized, such that they become part of our cultures, the way things are. Bowker (1997) observed that religions 'are a constant force for change, despite the fact that they are also, as systems, necessarily conservative' (p. xxi). Concerning the negative and positive impact of religion, he said:

> There is no doubt that one can point to many kinds of damage which religions have done, in terms, for example, of spiritual terrorization or the subordination of women, in most aspects of their lives, to the decisions and determinations of men. But religions also remain now as they have been in the past, the major resource for the transformation of life and the transformation of art ... (p. xxiii).

In Nigeria, amidst the need that women and men have to honour their spirituality through religion, and amidst a lot of religiosity, those who want to preserve dominant power, those who are looking for easy and lazy explanations, those who want to subordinate women to their will so that they can exploit them, appeal to 'the will of God'. According to this manner of thinking, a fatal accident, caused by a careless driver, and a building that collapsed and killed inhabitants because the builders had cut costs, were pre-destined, they were the will of God. This was what Freire (1973) referred to as magic consciousness. That is, non-rational consciousness, which 'simply apprehends facts and attributes to them a superior power by which it is controlled and to which it must therefore submit'.

Also in Nigeria, religious beliefs and practices are taught and learned through informal and non-formal education, and whether or not they appear in the curricula of formal educational provisions, they are almost always present as hidden curriculum. The question then, is not whether education practitioners are aware of the presence of religion within schools and classrooms. The question is whether they assume its positive impact all the time, because religions are thought to be about 'the will of God'.

So, while persons who are concerned that Nigerian women should have an important power resource continue to advocate for increased access to formal education for Nigerian children, women, and persons with disabilities, including literacy training especially for women; religion, with its patriarchal norms and values, pervades the private and public spheres in Nigeria, including institutions of higher learning. Meanwhile, educators in the formal school system have focused on the implications of socialization for learning and for negative and deviant behaviour, ignoring the more insidious effect of socialization and informal learning, especially in higher education, except as it relates to cultism, examination malpractices and other deviant behaviours; apparently because cultism, for example, is disruptive and costs human lives. Adult educators who are best placed to apprehend informal learning as day-to-day experiences in non-formal education and in higher education, had their sight elsewhere. They focused on religious institutions as providers of non-formal adult education activities, not on the teaching and practices of religion as, themselves, educative activities.

This is hardly surprising. In Nigeria, the colonial experience resulted in the formalization of education, in a non-indigenous language (Obanya 2004). The result was that formal and, to a lesser extent non-formal education, have displaced the system of education where persons, young and old, acquired knowledge, skills and attitudes required for everyday living and that shaped their character (Fafunwa 1974) in informal ways, through intuition, observation, imitation, and socialization (Hrimech 2005), reflection on experiences, and through oral tradition. Marsick and Volpe (1999) described informal learning as 'learning that is predominantly unstructured, experiential, and non-institutional' (p. 4). It is 'the acquisition of new knowledge, understanding, skills or attitudes, which people do on their own and which has not been planned or organized in formal school settings' (Hrimech 2005:310), nor in non-formal education settings, and involves action and reflection on experiences (Larsson 1997; Marsick and Volpe 1999; English 2002).

The discourse of informal learning has focused on: the different types of informal learning that are observable – tacit and explicit informal learning (Evans 2003; Hrimech 2005), self-directed learning and auto-didactic learning (Hrimech 2005), and the hidden curriculum (Garret 1987); the settings where informal learning takes place and activities that result in informal learning – income generating activities or work (Marsick and Volpe 1999; Marsick, Volpe and Watkins 1999); household, leisure, voluntary and community activities (English 2002; Findsen 2006); social movements (Hernendez 1997; Lander 2003); reading, travelling, exposure to the mass media, and socialization, and reflection on experience; the content of learning (English 2002), the theories of informal learning, the conditions that support and limit learning, and the role of intentionality in enhancing informal learning (Marsick, Volpe and Watkins 1999; English 2002).

Unfortunately, in Nigeria today, informal learning has become shadowy; it is unnamed, and seldom researched, even though it goes on within formal and non-formal educational institutions and teaching-learning contexts (as incidental and or explicit learning); and during teaching-learning interactions in formal and non-formal education (as hidden curriculum and incidental learning) (Fashina 2001).

I hope that I am able to show readers that the teaching-learning processes in higher education, and religion, taught and learned through formal, non-formal, and informal education/learning (or the hidden curriculum), and also socialization within and outside the formal school system, all interface to determine the persons that women become, that is, who they are; and how who they are, then enhances or limits their capabilities, whether in the civic-political sphere or in their attempts to resist violence. The research method that I adopted for this purpose spans both the interpretive and critical paradigms, given the feminist pedagogy framework that I chose to undergird the study and my research strategy, which was a phenomenological reading of the lived experiences of the women that I had targeted in the study. It seems clear from my framework that the study reported here is a feminist research. This book, then, is as much an academic pursuit as it is a project of the politics of identity.

In Chapter One, I describe the theoretical framework adopted for the research study, and provide detailed information about the procedure that was adopted for data collection. I also provide information about the participants in the research, and the strategy that I adopted for analyses of data. In Chapters Two, Three, Four and Five, I present female and male respondents' and religious leaders' views, beliefs, opinions and experiences on, and about, women's civic-political participation; the role of women in the private and public spheres of life; women's identities; and women's experience of violence, and what they should do when they have experienced violence. Also in all the four chapters, I examine women's analyses and their understanding of their roles in the public and private spheres, their experiences /others' experience of violence, who they believe themselves to be, and who others believe they are. I also interrogate male respondents' views and religious leaders' positions about all the issues raised. In Chapter Six, I interrogate the impact of the identities of women that have emerged from the previous chapters on women's abilities to gain power, reorder unequal power relationships, and resist oppressive power. In Chapter Seven, I explore how formal education, religion and informal learning/socialization interact to construct the identities of women who have gone through formal education, especially higher education, and I try to determine whether the identities of women that have emerged from that process are empowering or disempowering.

1

The Methodology

This chapter describes the theoretical framework that undergirds the study reported in this book, and the research tools that were employed for data collection and analyses.

Theoretical Framework

One broad theory that takes a full view of the character of the teaching-learning process in schools; what is taught, the hidden curriculum and the effect of religion on the formation of consciousness, and the cumulative effect of all these on the female identity, is the feminist pedagogy. This theory has a vision of what education might be, but is frequently not. Feminist pedagogy, according to Schrewsbury (1998), is

> a theory about the teaching-learning process, that guides our choice of classroom practices, by providing criteria to evaluate specific education strategies and techniques.... The evaluative criteria include the extent to which a community of learners is empowered to act responsibly toward one another and the subject matter and to apply that learning to social action (p. 167).

Feminist pedagogy focuses on the experiences and, in particular, the oppression of women in the context of education (Merriam and Cafarella 1999).

Two models of feminist pedagogy have been pulled out of the many strands of feminist pedagogies. They are the liberatory and the gender models. The liberatory model is said to draw from structuralist, postmodernist, Marxist and critical theories. It is the view that institutions of learning and the classroom itself reproduce the power structure that is found in the larger society, and so, liberatory feminist educators 'attempt' to recover women's voices, experiences and viewpoints, and use these to make systems of privilege, power and oppression visible. They also pay attention to the structured nature of power relations and interlocking systems of oppression based on gender, race and class, which are reinforced by education (Merriam and Cafarella 1999). In the gender model, attention is on how female identity has been socially constructed to be one of nurturer and how the individual woman can find her voice, becoming emancipated in the personal psychological sense. Educators therefore look at how the educational environment and the learning transaction can be constructed, so as to foster women's learning. In this model, a connected approach to learning is advocated, where life experiences are valued, where a woman can have a voice, and hence an identity.

Merriam and Caffarella indicated that Tisdell identified four recurring themes in feminist pedagogy: how knowledge is constructed; the development of voice; the authority of the teacher and students; and dealing with difference. They also observed that Tisdell found the liberatory model to be strong on differences based on race, class and gender, although she also thought they focused too much on structures, and did not account for the individual's capacity for agency, the capacity to have some control outside the social structure. Tisdell thought that the gender model, on the other hand, tended to emphasize similarities among women and did not take account of differences in power relations based on class, race, sexual orientation, etc. Tisdell further indicated that the way to take account of the recurring themes in the feminist pedagogy literature was to have a post-structural feminist pedagogy, which synthesizes both the psychological model with the structural factors of the liberatory perspective.

It is from the post-structuralist feminist pedagogy framework that this study proceeds. This is because it appropriately addresses our concerns about: institutions of learning as some of the social institutions that reproduce the power structure in the larger society; power relation in the teaching-learning situation and the construction of female identity; women's internalization of these constructions; and, resistances to the constructions.

Finally, the vision of feminist pedagogy gives hope. It throws up the possibilities that formal education may, at some point, begin to serve women better because 'it ultimately seeks the transformation of the academy, and points toward steps, however small, that we can all take in each of our classrooms, to facilitate that transformation' (Shrewsbury 1998:168).

Research Method

This research was undertaken mainly from the qualitative perspective. Our strategy was a phenomenological reading of the problem of the low social status of Nigerian women. Bakare-Yusuf (2003a) made a strong case for a phenomenological reading of African women's everyday experiences. Drawing who drew from the phenomenology of embodied existence developed by Simone de Beauvoir and Maurice Merleau-Ponty, she opined that phenomenology 'seeks to analyze existence and lived experience outside of the distorting influence of normative patterns of description' (p. 6). She indicated that it is through lived experience in concrete situations that an African woman, for instance, comes to understand what her context has contributed to her identity as an African woman; that a woman's lived experience alludes to the complex layers of socio-historical (personal and collective) and cultural context that makes an African woman who she is. The respondents in this study were therefore invited to take part in the identification of the processes that resulted in women's (especially literate women's) current low social position through the respondents' own lived experiences and the experiences of women around them. Fortunately, given the instruments that were used to retrieve information from respondents (interviews, open–ended questionnaires, observation and focus group discussions), respondents not only identified the processes that resulted in women's current social status, they shared their own understanding of the issues involved, and also proffered solutions to the problem of the low social status of Nigerian women.

Interviews were held with seven female and male lecturers selected from seven schools/faculties in two institutions of higher learning, the University of Ibadan, located in Ibadan, which is in Oyo State, in the south-western part of Nigeria and the Kogi State Polytechnic, Lokoja, located in the area that is referred to as the Middle Belt, in the central part of Nigeria. The criteria for selecting lecturers for interviews at the two locations were, first, that the lecturers had to have been teaching for a minimum of six years; second, that they would be willing to grant the interview; and third, that they would probably be available for the interview. Nine female and male religious leaders, representing the three main religions in Nigeria, Christianity, Islam and Traditional Religion (the worship of Sango[1]), were also interviewed in the two locations of the study. With the help of my research assistants and long-time inhabitants of both towns, we identified religious leaders who appeared to have the largest following (largest number of adherents), and who were also widely known.

Lecturers were asked: whether gender relations play any role in their analyses and illustrations during lectures; whether they take an interest in the totality of the development of their students; whether female students complain of sexual harassment, and/or that lecturers have tried to put them down; and, about the values that they take to class. Religious leaders were asked questions in relation to how they view women – who they are, what ought to be their interests, and their expected roles in the private and public spheres of life. Specifically, the religious leaders were asked to state the position of their religions on: women's participation in politics; the education of women in the Western sense; the leadership roles that women play in the different religions; and violence against women.

Except for a few of the interviewees who were passionate about the issues raised during the interview, and whose interviews lasted about two and a half hours, most of the interviews lasted between one and one and a half hours and were recorded on tape. All the interviews were conducted in the English language, except the two with the traditional religionists that were conducted in the Yoruba language. Yoruba language is the language of the Yoruba people, who inhabit the south-western part of Nigeria.

Six open-ended questionnaires were designed, and administered to respondents who were selected through purposive and convenience sampling techniques. We targeted women and men in the formal sector of the economy who were graduates of tertiary institutions, and were journalists, lawyers, teachers, and civil servants in the two locations of the study; as well as women in the informal sector of the economy who were tailors, hairdressers and traders. We also targeted female and male students from the schools/faculties and departments from which we had selected lecturers that we interviewed in the two locations; and sought out the female apprentices of the women in the informal economy who had shown willingness and readiness to take part in the study. We had hoped that we would get a good mix of illiterate and semi-literate interviewees among the women who work in the informal economy and their apprentices. We then administered the questionnaires to persons in our target groups, who were willing and ready to respond to the questionnaires once we got to a media house, a state secretariat, a salon, the market place, etc.

The question may be asked: but why were semi-literate and illiterate men not sampled? The focus of this study was essentially literate women. However, having bracketed formal education, religion and informal learning in the quest to understand the processes that shape the identities of this group of women, we suspected that like female and male lecturers, male students probably had a role to play in shaping the identities of different groups of women whom they interacted with on a daily basis, for at least eight out of the twelve months of a year (while school was in session), and for at least eleven to twelve years of formal schooling that they had experienced. Literate men in formal work settings were sampled for the same reason and more. They continued to interact with literate women at work (and also out of work), at least eight hours a day, and for at least five days in a week, after at least fourteen years of formal schooling. Of course, this is not to say that semi-literate and illiterate men that highly literate women interacted with on a daily basis, especially outside formal schooling and formal work, did not contribute to shaping the identities of the women. On their own part, semi-literate/illiterate women were sampled because, first, we wanted to compare the identities that highly literate women who had had at least fourteen years of formal schooling favoured, with the identities favoured by semi-literate/illiterate women who had experienced only a few years of formal schooling, or had no experience of that setting at all. Second, we wanted to know whether a real difference existed in the empowering potential of the identity(ies) that highly literate and semi-literate/illiterate women favoured.

At the end of the data collection exercise, we were able to retrieve information from: forty-two women and twenty-nine men who worked in formal work settings as lawyers, journalists, civil servants and teachers; forty-six female and thirty-two male students in the two higher institutions of learning where lecturers had been interviewed; and fifty-six illiterate/semi-literate women and thirty-nine semi-literate female apprentices who worked (and were training) in the informal economy as hairdressers, tailors and traders. All the questionnaires basically asked the same kinds of questions from all respondents, but required that female respondents volunteer more detailed responses to some questions. The questionnaires for the four categories of women that were involved in this research asked detailed questions about their participation in politics; roles of women in the private and public spheres; women's experiences of violence; their advice to victims of violence; and the associations, organizations/groups to which they belong. Questions were raised about: how women think men see women; how women see themselves; how women are similar to, and different from other women and men; the benefits of higher education/apprenticeship training and the changes that should be effected in the two types of education; the role of religion in the individual's life; and the critical question of whether women will vote for women who aspire to the highest political offices at the federal and state levels of governance, and top leadership positions in groups that have male and female members.

All women and men who work in formal sector settings, and female and male students, completed the questionnaires by themselves. The researcher and two research assistants, one each in Ibadan and Lokoja, wrote the responses of the semi-literate women in the informal economy in their questionnaires. The interactions were actually interviews. One hairdresser, and an apprentice tailor, who is also a Junior Secondary School Three (JSS III) student, completed their questionnaires, and their responses were comprehensible, although with great difficulty. The interviews with semi-literate women in Ibadan were conducted mainly in the Yoruba language, which is the language of the majority of the people who reside in Ibadan. The people who reside in Lokoja, the capital of Kogi State are not homogeneous, as they comprise about twenty-one ethnic groups. However, it appears the languages of three groups (Igala, Okun and Egbira Okene) are widely spoken. Fortunately, the research assistant in Lokoja is an Igala, the one at the Ibadan end of the research is Yoruba and, this researcher is an Okun who speaks Yoruba well. All three conducted the interviews with semi-literate women in Lokoja in Pidgin English, Yoruba and Igala, depending on which of the three languages the interviewee was comfortable with and the languages that the interviewers could handle.

We observed the interactions of: two lecturers with their students in class, and three female religious leaders during interactions with adherents of their religions. The observation of lectures took cognizance of the teaching-learning environment, the teaching methodology, the responses of students to the lectures, who was responding the most, and how the students related to one another and to their lecturers in class. At the end of one of the lectures, the lecturer introduced us to her students, and asked whether I would like to speak with them. I spoke to them about my research, which was the reason I was in their class on observation. I implored the few that would be called upon to complete the questionnaires to do so truthfully, and I also raised the matter of the noticeable silence of the female students whenever the lecturer asked questions, and she did ask a lot of questions. The observation of the interactions of religious leaders with adherents paid attention to the message that was being passed on, and how the message was received by the adherents, that is, the expression on their faces, signs of agreement/disagreement, etc. We were not unobtrusive observers at those interactions.

In five Focus Group Discussions (FGDs), four with all groups of women in Lokoja, and one with female apprentices in Ibadan, we explored the Appreciative Inquiry '4 – D' Cycle. In the groups, we: identified individual participants' strengths, assets, talents, and their contributions to a successful group project; and, got participants to envision who and what they (personal) and other Nigerian women (collective) would be in future. We moved to the design stage, which is about planning and also got promises from members of groups about linking up with one another to act on their dreams and visions (the delivery stage) in future. The FGDs had between five and nine participants, lasted between one and one and a half hours and they were recorded on tape.

Apart from primary data that were retrieved from respondents as indicated above, also available were: audio and video cassettes of the sermons of a Christian female religious leader who I could not observe; and secondary sources of data, such as books, journals, magazines and programme pamphlets that some well-meaning respondents gave to me in the course of collection of data. All the data, except the observation of a retired female professor who is also a religious leader, were collected in the second half of the year 2004. The observation of the professor took place in March 2005.

The Respondents

Most of the women in formal work were married (only four were unmarried), and were between the age bracket 30 to 39. There were a few others in the other age brackets – 20 to 29, 40 to 49, while only one respondent was above 50. Seven women, six of whom were from Ibadan and one from Lokoja possessed Masters degrees. Only one woman possessed the Higher National Diploma (HND) while three possessed the National Certificate in Education (NCE). All the four who held the NCE and HND certificates were from the Lokoja end of the research. All others in both Ibadan and Lokoja possessed Bachelors degrees.

Most female students and female apprentices were unmarried, and only a few were above age 30. Most were in their early twenties. Among female apprentices in Lokoja, half of the respondents were less than 20 years. The difference in age between apprentices in Ibadan and Lokoja is traceable to the fact that half of the apprentices in Ibadan were in school up to Senior Secondary School, whereas half of those in Lokoja were already out of school after primary education or Junior Secondary School education.

Among women in informal work and female apprentices, most were semi-literates. Some could read but could not write, but most said they were unable to read and write, despite the fact that they had been in school. Four out of 56 women in the informal economy could read and write with understanding. Seven in the same category had never been to school. The researcher was going to analyse data for the three groups represented in informal work, but it was discovered that there were not many differences in the responses of the three groups.

Following from these, we refer to women in the informal economy and female apprentices as semi-literate women, and sometimes, illiterate/semi-literate women, while women in formal work and female students are referred to as literate and, sometimes, highly literate women.

Most (42) of the women in the informal economy were married; five were single parents, two from Ibadan and three from Lokoja; and eight were single, five from Ibadan and three from Lokoja. The women were between ages 20 and 39. Nine were between ages 40 and 49, while three were above 50.

Like female students, most male students were not married, and were between ages 20 and 29. Most of the men selected from formal work settings were married. Four were single, and one was a single parent. Most of them were between the age range of 30 and 39. Five were above age 50, and one below age 30. Five of them possessed the Masters degree while one possessed the HND. The rest were Bachelors degree holders.

The question may be asked: why the decision to label journalists, lawyers, teachers and civil servants who work in formal settings as literate/highly literate, and tailors, hairdressers and traders, who work in the informal economy as illiterates/semi-literates? The reason is linked to the key question that was raised in the introductory part of this book, which is: why has the social, political and cultural status of highly literate Nigerian women not improved in spite of their education when their status is compared with that of men?

Some conceptual clarifications are required here. We will then tie them up with the key question that we are trying to answer in this book. The definition of a literate person that I would like to adopt is: someone who possesses the ability to read, write and perform basic numeracy tasks (Quigley 2005) with understanding, in either his/her mother tongue or an official language (that is, the language of formal institutions in one's context), and who is able to employ those skills for functioning in daily activities. Conversely, an illiterate is someone who cannot read, write and perform basic numeracy tasks, in either his/her mother tongue or the official language of his/her context. Because I am interested in why the status of highly literate Nigerian women, women who are literate in the English language, have not matched that of men, I have adjusted the definition of literate and illiterate persons. A literate person is therefore someone who possesses the ability to read, write and perform basic numeracy tasks, with understanding, in the language of formal institutions in Nigeria (the English language), and who is able to employ those skills for functioning in daily activities. An illiterate is someone who is unable to read, write and conduct basic numeracy tasks in the English language.

The reason here is that it is through the English language that Nigerians interact with official institutions. If they were literate in their mother tongue alone, they would have to seek assistance from others, when interacting with officers of formal institutions, and this limits their autonomy and independence. Linked to this is the fact, for example, that the Nigerian Constitution prescribes a certain formal educational attainment or literacy level for persons seeking elective office, which is, a minimum of Secondary School Certificate or its equivalent. Equivalents include: Grade II Teachers Certificate, the City and Guild Certificate, ability to read and write, understand and communicate in the English language to the satisfaction of the Independent National Electoral Commission, the body responsible for conducting elections in Nigeria (Federal Republic of Nigeria 1999). The rights and wrongs of this constitutional requirement notwithstanding, its implication is that women who would like to occupy elective positions, for example, must possess some formal educational qualifications. At any rate, they have to be literate. In Nigeria, formal educational qualifications, recognized in formal institutions across states of the federation, are acquired in the English language. For the purpose of the study reported on in this book, we define a semi-literate person as a person who can: read in the English language but cannot write; only write his/her name/append his/her signature to documents; read and write but not with understanding, such that those limited skills cannot then be applied to a wide range of daily activities.

In this book, the terms illiterate, semi-literate and literate are therefore descriptors, and the possession, or a lack, of literacy skills is a mode of identification of the categories of respondents in the study reported on.

Identification of Participants in the Research and Analyses of Data

The research study reported on in this book, explores the processes that shape women's identities, and how the identities that result impact on women's power to become persons who are full citizens, through a phenomenological reading of their lived experiences. It therefore became imperative that certain processes of identification of participants be adopted, and also inevitable that one would associate specific forms of identities (identities which the participants value and have self-identified) with the participants. So, one had to give participants names and initials, so as to be able to keep track of the beliefs, opinions, attitudes, voices and experiences of individual respondents and interviewees. The names and initials of all the respondents and interviewees in this book are therefore not real. However, the identities associated with them are real.

In addition, before data collection, some prospective interviewees, and institutions from which respondents and interviewees were going to be drawn, were wary of granting interviews and allowing the researcher access to prospective respondents and interviewees. Some of them made it clear that they did not want to be misquoted, and they did not want information they would provide mangled. They asked the researcher to write formal requests for the interviews, which she did, after which she was given access to interviewees and respondents.

This accounts for why large portions of the interviews with religious leaders were reproduced verbatim in this book. At any rate, the purpose of the interviews with the religious leaders was to draw them out on their position, beliefs and teachings about the roles of women in the private and public spheres, their identities, their relationship with formal western education, and their leadership roles in the new religions. Reproducing those portions of the interviews that are relevant to this study on the pages of this book appears to serve the purpose. In addition, at the beginning of all the interview, there was an agreement reached between the researcher and the interviewee that we would pause the tape recorder when the interviewee did not want an opinion or information out in the open, in the public sphere. This was strictly adhered to, so even if an interviewee could identify himself or herself in this book, the views associated with him or her cannot be contradicted.

I am convinced that many of the respondents and interviewees were conscious of the process they were engaged in when they agreed to be interviewed, complete our questionnaires, and/or participate in focus group discussions. I therefore believe that many were forthright, but also strategic in their responses to my questions. I sensed that some of them used the opportunity of the interviews and completion of the questionnaires to comment on issues that were already in the public sphere that they thought they needed to: add their voices to; correct misrepresentations about; and provide information about. Again, in cases such as these, there were specific references to specific events and personalities in our history. I have taken out names of the personalities, if the reader's knowledge of the name would not add to an understanding of the subject.

Before fieldwork, the researcher assumed that because respondents in Lokoja resided in a multi-ethnic town, their responses might be different from those of respondents in Ibadan, as Ibadan was a predominantly Yoruba city. Analysis of data has not shown major disparities in results, hence the decision to draw inferences from results without reference to the location. There are references to locations only when a real difference appears, or when a result displays the character of the location from where data were collected.

Quantitative analyses, mainly frequency of occurrence and percentile scores, were used only when we thought it would give a clearer picture of the point being made. Otherwise, we looked for the typical and atypical responses, and also looked out for slight deviations from both types of responses. We looked at relationships between sets of responses, even though attempts were made to avoid putting responses in straitjackets or neat categories. Just as we had suspected, we were able to pin most of the available data into the different traditions that are represented in the discourse of identity – essentialism, social constructionism, deconstructionism, and an eclecticism of two or all the traditions (Calhoun 1994; Mejiuni 2005). This is understandably so because women's identities, or the identities that women favour at different points in their lives, and that affect their view of their roles in the public and private spheres of life; all forms of violence on women and what to do about them; and the participation of women in political and community life, are, in reality, based on essentialism, social constructions, deconstructions and an eclecticism of the traditions.

I have tried to ensure that the real-life experiences and the voices of women who provided information for this research on the field are shared and heard. Concerning the experiences and voices of women, while some women appear silent, for they would not respond to some questions, and others appear to exaggerate their positions, I think the respondents were generally forthright. Even when some of the responses appear to contradict earlier positions, such can be a result of the dilemma that women face as a result of their social position and also due to the fact of the multiplicity of the identities that women inhabit.

In the chapters that follow, we look at the processes that have resulted in the present level of women's participation in civic-political affairs and the dominant discourse around women's experience of violence, and try to explore the possibilities that – that women will participate in civic-political affairs at the topmost levels in future; and that women will be able to resist and take decisive action against violence in future, in spite of, and/or because of their identities.

Note

1. According to Idowu (1962), Sango is one of the divinities (the Orisa) of Olodumare (God). It is believed that the Orisa were brought forth by Olodumare; they were His ministers, who look after the affairs of His universe and act as intermediaries between Him and the world of men. Idowu indicated that, to the believing, worshipping minds, the divinities are real, 'so real to the worshippers that they have, for practical purposes, almost become ends in themselves, instead of the means to an end, which, technically, they are according to Yoruba theology' (See E. B. Idowu, *Olodumare – God in Yoruba Belief,* Ikeja, Longman Nigeria Ltd, 1962:63, for more information about how Sango came to be associated with 'the wrath' of Olodumare).

2

Women's Civic-Political Participation Towards an Equitable and Humane Democratic Order

The kind of governance that Nigerians experienced since the pre-independence period has been criticized for, among other reasons, having been characterized by low-level citizen participation. Key aspects of this governance range from the provisions made for participation in the 1922 Clifford Constitution; to those in the 1947 Richards Constitution; to those in the Macpherson Constitution which took effect in 1952; to participation in general elections beginning from 1951(I-IDEA 2000a), which a colleague described as 'constitutional despotism';[1] and to the competitive model of democracy which Nigeria practiced just before independence and immediately after independence in 1960, between 1979 and 1983, and which it is practicing now. With the benefit of modern governance parameters, social development practitioners would tell us that low-level citizen participation and social inequity are inextricably linked. In this context, the next line of argument would then be that, in order to have a more equitable and humane society, there is a need for a more participatory political system. Macpherson (1979) warns that a more participatory system would of itself not remove all the inequities of society, but he assumes that a system that offers more citizen participation than the competitive model of democracy is desirable. However, even participatory democracy which is thought to be an advanced theory of democracy that focuses on how class inequalities undermine formal political participation, has been critiqued for paying little attention to sexual inequality and the effects of patriarchy on democracy (Pateman 1983).

Many obstacles have been identified as affecting women's participation in politics and women as politicians, not only in Nigeria, but also across the African continent and around the world. From the identified obstacles, solutions are usually suggested and strategies adopted by non-governmental organizations and development agencies (Longwe 2000). The often mentioned obstacles include: masculine models of politics; education and training; women's poverty and unemployment; women's dual burden and their traditional roles; lack of confidence; the perception of politics as dirty, given the high level of fraud and corruption; and the role of the media (Shvedova 1998; Akiyode-Afolabi and Arogundade 2003). As earlier indicated, however, access to resources, money and education are more frequently cited as factors that hinder women's participation in politics. Longwe apprehends many of the 'reasons' given as affecting women's participation in politics as 'blaming the victim'. She argues that women's education does not lead to political empowerment. She states that there is 'absolutely no correlation between the percentage of women in university in a particular country, and the percentage of women in parliament or in the higher levels of government'. Longwe (2000) identifies the key problem as 'the covert and discriminatory systems of male resistance to women who dare to challenge male domination of the present political system' (p. 24).

A recent work that documented the narratives of Nigerian women who had participated in the political party primaries preceding the 2003 elections in Nigeria supports Longwe's position. One of the authors of the report, J. Ibrahim, observed from the narratives of the women that 'it soon became clear that there was a near systematic process of the exclusion of women from, and indeed the subordination of women in the party political process' (Ibrahim 2004:1). The report noted twelve recurring issues in the narratives of the women, and they were all directed at the exclusion of women. A few of the issues cited included: male-centred interpretations of culture and religion such as perceptions that only men can aspire to public office; organized campaigns to slander unmarried aspirants as lacking in morals; high level of violence which characterized the electoral process, including the use of security forces to intimidate women aspirants and their supporters; and claims that some female aspirants were too assertive and independent, and therefore could not be team players.

Given the observations above, we sought to gain insight into: the nature of women's participation in politics and community life/group activities; why women participated in politics and civic life the way they did; and the possibilities for women's increased participation in, especially, politics. Specifically, we reckoned their participation as: candidates in elections; voters, both in recent times and in the past; supporters of female political aspirants, and elected/appointed leaders. We also wanted to know whether women and men would vote for a female politician/leader in future.

Participation as Voters

Literate women in formal work settings, semi-literate women in informal economy and female apprentices were asked whether they voted during the 2003 General/ Local Government elections and why they voted. Seventy six point two (76.2) and 76.8 per cent of women in formal and the informal economy, and 53.9 per cent of female apprentices said they voted. The reasons that women in the formal economy gave for voting ranged from: exercise of their civic rights; to hopes that politicians would deliver dividends of democracy; and the thinking that a vote may be important and the country will be the better for it. Omolade said:

> I detest the idea of anyone who has refused to vote, complaining about anyone in Government who is not performing, so I didn't want my not voting to be a reason for the wrong candidate to be in position by a difference of one vote.

Literate women in formal work who voted during the general elections but did not vote during the local government elections said they did not know any of the candidates and they were of the opinion that people were not being sincere. Adetutu said: 'The average Nigerian was raped during the general election; so, I did not see the need to waste my time during the latter'

Different reasons were given by women in formal work who did not vote: there would not be a conducive atmosphere for free and fair elections and they did not want to risk their own lives; either lost their voter's card or name did not appear on the final voters' register; and could not see the essence of voting in Nigeria where, after the exercise, the ones voted in fail to provide for the needs of citizens. One woman said she could not register in her place of domicile as there were no voters' cards, and she could not travel to the place where she had registered on Election Day, since travelling was prohibited that day.[2] Aanwo said she did not vote because, 'I had and still do not have any believe in the PDP[3] government, and I also knew the election would be rigged'.

Semi-literate women in the informal economy typically voted because they wanted peace and progress for Nigeria. Some wanted a change, others, a better future, while yet others wanted good leadership, good government and a government that would favour the masses. The responses were mostly optimistic, although some were opportunistic. While some were about security, others were about going through the motion. A few women indicated that they were asked to vote, so they did, hoping that things would get better in the future and their children could go to school. Two women said they voted in case government asked that citizens should produce their voters' cards before they could access social services.[4] One woman said she voted because she is a member of a political party; another said she wanted to vote for her favourite candidate; yet another said she thought she should play her part, while another said she voted because others were voting.

For those who did not vote, it was either because they could not locate their names on the voters' register, even though they each had a voter's card, or they had lost their voter's card. Most, however, said they did not vote because voting was a waste of time, as politicians would rig anyway and they did not have the time to waste, and they could better expend their time in search of their daily bread. One woman said they harassed them when they went to vote. This was an apparent reference to political thuggery. Adunola in Ibadan said: 'I don't have the time, the queue was even long and I needed to go and look for my daily bread. After all, we do not gain anything from voting'. According to Niniola in Lokoja:

> I don't like voting. I will support anyone that will do good. The problem is that we vote for people who get there and start doing what they like. I believe say we use our hand find trouble for ourselves.[5]

Female apprentices voted: so as to move the nation forward; because they wanted peace to reign; because everyone was voting; and, because 'I just like to vote'. One woman said she voted because of the future of her children. Other responses were that: 'it's a right'; 'it's compulsory'; 'to effect change of government because incumbents were not doing well'. One woman said she wanted a particular candidate to win, while Towoju, a 16-year old, obviously under-age, said: 'They said I should vote'.

Those who did not vote said: I took ill; not interested; could not locate card; no time; and was busy. Three in Lokoja indicated they were under-age. A respondent said: 'I was too busy and the queue was too long, so I had to go back home to finish up what I was doing'. This respondent was a single parent. Amina said: 'I could not leave the shop because my madam went to vote and there was nobody at the shop'.[6]

There are similarities and differences in the reasons literate and semi-literate women gave for voting, or not voting. Most of them voted because according to them, to vote was their right, and by voting, they were hopeful that things would get better, both for them as individuals and the country. One point that semi-literate women made, and which no literate woman made, was that they voted so they could tender their voters' cards to access social services. That was on the assumption that voting was compulsory. Literate women also did not say they were just going through the motions. Semi-literate women were time-conscious. Some mentioned long queues and their implications for time. We have to note that these are women who work in the informal economy, and so earn their living on a day-to-day basis. For them, the long-term benefits of participation as voters in an election are not obvious. What is obvious is the time or, more appropriately, the money they lose queuing at polling booths, or the domestic work that will remain undone until they get back home. In cases like these, women are unable to partake fully as members of the community because of their other roles as bread-winners and care-givers.

Literate women were asked whether they participated in or had participated in Students' Union/Association elections while in school and why. Seventy-one point six (71.6) per cent of the female workers said they did, while 61.0 per cent of students said they did. The reasons that women in formal work gave for voting while they were students varied, but four reasons were often cited: to elect credible leaders who could represent students' interests; voting was a right that they thought they needed to exercise; they were interested in particular candidates/friends; and they thought they needed to choose student leaders who could present students' opinion and position to the authorities of their institutions. Aanwo in Ibadan said it was usually free and fair and there was little chance of rigging, while Hauwa in Lokoja said: 'I wanted a situation where as students, we could speak or dialogue with the school authority as a body and not as a person'.

The reasons that female students gave for voting in Students' Union/Association Elections in both Ibadan and Lokoja were very much the same, although there were slight differences in a few of the responses from Lokoja. The students said: they had the right to vote, and choose good leaders who would represent their interests; they loved politics; loved to participate in the activities that took place around them; and, they thought their votes would count. The female students in Lokoja added: to encourage democracy among students and allow students to air their views. Jumai in Lokoja said she voted because it was the turn of her ethnic group to pick the presidency of the Department Association, a reflection of the ethnic configuration of the state that owns the polytechnic.

Some of the women in formal work who did not vote did not give reasons for not voting. Two women said they were just not interested in voting; another said she was not active in campus politics; and yet another woman said she took an interest in a particular election but found out she did not like the character of about six candidates who contested in that election, so she gave up on Students' Union elections. Again, Adetutu in Ibadan said:

> I knew elections were rigged and won before votes were cast. I remember voting only once, and it was because Christian Fellowships on campus came together to support our own people who did not do any better than the so-called unbelievers.

Adedigba said, 'I was living out of campus and in fact feeling too old to be part of the system'.

The reasons female students in Ibadan gave for not voting included: lack of interest in Students' Union elections; and, inadequate knowledge of candidates that contest elections. Modupe said: 'I feel whether or not I vote, persons will be elected and, hopefully, they'll perform well'. Kehinde said she did not believe voting represented the true collective wish of the majority. One reason that

Ajoke in Ibadan gave, and that got support from another student in Lokoja, was lack of trust. She said

> I don't trust them. They are just as corrupt as the school authorities and Federal Government that they say they fight against and I don't see them really representing the students.

The reason that stood out as being responsible for female students not voting in Lokoja was the fact that the Authority of the Institution had prohibited the umbrella Students' Union, although departmental associations existed. The students were of the view that: the departmental associations did not run well; too often candidates had no opponents and at times, a winner was known before the elections, so they could not see why they should vote. Omotayo's reason, however, stood out. She said, 'I do not vote because of the time constraint. The period of election is usually weekend that I have to do other things'.

A number of interesting issues have emerged from the responses in respect of women's participation in politics in educational institutions. Students' interests appear to be well cited as a reason for their partaking in elections, and a woman extended the matter appropriately when she noted that 'power with' one another was important when trying to get across to the school authority. It is interesting that students in Lokoja who had no umbrella Students' Union were the ones who articulated the point about encouraging democracy among students, perhaps, appropriately, because of its absence in their own institution. Also important are the testimonies of Jumai who was still a student and Adetutu who is a lawyer. They spoke to the matter of ethnicity and religion in politics in educational institutions, a reflection of how identity politics is played out in the Nigerian (macro) society (I-IDEA 2000a). These two women who obviously inhabit multiple identities participated in the politics of ethnicity and religion. By her testimony, Adetutu was not satisfied with the outcome of the politics of religious identity that played out in the Students' Union election. Unfortunately, going by her responses to all the questions posed, Adetutu took her religion seriously. Another issue that came out is that of rigging, again a reflection of the problem that afflicts elections in the macro society. Aligned to rigging is the matter of distrust, specifically with regard to corruption in government. Ajoke's point will resonate again, in this study, when women and men speak to why they would vote women into leadership positions. A problem of a slightly different nature is the one Adedigba pointed out, and that is how some people feel alienated in schools (Maduka 1991; Luttrell 1997) For Adedigba, the problem was her age.

Active Support for Female Candidates in Elections

Again, literate women in formal work settings, semi-literate women in informal economy and female apprentices were asked whether they had ever supported women who were candidates in elections and why they did or did not support them. Seventy-six point two (76.2) per cent of literate women said yes; 26.8 per cent of semi-literate women said yes, and 15.4 per cent of female apprentices said yes.

Six of the nine women in formal work who had indicated they had never supported any female contestant did not give reasons. One of the three who responded, Adetutu, said 'I have never supported anyone on the basis of gender'. We recall of course, that Adetutu had supported someone on the basis of religion. Another woman said she had not had the opportunity, while the third woman said 'it is because the female contestants were usually utilized', whatever this means.

Sixteen of the 33 women in the informal economy who said they had never encouraged/supported a female candidate said they had never come across female candidates. However, two of the 16 said they would support female candidates, if they step out for elections anytime, and they added, 'for the sake of Nigeria'. There were other responses. One interesting one was Alake's who said, 'I believe it is against God's will, so I can't support or encourage anybody, be it female or male'. It is important to note that although this woman had indicated that she did not vote during the last General/Local Government elections, the reason she gave was that her voter's card got lost. Much later, as we will show, she was more categorical, and her position became clear.

As for female apprentices, the main reason they had never supported female contestants was that they did not know about female contestants in their area. Another woman said, she just voted, she did not know whether the candidates were male or female. It is important that we do not lose sight of the fact that this group of respondents were the ones who participated the least in voting during elections.

For women who had supported female contestants, they were asked to indicate the nature of support that they gave. Many women in formal work indicated they supported contestants in more than one way. They said they engaged in open campaigns at rallies; one-on-one campaigns; and sought other women's support for the candidates. Some said they did 'underground campaigning', while others said they gave spiritual support in form of prayers. At least, one woman was involved in planning a candidate's campaign, while many gave moral support in the form of words of encouragement. Many indicated they voted for the women, while others said they put their moneys into production of campaign materials. Grace in Lokoja said she encouraged a contestant by letting her know she could make it even in the presence of many male contestants. Adedigba, who is a journalist, said: 'I printed postcards and as a media woman, I gave her publicity on my programmes'. We recall that Adedigba is the woman who did not partake in Students' Union elections because she was feeling too old in the system.

Women in the informal economy who had supported female contestants said they did so mainly by campaigning for the women. One woman said she spoke on a contestant's behalf to the Hairdressers' Association in Lokoja. At least, two women said they assisted a contestant in putting up posters, while one woman said she gave moral and financial support. Yet, others said they voted for the female candidates.

The few female apprentices who had supported female contestants said they campaigned for, and voted for the candidates; prayed for her, and wished her well.

The reasons women in formal work gave for supporting female contestants while in school, and as workers, were diverse. Some said it was because they knew that the women were competent, capable and, would deliver. The other reasons that women gave for supporting women were about women believing more in women, and women affirming women. Itunu in Ibadan said:

> I believe in women emancipation. I believe that a woman has equal right to vote and be voted for. Also, I am of the opinion that women, due to their role as homebuilders, will offer quality service if elected into office.

Deborah in Lokoja said: 'To encourage female participation and empowerment in politics, so that better policies for women and children can be made.' Rukayat in Lokoja said, 'Women can be better in politics than men because they are tender hearted, can manage their resources, they are good and fully focused on whatever they do'.

Although one woman in the informal economy said she supported a woman because she was capable, quite a number of women said they encouraged and supported female candidates because: women would listen to women; women needed to get into the positions that men now occupied so as to lift Nigeria up; and what men could do, women could do better. Nkechi said although the woman she voted for in the last election lost, she voted for her because, 'She is a woman like me and she went to school. So, if my children go to school like her and contest election, people will vote for them'. Modinat, who voted for a female candidate that won an election, said: 'We need women to govern us, we are tired of men ruling us, and I believe women can do it better, since they have feeling'.

Tanwa, a female apprentice said she voted for a woman because, 'she is a woman like me and I believe in her capabilities'. Another said she supported a female contestant who was a well-known presenter on TV with prayers because she liked her personality. Interestingly, the presenter contested elections in a constituency that is about seven hours' drive from the respondent's own constituency/place of abode. For Zainab who supported a female candidate who lost the election, she felt that if she had won the election, the chances that more women would get into such positions would have improved –'if she is there, other women will also get there'.

From the foregoing, it would appear that women in formal work settings support female contestants in elections more than semi-literate women. This may not just be an appearance, it may be a fact. The reason may be found in the fact that literate women were accounting for the support for female contestants while they were in school and as workers. Higher education ensures that persons are together on a regular basis for at least three years, and so, more than women who had never been in that environment, women who had been in tertiary institutions had more opportunities to support contestants in electoral processes. Important too, was the fact that Students' Union elections represented students' own operation of democratic principles.

Women as Candidates in Elections and Appointed Leaders

Among women in formal work, 14 (33.5%) had been candidates in elections. Medupin said she did not follow through with the elections because 'another female was contesting, so I stepped down for her to give her my total support'. Ruth said she had held positions of responsibility such as: class representative (twice), chairperson, Local Government Caretaker Committee and President of her Old Students' Association. Out of the fourteen women who had contested elections, five women had contested for the position of the overall head (president/chairperson) of their group. Three of the groups clearly comprised female and male members. Two of the three groups were a social club, and a cooperative society; one was not quite clear about the gender composition of the third group. The positions that the other nine women contested for were: vice president/chairman; treasurer; general secretary; assistant general secretary; and director of publicity and information. The groups/associations in which women had contested elections included students' union/departmental associations; professional, ethnic; cooperative thrift and credit unions; and religious groups.

Two of the five women who contested for the presidency of the groups to which they belonged (a Students' Union Government and a cooperative thrift and credit society) did not win. The reasons they adduced for losing the elections were: rigging of the election and dishonesty and disunity among members. All except one of the other women who contested for positions other than the overall head won the elections. The woman who lost the election believed she lost the election due to discrimination relating to her state of origin. The reasons that persons who won gave for winning varied. They included that: people believed in their competence, ability and integrity; God was in support; did a lot of homework and campaigned hard; and that there was overwhelming support from all members. Esther, who had won the presidency of a Christian Fellowship at school said: 'I cannot tell, the people might know better. All I can say is that I have a heart to serve God'. Abosede, a journalist, who possesses a Masters degree, said: 'The other members wanted a female vice chairman to assist the chairman who was male'. Women indicated that the reasons they contested for, and aspired to elective positions were because: the individual wanted to contribute to the progress of the group; members wanted ladies in the executive committee; she wanted to change the status quo; God wanted the individual; and the individual was the people's choice. Aanwo said she was confident she could do well if elected. Hauwa said: 'I believe women too should aspire to the positions that their male counterparts feel are meant for them alone. As a woman, I believe in the saying that what a man can do, a woman can do better'. Four of the fourteen women who had contested for elections did not respond to the question that asked them to state the reasons they contested for the position.

Only twelve female students had been candidates in elections, and there were more of them in Lokoja (8) than Ibadan (4). In Ibadan, a student said she contested because she was passionate about the association, and two others said it was to help their association make progress. In Lokoja, the students said they wanted to serve to effect possible and necessary changes among staff and students; and wanted to work for the progress and success of the union. Rachael said: 'My course mate wanted me to take part as the only lady in HND 1 Public Administration Department'.

Forty out of the 56 women in the informal economy sampled in this study were members of community, religious and trade groups/bodies, and cooperative thrift and credit groups. Only eleven (19.6%) women had contested elections or had been appointed to various positions in religious, community groups and trade guilds. The positions that the women had occupied included: President, Kogi State Hairdressers' Association; Director of Socials of Rivers/Bayelsa States Community Association in Kogi State; Provost of the women's wing of Igbo Community Association and, deaconess of a church. The associations/ groups in which these women took up leadership positions were groups that were composed of predominantly female members – Hair Dresser's Association and women's wing of Igbo community; and those that had male and female members – Rivers/Bayelsa States Community Association, Tailors' Association and the church. The reasons that most of the women were appointed, or elected, were that they were seen as capable of moving the association/group forward. For Hassana, it was that 'They are afraid of me because I will tell the truth, I respect myself, I am hard working, and I don't hide my feelings'. Another woman said: 'People like me, and majority of them told me to contest and I did'.

Some of the women in the informal economy who were not members of groups and/or who had never contested elections or been appointed to positions gave reasons. Toun said: 'My husband doesn't like it and I don't want to go against his wish'. Even then, she was a member of a religious group – Good Women Association. One woman in Ibadan said older persons should not be seen to be joining unnecessary groups. The woman, a trader, is above 50. Two women who belonged to religious groups and their town unions said they were unable to contest because they were not literate.

An overview of the groups to which these women belonged showed that many who belonged to groups/associations participated mostly in activities of women's societies/groups. In the church, for example, only two women indicated they were deaconesses, and that is how far they could move up the ladder of leadership in some churches. Interestingly, women in the informal economy mentioned their affiliations to religious groups more than they did other groups. In the town's associations, women were mostly in the women's wing except for Yime who was the Director of Socials of her community association. Only two women, one each in Ibadan and Lokoja, said they were members of the ruling People's Democratic Party. A woman in Lokoja said she joined the party because her brothers were involved in it. A woman in Ibadan said she also belonged to a group of women called Delta Women in Politics, and she joined because she was planning to contest for a position in the year 2007.

Most of the female apprentices in Ibadan said they did not belong to any religious, ethnic, political, cooperative thrift and credit group because they were still apprentices and were not allowed to join any association until they had graduated. However, the reason Aina gave was, 'My husband did not like me associating with people'. Only five female apprentices in Ibadan and six in Lokoja said they belonged to religious groups, cooperative thrift and credit societies, social clubs and youth movements. Some of the associations to which the women in Lokoja belonged were: Islamic Sisters' Society and Muslim Students Society; Drama Club, and Community Youth Development Associations such as Ajobaje Youth Development Association, Adankolo Youth Mass Movement and Youth Association of Mopa.

Most of the eleven respondents who indicated they were members of groups said their groups did not have elective positions. Positions were held mainly by appointment. Only one was elected as a youth leader, and she was elected to the position of the General Secretary of the Youth Fellowship of Christ Apostolic Church. Four of the eleven had held positions of: financial secretary; marshal; chief and assistant chairlady. The groups to which these women belonged were groups comprising both male and female members and female members only. Two women gave the reasons they got into the positions. Mariam said, 'because I be better person, and I don te for the association'.[7] Mary stated: 'because I'm playful and friendly with all'.

Would Women Vote for a Woman who is Contesting for Governorship/ Presidency or Head of a Group with Female and Male Members?

Eighty-three point three (83.3) per cent of literate women in formal work, 92.9 per cent of semi-literate women in informal economy and 87.2 per cent of semi-literate female apprentices said they would vote for a female who is contesting for the overall leadership of the country, the state or other groups with male and female members. Female students were asked the same question, specifically in relation to their students' union/departmental association elections and 84.7 per cent said yes.

Among women in formal work, two women said they would not vote for a woman as overall leader, while five did not respond. Interestingly, among the five that did not respond, two, Aanu and Abosede, both Masters degree holders, had themselves sought for, and won elective offices. The reasons given by the two who would not vote for a woman varied: according to Omolola, 'women are always humiliated in the society, even if she's doing her best, she may be sabotaged'; but for Kanyin the reason was that, 'women are too harsh'. Among women who said they would, eight added provisos: will vote for anyone, male or female who is qualified and will achieve; will vote for the woman if she is capable, eligible, qualified for the position and if she's God fearing, have people's interests at heart, honest and hardworking. Adetutu said: 'certainly not because she happens to be female, but if I felt she were deserving of my vote'. And Aanwo affirmed: 'If she is competent and up to the task of doing a successful job of it, yes I would, not because she is a woman, but based on merit'. Two of the eight women who had said yes with provisos had also sought and won elective offices.

While these women appear to be cautious about the kind of women they would vote into topmost leadership positions, many women want women without provisos and they gave a lot of reasons. The reasons include: a need to have more women in leadership positions; the women will be representing women, and women political office holders are pulling their weight. Others are that women are sincere, dedicated, honest, prudent and hardworking. Idiat said: 'Women are meticulous, mild, God fearing and they account for whatever they spend well, though there may be exceptions, they are few'. Oyinade submitted: 'Everybody is born with wisdom and knowledge to administer, if given the opportunity'. Rebecca added, 'Women are hardworking, honest, intelligent, straightforward and lovely: see Dora Akinyuli of NAFDAC'.[8] Hauwa said: 'as a woman, I look forward to the day that a woman leader will emerge as a governor or even the president of Nigeria, it has been men all along, so why not women now'. Rukayat said: 'A woman has natural endowment – love, kindness, patience, tolerance. These attributes are required to be an effective leader, and they are found in women'.

Twenty female students in Ibadan said they would vote for a woman as leader, while nineteen female students in Lokoja said yes, they would. Two students each in Ibadan and Lokoja said they would not. Twelve of the students in Ibadan said they would vote for a female with provisos, while only two of the women in Lokoja would do the same. They said they would vote for a female president at school if she was: committed; not a figure head; up to the task;

capable (it is the office not the gender); academically and morally sound; and intelligent, honest, brilliant and can think fast. Enitan said: 'If she knows what she is up to, and not just a figure head, with some people calling the shots behind the scene'. Modupe posited:

> If I believe she is committed, I will. Gone are those days when people thought women could not deliver the goods (they are too weak, too fragile, they said), but women continue to prove them wrong by holding important positions.

Chigozie said, 'I will, if I feel she is capable of doing it and I know definitely there will be a difference in their way of ruling because females are more considerate than their male counterparts'. So, even among the students who were demanding that female candidates have sterling qualities, they were still of the opinion that women are better leaders.

For those who would unconditionally vote for women, the reasons they gave were: men and women have the same capabilities; they just believe in women; women are better managers of resources; men have not met up to expectations; women shun bribery, corruption and always seek the way forward; they are mothers; would like to erase the notion that only men should rule; men and women have equal rights to rule and women are more reliable, have human feelings, and are not corrupt. This category of respondents displayed a lot of confidence and excitement when they spoke about their belief in women. Fullerat said, 'I will vote for a woman president in my department because I believe so much in women and I believe women are better managers of resources than men'. Jumai submitted: 'Well, I would vote for her even if she does not have more supporters than the male contestant. I prefer womanhood'. Omotayo argued, 'I believe a female student will perform better than their male counterparts because of the wisdom bestowed on ladies by God'.

Those who would not vote for a female president would not do so for the following reasons: 'I hate politics'; 'Because I don't believe in voting. Voting, as I said, does not represent the interest of people' – Kehinde; 'It is preferable for a female to contest for the post of Vice-President of a Students' Union/ Departmental Association than a president. She won't be able to cope at times, so it is better she is assisting someone' – Apeke; while Tolani said, 'Since she is a woman, other members of the association may not want to cooperate, thinking that a woman cannot rule or dictate to them'.

An overwhelming majority of women in the informal economy said they would vote women into the highest offices in the public sphere. Only three said they would not. The reason one of the three gave was that 'It is against the will of God'. This is Alake who said she had never encouraged nor supported a female candidate, and who also said, 'I can't encourage anybody female or male'. Now, she has come clear and she concluded by saying 'God has made them the head so they are the one that is suppose to hold the position of authority'. Maimuna said women 'can't supervise people. Anything wey woman say im wan do, e go take am wicked'.[9] Another woman said, 'What a man can do as governor or president, a woman cannot do'.

The reasons so many semi-literate women would vote a woman to the topmost position vary. Fadeke said: 'Women are wonderful; they will use the brain God has given them, to normalize things'. Some women said they wanted a change and they thought women could bring about the desired change. Many said what men could do, women could do better. Adedotun referred to Deborah in the Bible. She said: 'Look at Deborah in the Bible, what was difficult for men to do in her time was done by Deborah easily. So, a woman can do better than a man at any point in time'. Oreoluwa wondered why men thought women could not do what they could do. She said, 'After all, there is no special role for the penis in those jobs, and some women even attain higher than men'. Other women said women were: 'kind-hearted, they will listen to fellow women'; 'they know where the shoe pinches'; 'women can discuss with women'; and 'women are not money conscious, selfish, callous, stingy, arrogant and dictatorial like men'. Some others said women 'know how to manage things and because they are mothers, they cannot but respond to the yearnings of people'. Anike said: 'Women have feelings as mothers. If women were up there, since we've been grumbling, their breasts would have reacted, because they will remember the day they put to bed'. Caroline said: 'Women stand by their words to ensure that things go well. Their yes is yes and their no is no'.

Although some women had indicated they would vote women as governors, presidents and heads of groups, they were cautious, and not as optimistic as the majority. Hassana said, 'If the woman will be able to do it, because I know it's not easy and I cannot'. Another woman said she would want to know what a woman could do: 'at least we've seen what men can do'.

Among female apprentices, the five women who said they would not vote for a woman as overall leader gave the following reasons: 'it's against my religion'; 'I don't believe that women can do the job, and they will only waste peoples time during the voting exercise'. Another said a woman would not be taken seriously; she could be cheated and she wouldn't know, adding 'no good make woman dey contest'.[10] Another just said she would vote for a man. Interestingly, the respondent who did not believe that a woman could do the job had held the position of Financial Secretary of the Youth Fellowship of her church. Well, she wasn't president, one would say.

Female apprentices who would vote for a female head also gave reasons why they would, and they were not really different from those that literate and semi-literate women had given thus far. Olonade said: 'Women are sympathetic, they think deeply and they will listen as they would to their children'. Another woman said women have milk of kindness, and since they are mothers, they will do better.

There were also those who would vote for women, but with provisos. Abike said:

Table 2.1: Women's Civic-Political Participation

	A				B				C				D				E			
	Yes		No		Yes		No		Yes		No		Yes		No		Yes		No	
	Frequency	Per cent age	Frequency	Per cent age	Frequency	Per cent age	Frequency	Per cent age	Frequency	Per cent age	Frequency	Per cent age	Frequency	Per cent age	Frequency	Per cent age	Frequency	Per cent age	Frequency	Per cent age
Literate Women in Formal Work (42)	32	76.2	10	23.8	30	71.4	10	23.8	32	76.2	9	21.4	14	33.3	28	66.7	35	83.2	2	4.7
Female Students (46)					28	61.0	17	37.0					12	26.1	32	69.6	39	84.7	4	8.7
Semi-Literate Women in Informal Economy (56)	43	76.8	13	23.2					15	26.8	33	58.9	11	19.6	45	80.4	52	92.9	3	5.4
Semi-Literate Female Apprentices (39)	21	53.9	17	43.6					6	15.4	32	82.1	5	12.8	33	84.6	34	87.2	5	12.8

Key:

A: Did you vote during the last General/Local Government Elections?

B: Did/do you vote during Students' Union Elections?

C: Have you ever supported a female candidate in an election?

D: Have you ever been a candidate in an election?

E: Would you vote for a woman who is aspiring to the position of President/Governor or the overall head of an organization with male and female members?

Source: Data generated from the open-ended questionnaires completed by (or for) all four categories of female respondents who provided information during fieldwork.

'It is only if I know the woman and I can see and sense that she is capable, then I will vote. But if I sense that she will just be there for the sake of it, I will not'.

Inunkan will vote for a woman who believes in God because, according to her, the woman will do whatever she promises.

Literate Men and Women's Participation in Politics

When asked whether women should contest elections into public offices, twelve of the fourteen men in formal work in Ibadan said yes, while two said no. All the men in Lokoja (fifteen) said yes. One of the twelve (Abayomi) who said yes in Ibadan said: 'provided she has her husband's permission'. When asked whether female students should contest for students union/departmental association elections, all the students in Ibadan and Lokoja (sixteen each), said yes, female students should contest.

The men were asked to specify the positions that women should aspire to occupy. Among the men in formal work who said women should aspire to occupy public office, only five thought women should occupy offices lower than the presidency. They said women should aspire to be senators, councillors, deputy governor, commissioners, vice president and members of the National Assembly. The reasons they gave are: 'these are the areas where their roles can be well displayed by virtue of their natural gift and intellect' – Abayomi; 'women are to take supportive role' – Ade; 'certain women have left indelible prints in this nation. The lady in charge of NAFDAC and the Lagos Stock Exchange are clear indicators that women can hold such positions' – Adamu; 'because the fear of God is in most women than men. They do not have the love of money at heart as men do' – Alonge; and,

> Brilliant women can even deliver more goods than some men. However, care should be taken in electing women into public offices because of their peculiar position in the family – Audu

Out of the five who thought women should occupy positions that are lower than the overall leader, three – Abayomi, Ade and Audu said they would not vote for a woman who is contesting governorship or presidential elections. The reasons they gave were consistent with their position that women should not aspire to the highest position. Abayomi who is a lawyer said, 'I don't believe in women leadership except where there is no capable and fit man'; while Ade said, 'They are to advise or support their male counterparts'; and Audu argued, 'Official functions of a governor or a president does not only require intellectual ability but also combine physical ability that women may not possess'. We observe that Adamu and Alonge, who had earlier indicated that women should occupy positions less than the overall head, said they would vote for women who are aspiring to be governors or president. Alonge reinforced his earlier position when he said,

'They will not be partial in their decisions. They will rule with the fear of God at heart'. The two men who said women should not contest elections to public offices stated that:

> Without prejudice to the right of women to hold political offices, such positions tend to have negative effects on the home, especially the children who are the victims of broken or unhappy homes. Society suffer for children without home training – Ola.

'The woman may not have time for her family since she may have to attend so many meetings which may occupy much of her time', argued Oni. When Oni was asked whether he would vote for a woman who is contesting for governorship or presidency, he said yes, provided such a female would not misbehave when she gets to power, and that as the adage goes, what a man can do, a woman can do it as well. His concern shifted from the family to whether or not the woman would misbehave in office. Somewhat consistent with his earlier position, Ola would not vote for a female who wants to become governor or president, but he also shifted ground a little on the concern for the family. He said: 'Women are not mentally and emotionally stable to be effective in such offices. Her home will also suffer for it. Society too will suffer'. This is an interesting point that Ola has made here. The surprise is that if women were that mentally and emotionally unstable, why would men like him be willing to commit children to the care of such women, such that children will suffer when the mentally and emotionally unstable women are not there?

One respondent, Fola, said women should aspire to occupy 'positions that their educational background fits'. His reason is that, 'no one should aspire to public office on quota basis'. This is an obvious response to women's demands for affirmative action. Fola further stated that he would vote for a female governorship aspirant, 'if she's sound, balanced and not overtly feminist'. Fola is clearly resisting the women's movement.

The other men who thought women should aspire to occupy any position said: 'women and men are equal before the law and the Lord'; 'women have to sit up because they have been relegated to the background'; 'they have equal right with men as entrenched in the constitution'; 'they are human beings like men and should be given the chance to thrive for ability to rule is about intelligence, not sex'; 'not aware of any law that confines women's aspirations to particular positions'; 'perhaps things will be better if women were at the helm of affairs'; 'have confidence and trust in women's service delivery, especially if given the opportunity to be in government'. Specifically, Shola said: 'Women are better managers of resources and good listeners.' Joshua indicated that, 'Men and women are endowed equally by our Creator'. Zaki affirmed that, 'Women are equal to men in intellectual capability and even more suited in discharging official functions than men'. Haliru said, 'I sincerely believe that women are more dedicated to their jobs than their male counterparts, they are not easily influenced to perpetuate evil in the office and, above all, they are mothers, therefore, they have love for all and sundry'. Yemi posited: 'The society is made up of men and women. The knowledge acquired for both sexes are the same from same institutions'.

All the men who said women should aspire to any position also said they would vote for a female governorship or presidential aspirant. While a few of them added provisos, most reinforced their earlier position about the reason a woman should aspire to occupy any position. A man cited the examples of Margaret Thatcher and Benazir Bhutto.

Male students in Ibadan were split in equal halves about the positions that they want women to aspire to. Eight felt that they should aspire to any position, while the rest eight felt that they should aspire to occupy positions such as vice president, general secretary and treasurer. In Lokoja, the majority of male students said women should aspire to the positions of vice president, general secretary, director of welfare/socials, and according to Mejabi, 'any position apart from the president'. Taiwo in Ibadan said: 'They could aspire for any position, publicity secretary, treasurer, social secretary and vice president'. Yele in Ibadan said: 'sensitive positions like financial secretary, treasurer and so on'. Fijabi said, 'They should vie for relatively feminine offices like treasurer, financial secretary, assistant to any office, general secretary, etc.'

The reasons they gave for specifying that women aspire to occupy positions that are less than the overall head were that: 'women are light-hearted as regards stealing and corruption: they are good custodians of funds as they have no courage to mismanage money in whatever form'; 'they can manage money better than men'; 'they care more than men'; 'they hate cheating and have good and legible handwriting'. They also said some tasks are easy to handle, and the risks involved low, so it is better that women attend to those tasks, given their fragile nature. Also, women should support the president, for example, by giving him advice. In Ibadan, Taiwo said, 'Ladies know how to handle financial transactions and social activities more than men'. Odedele said:

> Some positions are culturally defined and women can easily succeed in these regard. Women tend to be more accountable and transparent than men. Other positions are usually demanding as president and secretary and also because of the cultural factor, people don't always vote women into such positions.

While Yele said, 'It would be safe to keep your money and finance in care of a woman', Fijabi said:

> Certain offices are feminine relative to others. Also, women can hardly undergo the rigours associated with certain offices and the dangers therein and women are often not able to harmonize certain key/very demanding offices with their private/domestic responsibilities.

In Lokoja, Joshua, Yisa, Zubairu and Daniska gave the following reasons: 'The fact is that female cannot be head Biblically (Adam and Eve)'; 'They might not be able to cope with attendant problem of being a president. But as secretary general, all they need do is to take minute of meetings and be in charge of all correspondence. Again, they are more financially prudent than men'; 'Due to their nature women cannot take positions like the presidency, so it is better for them to act as an assistant'; and, 'As stated earlier, women are tools to support men and with this position they can assist the men if the need arises or in absence of the men they can deputize'.

When male students were asked whether they would vote a female as leader, eight students in Lokoja said no. Joshua was one of them and he reinforced his earlier position that women cannot be head Biblically. Zubairu said, 'This is because women can easily be influenced by the management. Women are meant to help male and not be leader'. Mejabi argued, 'She would always be controlled by her spouse and so decisions will not be completely on her own'. Daniska said, 'I wouldn't vote for a female student, the reason is that if given a chance and she probably wins the election, men are in trouble; they would whip the arse of every man and oppress men and their fellow women'. Positions were pretty hard in Lokoja where more female students had contested elections than in Ibadan. To the same question, all the students in Ibadan said yes, apparently consistent with their earlier response that female students should contest students' union/departmental association elections. All the students who said women should contest for any position in Lokoja also said they would vote for female candidates. The reasons they gave were that: 'gender discrimination should be discouraged, women are more responsive and attentive to issues than their male counterpart' – Gafar; Ayodele avowed that 'even in the class, some ladies do better than their male counterparts. Because research has shown that women make good managers as they can be meticulous', and added 'When God said women should submit, He did not say that they should not aspire. Everybody has a right to become anything'; and, Daniel said:

> I doubt if there is any constitution that limits the leadership aspirations of women be it union/association or even the government circle. Therefore all positions are opened to anybody, anywhere in the world as far as I am concerned.

Male respondents were asked to indicate whether they had ever encouraged female members of groups to which they belonged either to contest elections, and/or supported them during elections. Most of the men in formal work said they had encouraged and/or supported female candidates during elections. One of those who said he had never encouraged or supported female candidates, Zaki, who belonged to a Church group said, 'by doctrine of my church, women are only ordained as deaconesses, they cannot go further'. When those who had encouraged women to contest elections were asked the reasons they did so,

Abayomi, consistent with his position, said: 'This is because there are posts that trustworthy, honest and sincere persons should occupy, and women qualify for such positions'. Fola, the man who appeared to be resisting the women's movement, said: 'There was a post for which the most preferred person was a woman and it would be retrogressive not to encourage the woman'. Somewhat consistent with his earlier position, Haliru said, 'I believe they can manage the resources of our club more than men, that is why I encouraged one to be our treasurer'. Audu, also consistent with his position of not supporting a female for the highest office said, 'I have always encouraged women to be elected as either treasurer or vice chairman of executive committees'.

Only seven male students from both Ibadan and Lokoja said they had never encouraged female students to contest elections or supported female students during elections. One man said he was actually not politically active, while another said he had not had the opportunity to do so. Zubairu, who was the auditor general of a departmental association said: 'This is because women are not good in keeping secret. Women are too tender for holding executive position'. Remember, Zubairu had said he would not vote for a female leader because they can be influenced by management and that women are supposed to help men and not lead. In Lokoja, Chris, who was the director of finance of his departmental association, said he had never encouraged a female to contest because 'man is more competent in the area of agility, and they are also bold'. He had also earlier said he would not vote for a female leader because it involved rigorous exercise which could be too strenuous for women.

One wanted to know why those who had encouraged women did so, and took particular interest in those who said they would not vote for women as overall leaders, but had encouraged/supported women. Joshua, a Catholic, who had indicated that it was not Biblical that women should lead even though he conceded they could aspire to be vice presidents, and, who would not vote for a female as leader said, 'The fact is that women should take part in the call of leadership'. I think what Joshua objects to is women being the overall head. Mejabi, who is also Christian, who would like women to aspire to any position apart from president, and who would not vote for a female leader because she would always be controlled by her spouse, said: 'They have some good inputs to make and sometimes could be very sincere in their contributions'. Dauda, who thinks women should aspire to be treasurer of the union because they are light-hearted in respect of stealing and corruption, and who would not vote for a female leader because 'it would amount to waste of vote, as I do not believe that women have the driving spirit to lead a union like men do. They may not be able to face harassment from members of the association'. He said he encouraged a woman to contest, 'because I do not believe that women should be kept out in the executive committee of the union'. It appears Dauda is also concerned that women should not take on the overall leadership of the group.

Daniska, who had earlier indicated that he would not vote for a female as leader because if she won, men would be in trouble, and who had also said his association, the National Association of Kogi State Students did not have female members, said: 'I once encouraged a woman and my reason is because we discovered that the association is financially backward and I for one suggested that with a woman in our midst we can use them to source funds from our Kogites rich men'. It is strange that Daniska said they did not have female members. In Ibadan, Odedele who had favoured women to occupy the position of vice president and treasurer was coincidentally, at the time this data was collected, the President of the University of Ibadan branch of the National Association of Kogi State Students, and he had indicated that two of their female members held the positions of Vice President and Treasurer. We recall that Lokoja is the capital of Kogi State, and so Daniska who said they did not have female members is talking about the same association, that had a branch in Ibadan. Perhaps it was the Kogi State Polytechnic branch of the association that did not have female members, and this would also be strange. If this is indeed true, the reasons may not be far-fetched. Given his views about women, with males like Daniska in the association in Lokoja, female students in the institution who were indigenes of Kogi State would most probably give the association a wide berth. This may be one of the reasons that female students in Lokoja identified with, and had given the indications that they were committed to religious groups.

In Appendix I, we will find an overview of the assessment of women's potential for participating in politics (public life) and the assessment of their performance in public life, as stated by literate women, semi-literate women, and literate men.

Discussions

We note that although all male students in Lokoja conceded that women should contest elections, the majority thought women should aspire to positions other than the overall head. When asked whether they would vote for a woman as overall head, half the male students in Lokoja said no, they would not, while all the male students in Ibadan said they would. As we had earlier observed, it is interesting that positions are hardened among male students in Lokoja, where more female students had contested elections, than in Ibadan. Given the reasons that the students proffer, we are supposed to believe that women are incapable of handling positions of leadership, particularly overall leadership in the public sphere.

The picture is not so gloomy though. On aggregate, many men were positive that women should, and could, take up leadership positions, including the topmost jobs; and only a few women said no, women should not take up leadership in the public sphere. The men and women who said no appear few, but influential, given that women are still few in political offices. Another way to view the seeming low resistance to women's participation in public life is to say that the big yes to women's participation in politics is a recent decision to say yes to women, and so we can sit back and relax and assume that women will contest elections, and that when they contest, men, in particular, will not get in their way with determination (Longwe 2000; Ibrahim and Salihu 2004).

It appears better that one takes the decision to be cautious, and this includes the decision not to underrate the determination of those women and men who said no to women's participation in the public sphere, and so take them seriously. The reasons they are saying no are the reasons we have to take them seriously. The reasons/arguments – that: they are more suited to handling certain positions; they can't cope in certain positions; their children/family will suffer; they are not mentally and emotionally stable; they will not be taken seriously; they will be wicked; it is against the will of God; and religion forbids it – all suggest that either women should look on while men take charge of public affairs because men are more suited to govern, or born to govern, or that women should play the subordinate roles that men assign to them in the public sphere. While it is clear that men put forward and proffer self-serving reasons and arguments, the reasons women give often border on fatalism.

The position of some literate men and very few literate women on the involvement of women in civic-political affairs, therefore, shows that their views are tied to the 'nature' of women; the 'femininity' of women; religion; the structure of power and 'natural' structure of duties and responsibilities in the private sphere; the type of political office that is sought by women; an uncritical sense and account of the African culture; and the feminization and masculinization of certain foci of power and office. These, no doubt, stem from how men, and, to a lesser extent women from the above data, perceive women. It is a reflection of their understanding of who women are, and what women ought to believe in; not necessarily what women believe in.

Although our data show that, in the main, women (and many men) affirmed women by expressing confidence that women have the potential to handle public affairs well, like some women are currently doing, we also cannot ignore the fact that many women, especially among literate women (and a few men), said they would vote for women as overall heads with provisos, that is, if the women fulfilled some requirements. Clearly, women are correct to demand that women who they vote into positions of responsibility meet certain standards, for we do not want to vote in women who will mess up the reputation of women, given that we desperately need to show other women and all men that they can trust us with those positions. However, knowing as we do that most of the women who said they would vote for women if they fulfilled certain requirements voted during the 2003 General/Local Government elections, one has been wondering whether they made the same demands of the men that they voted for one and a half years before they were asked these questions. We have raised this because we want to be sure that the demand that women meet certain standards is not a mask to conceal resistance to women taking up positions of responsibility. As earlier observed, most of the yes with provisos came from literate women, both workers and students.

We know that persons who are literate like to convince themselves that they take decisions from a rational and objective point of view, even if we fail to acknowledge that normative ideologies that prevail in our contexts affect our rationality and objectivity (Clark and Wilson 1991).

One of the reasons/arguments put forth by those who would neither support nor vote for women as overall leader is that which supposedly takes its root from religion. Semi-literate female respondents and highly literate male respondents cited God, their religion and the Bible as part of the reasons they would or would not vote for female leaders. We therefore decided to ask female and male religious leaders to tell us what the will of God is, in respect of the participation of women in politics. Specifically, we asked that they speak to the position of their religions on women's participation in politics, and tell us what they preach to their followers about women and politics.

The matter of religion also had to be taken seriously because, in this study, respondents made a lot of references to religion, God, the scriptures; and so, we thought we should check how seriously they took their religions, and determine the amount of religiosity that respondents displayed. We therefore took, per category, the percentages of respondents that made references to religion. There were two items in each of the open-ended questionnaires that were administered that required that respondents speak to religion, so those two items were not reckoned along with other items in the questionnaire. We found that: thirty-two literate women (68.1%) in formal work made references to religion, and half of this percentage referred to religion more than twice. Thirty-two female students (69.6%); 91.1 per cent of semi-literate women in the informal economy; 39.5 per cent of female apprentices; 31.03 per cent of literate men in formal work; and 37.5 per cent of male students, made obvious references to religion. References to religion were high among literate women (workers and students) and semi-literate women, but more so among semi-literate men.

Religious Leaders on Women's Civic-Political Leadership

Islam

Male Muslim Leaders (MM) – Lokoja

OM: What is the position of Islam on women's civic-political participation?

MM: Women are given political positions in their own right and in accordance with what the Qur'an and the Suna of the Prophet have prescribed.

OM: Do you encourage women to contest elections? What do you preach to and teach your followership about women's political participation?

MM: What Islam says is very simple. Give them what is due to them in accordance to what Allah has prescribed. A woman can become a leader among her womenfolk. A woman will be the spokeswoman, the leader who will be the connecting point between the other stream and this stream, because women are supposed to be brought into direct enlightenment, because the Prophet said seeking knowledge is compulsory for both men and women, so you don't relegate them. But the situation as the West has it today, although not diabolical as such, but an affront to human arrangement as divinely put in place by Almighty Allah. Because women know who they are, you can see, if Islam has outrightly said women should become leaders, today, like we have in some churches prophetesses, pastors and so on, but we have never heard of a woman Imam for obvious reasons (laughs). Is that okay, because the Prophet has told us the position Allah has put women – they are feminine in nature, they are weak, and we should relieve them of the burden of that leadership.

Prayer is not a play thing it is something of concentration, it is something spiritual and it is something of commitment. Where a woman is leading and the child is crying wen wen, and she is running to give breast to the child, how about that? Again, a woman is just standing Alahu Akbar!!! Before you know it, the menstruation just blow up gbam, she is gone. Again the femininity, the fragility of a woman, tender heart/mind does not build her up to withstand the rigour and shock which go along with the present chaotic leadership system. You see, the government should as a matter of fact ask these women to do what they are supposed to do in their rightful places. You know, if you look at education, for instance, and you look at women in the teaching profession, they almost take a lead because they act as mothers, they nurture, they tutor, they have the feeling of mothers, the tenderness. But I as a man will just shout at them, you know that type of thing. Then, medically, when you see the female nurses, they are more tenderly, more caring just because of the nature in which Allah has built them.

OM: Would you support a woman who wants to run for the chairmanship of a Local Government?

MM: Well, as far as I am concerned, going by divine injunction, I will not, because Allah who created her has already assigned her a job which befits her, which is good for her, and is more comfortable for her. For me to ask her to go and do anything outside that, I must be doing a wrong thing.

We are not ruling out the fact that some countries have women leaders like we have today – Megawati, she is having problems there…

OM: The woman in Pakistan

MM: Benazir Bhutto, the former Prime Minister. When you come back to Nigeria, we have Queen Amina of Zaria. She was an undaunted leader, but again, in spite of her prowess she had limitations. Of course, she cannot command and fight wars; rather, she put in place commanders.

OM: So she never went to war?

MM: She never did. She was only directing people to go to war because she never participated physically in war, given that she was a woman. Yes, we may be told, going by modern times, that it is an oppression for us not to allow women to become leaders; yes, but Islam has very much put in place so that nothing disturbs the woman, nothing terrifies her, and nothing makes the woman suffer because of her numerous tenderly job.

OM: What about voting, should women vote in elections?

MM: Yes, they can vote

OM: If they cannot contest elections, why would you encourage them to vote?

MM: Good leadership. A woman can be voted to represent women because in the society women are supposed to be represented; their suggestions, their voices are supposed to be heard, so they can be voted in that context. That is the context of the representation of the womenfolk, not representing men.

OM: What if we write it into our constitution that 30 per cent of the state legislators should be women, what would be your reaction? The logic of what you have said is that women should vote for women. So, perhaps women should vote for women, so women can go and legislate on all matters in the Assembly.

MM: Madam, when we talk of leadership, there are categories of leadership. You know we can have head of state, governors of states and local government chairmen. In these areas, women cannot come in, but they can go to the House of Assembly. That is representation, and you know why? Because they are not meant to represent men and women together, although women are more knowledgeable about a few things that concern them.

OM: If they go to the House of Assembly, why can't they be governors?

MM: You see there is an explanation for that. The process of legislation involves sitting and making contributions, and we put the contributions together and have a leeway out. But the governors, the whole legislature, the judiciary, the destitute, the criminals are all on his head; he is not in peace. It's too taxing.

OM: Are you saying it is too taxing for the woman or there is something underneath this, something about women not being exactly equal to men...

MM: No, No, No.

OM: ... so they should not come and boss us because God has destined us to be leaders over women and not women lording it over us.

MM: No, No, No. What you should understand here is that men and women are equal in the sight of God. The only problem is where it involves a husband and his wife. The man has an edge over her. The edge of maintenance because that is what God said. The responsibility is never assigned to the woman, it is always to the man. Secondly, in the area of spiritual development, men are supposed to be leaders. In the Mosque, we have never gotten a woman Imam.

OM: Because you don't want one.

MM: No, it is not allowed, since it is a divine injunction, and we cannot go against Allah's injunction.

OM: Show me in the Qur'an.

MM: Alahu Akbar!!!

MM: That what?

OM: That women cannot be Imams.

MM: The Prophet said it in the Hadith and he said it clearly, he said they can only lead women in prayer. If women are gathered together and one of them is learned, she can lead others in prayers, she can't lead men because of the nature of women. Women stay behind in prayers, they should not be mixed up with men. If I am standing and a woman is leading us in prayer, even if she is covered, we are weaker in lustfulness than women. The moment a woman stands before men even in ten minutes... It is the femininity of women; in fact their structure is enough to destabilize a man when she is leading a prayer. Then women are unclean during menstruation.

Female Muslim Leaders (FM) – Lokoja

FM: During the last general elections, FOMWAN participated actively as monitors because we believe in good governance. FOMWAN was like an umpire at polling stations, the chief judge, especially on procedures for voting; validity of some votes – to count or nullify. We made sure the polling booths were orderly, and no thugs were allowed to mess up at any of the polling stations. You know, the way people present themselves in most cases will determine how much control they can exercise over others. The Grand Khadi has also given a lecture on the role of Muslim women in politics. Because you see, he who wears the shoe knows where it pinches. If women don't participate in politics, how would they be given positions at decision-making levels?

In as much as I encourage women to participate in politics, I will not encourage women that are just coming up to go into politics. Women who have finished bearing children, those whose children have graduated from school and are alone, with the understanding and permission of your husband, you can go for elective position. The responsibility of rushing home to go and cook for the children will no longer be there. We encourage you to resolve with your husband before going into politics. Don't be confrontational with your husband. The support of the husband must be there for you to succeed.

Islam does not say women should not participate in politics; it is not stated anywhere in the Qur'an. I know that for leadership positions in Islam, like being an Imam, I will not support a woman to be an Imam. To be an Imam, you have to be fully clean to lead the congregation because during your menstruation you cannot enter the Mosque.

OM: What about when a woman has reached menopause?

FM: No please. You can lead a congregation of women. That is the rule and we all understand it. Even in the Christian faith, even though you have female pastors or reverends, it is an imposition.

OM: But there can't be uniform attitudes to these issues. Some women would say, for example, that they would rather vote and let men deal with real politics – the decision-making processes.

FM: Well, that is why we are not moving. We need to continue to sensitize and create awareness in them that women should participate at decision-making level, lest their views will not be heard. If women are not there at the decision-making levels, men will push aside their concerns. Look at what is happening to the Child's Rights Act now. It has been debates upon debates. If children were there, they could have insisted that this is our own issue, we want it heard. That is why we are saying women should participate at decision-making levels, so they can present their concerns adequately.

Female Muslim Leader (FM) – Ibadan

FM: There were examples of women in the time of Prophet Mohammed who were politicians. Some were leaders of market women who were consulted when the need arose. But here, a lot of things are intertwined with our culture. For example, why do people have to travel overnight because they want to campaign? I mean, no husband, whether Muslim or otherwise, would allow the wife leave home four or five days in the dead of the night because she wants to go and campaign. If things are done the way they should be done, if when we vote the results are fair and people who voted are convinced that the results are as expected... after all, in the US, Great Britain, the opinion polls would have projected results. And you know, to a very large extent, as women, women want to be honest. That is why some men, and even women, don't like to work with female bosses; for they say women are too strict – you want to do things the way they should be done. If things are done the way they should be, a lot of women will step out and vie for elective positions.

More importantly, the men who are at the helm of affairs today are some people's children. If they had been properly brought up to be honest, dedicated, loving, they will not behave the way they are behaving now, and things will work out the way they should.

Islam prefers that if women are going into politics, they should not be women of childbearing age. You cannot leave your children unattended and go out to campaign. FOMWAN members have had the luck of holding public offices in politics, and I am happy to say they did not let us down. And again, most of them are not of childbearing age. Their children have grown up, so they have time for the nation. Those who have lost their husbands, for example, whose children are grown up and scattered all over can, since they cannot be left to rot at home, they have to do something.

OM: What about female Imams?

FM: There should be no female Imams. If you observe, women pray behind men. There is the Islamic code for dressing for women. It is in the Qur'an that the entire body of a woman is naked, so anything that you will do to attract the other person out of the way of worshipping God should be avoided. Inside the Qur'an, women are asked to lower their voices more than those of men, because the gift of the Almighty Allah makes women have sonorous voices such that men can get carried away if a woman leads prayers. That is why a woman cannot go in front. Again, when a woman is undergoing the monthly period, she cannot go and pray until the end of the menstruation. If you are an Imam and have a period for five days, who will lead the congregation? God has stated the jobs that are to be done by each sex.

OM: The talk about women being attractive, their voices attracting and distracting men gives one the impression that it is taken for granted that men are not disciplined and that they lack self-control.

FM: I don't think it is because they are not disciplined. If it is because they are not disciplined, it would not have been said by the Almighty Allah because He created us, He knows what gifts he has given everybody. He knows if there is no attraction between the opposite sex, the question of love and marriage will not come in. It is the way he has created them. If they want to discipline themselves, there is a limit, the limit of elasticity. After that, the thing will break. Once the human aspect sets in, they get lost. So, to a very reasonable extent, we shouldn't harass them with whatever God has given us. Like you get to some public places, like a bus, you see a girl or a lady with mini-skirt or hot pants. She sits and suddenly begins to pull her skirt or dress down. She pulls a cloth that is not elastic. In some cases, you will see the colour of the pants they have on through their clothing. The level of discipline also varies in men. There are some that can hold themselves longer, but for others, immediately they see it they start shaking, and all sorts of things come into their heads. Along the streets you see these youngsters, when they see such girls, they start slapping them at the back, push them, draw them; they wouldn't do it to anybody who is decently dressed, and that is the difference.

Christianity

Male Christian Leaders (MC) – Lokoja

MC: Culture has been the problem from time immemorial. Women had been unfortunate to be maltreated in all ways and it is just maybe civilization that is now emancipating them. It is an inexhaustible action though, it will continue, it's an evolution and there is nobody that can stop it. I don't even think it can be slowed down; rather, it will continue to gain momentum. But then you see, the bulk of the whole thing now rests with the women. Unfortunately, women are used to attacking themselves and they find it difficult to come together and, because of that ... maybe it's a natural tendency, men always exploit that and we are able to sort of divide and rule. If women can learn to respect one another to the extent that they can come together irrespective of whatever level they are in the society, then it will be a beautiful thing because then the evolution will be faster and more concrete. When you look at women in politics now, and you look at the number of women in politics maybe some years ago, you don't find a lot of activists now, if I'm right. When they showed Mrs Margaret Epko on TV the other day, you know, the woman was still breathing fire and you have very few of them now. Who would you say is like Mrs Ransome Kuti now?

     They have been given more position in Government now...

OM: Or have more education now...

MC: Yes they have more education, but when you look at individuals, who are in government, are they activists? Are they? What do they stand for? So we need to, one way or the other, encourage them to come out of their shell. We need to let them know that the fact that you have education does not automatically confer on you the ability to convince the male that, listen, don't give dole outs to us. We can fend for ourselves to the extent that you will have to reckon with us. Instead of saying that, alright ministerial post, let us give them 5 per cent, or 30 per cent; they have not worked for it, but you just give them. Whereas if they have the attributes, people will respect them; and respect is very very important in politics, especially in this country. If we want to move forward in a democratic dispensation, we should encourage women activists positively so that we can have a continuation, not a situation where you have, unfortunately, women being afraid to come out and so they would rather hide and accept positions that are given to them, instead of mobilizing properly.

On the other hand, it might be that the men just know how to squeeze them up and silence them because now that money is the root of all intrigues in politics, if you don't have money you just say well, let me ally myself and make some money. Whereas in those days, the women never thought of money in the sense of leverage. No. They believed in something, they say it, and then mobilized people of like mind and get them to gently do something. But now, we count so much on money, as against principles. We don't fight for principles, we don't look at issues anymore, and that is dangerous even for democracy. And I hope and pray, you know that women who will stand up for principles will come out, irrespective of the money they are going to get.

My sister was very active in the North until her death. She was at one time the General Secretary of NEPU Women's wing when Gambo Sawaba was the President. And I kept asking the children... no one is inheriting their mother's activism. They say when we do that now, we won't get money and we will starve, which is the truth but it is because of misplaced priority, the thinking that money is everything.

OM: I think the Anglican Church in Kogi State has a female priest ...

MC: No we don't. What happened was, before the Diocese of Lokoja was inaugurated in 1994, this area was part of the Diocese of Kwara and the Bishop at that time ordained three women as priests. Among the three, two happen to come from here, and the third from Ilorin. At the time the Bishop made the dedication, the Church of Nigeria had not given authority for Bishops to ordain women. Although Bishops are autonomous within their diocese, when it comes to issues of this nature, Lambert Conference says each Church should go back home and decide what they want to do.

Up at Lambert, there is nothing wrong with ordaining women or making them priests, but you cannot just do it, go back to your Church because it is a very sensitive thing. The Church of Nigeria sat and they said it was too early. They were not against it, but they were looking at the division it has caused in the United States, in UK, in Australia. It is too early for us to introduce it, especially where our culture is even deeper in terms of man/woman relationship, worse than in the liberal cultures where the ordinations were already causing divisions. The Church then decided that we should take our time. The Bishop in Kwara then decided to emphasize the rights of the Bishop in his territory, given that the Bishop has considerable power in his diocese. Except that on this issue, a general consensus had been reached, and irrespective of what the individual thought, once a consensus had been reached, and the decision taken at the Episcopal level, that is the House of Bishops, all bishops of the Church of Nigeria will abide by the decision of the majority. Because if you don't, according to the law, you can be sanctioned by 75 per cent of the bishops. Even the primate, if the primate decides to do anything that is wrong, we just need four bishops to summon an Episcopal meeting ...

Female Christain Leaders (FC) – Lokoja

FC: As much as I would want our men to consider women, you know men generally... We encourage women to vote, and you know, women are more than men. You can even say it is because of our votes that they win. And then when it comes to positions, some will say women's position is in the kitchen. I am of the opinion, even as a clergy, that women be given more political appointments than we have presently, so that we would demonstrate our integrity, our ability. If women are in positions, because they are frank and they work hard, they would also want results. They would prefer that things are done the way they should be done. I believe women will not condone theft, corruption and laziness. Women are thorough. In the ministries, where you have women, they perform well except when men get in the way and frustrate you, especially when they want to spend money as they like.

I am of the opinion that we should still make effort, and insist that women should be put in positions of authority, and we will not fail them. Now we are even learning about how to better the lives of the majority, especially the poor people. The money in the country is presently circulating among those who are rich. If they put more women, the women can in turn pull up more women. But some men say that women are so strict, and that women may not want to work with other women. I have heard men saying that.

OM: I think they use that to divide us. They use that to set us against one another.

FC: After all, men who occupy positions of power, the ones at the top, do have clashes, much more than women.

OM: Do you preach against women who vie for political offices?

FC: No. In the Bible, a man was supposed to go to war, he felt lazy and Deborah said let us go, and they won the war. She led the war. It's in the book of Judges. Also, Esther too, delivered her people.

OM: You have said women should be submissive in their private lives and you have also said women will perform well if allowed to function in public life. Is there no problem with this? Some will say if you're going to be submissive, you're not going to be able to take part in public life.

FC: Thank you very much. Let me clear that area. In the family, a woman has to be submissive to her husband. But a woman is not competing with her husband when she wants to get into political positions; she is competing with other men.

OM: What if a husband objects to the wife's political aspirations? We are not talking about reaching the top position in a career or in the work place.

FC: I think only a few men will object to their wives being at the top. We have female commissioners whose husbands are in the civil service, and the husbands are not even of the rank of a director in the service. Yet, they are happy because at the end of the day their wives will bring 'brown envelope'. I mean the ones that they have worked for, not the ones they lobby and do all kinds of things to get. We cannot rule out the fact that some men may object. Look at the churches. I am a pastor in my church. In some churches, you don't have women as pastors or evangelists because of the oppression of women. But like the founder of my church would say, in heaven there will be no difference between man and woman. I am the district coordinator of my church. I have about eighteen or nineteen male pastors in my district. There are just five women clergy, and I am the head of all as the district coordinator. We can have a few cases where men would say I don't want my woman to participate, but what about what they, the men do? At any rate, a responsible woman will not mess herself up as a politician.

Submission to husband is about total respect for husband. Seek his advice. This is not to say that the husband will not seek advice from the wife. You know some men are dictators; they do not seek the opinions of their wives. That is not what the Bible is saying here. A woman should respect and honour her husband. You see, if the husband loves the wife, everything will be okay. He will not do anything that will harm the wife. When a man loves his wife, you can be sure that there is nothing that he demands from the wife that he will not get.

Female Christian Leader and Academic (Prof. W) - Ibadan

Professor W does not see any basic contradiction between her beliefs as a christian and the theory of evolution, for instance. As a matter of fact, she said she uses the history of palaebotanical studies to teach scientific ethics as there are lessons about humility, flexibility, dialectical thinking, honesty and hard work, amongst others, that can be drawn from this history. Alongside other women, she is leading the campaign for the ordination of female priests by the Anglican Church in Nigeria. She believes that practitioners of any religion who condone oppression of, and discrimination against particular groups are acting contrary to the spirit of their religion. She believes that there is much wisdom to be gained from Ifa, the traditional Yoruba god of knowledge. She reiterated the fact that Yoruba traditional religions did not just have priestesses; they had goddesses who were, like the male gods, intermediaries between the almighty One and the people. She uses this to question the view among those opposed to the ordination of female priests on the grounds that women cannot represent God to the people because God is male. Furthermore, some in the Church of Nigeria who oppose the ordination of women give as one of their reasons the fact that such a step is against 'our culture'. She then asks: which culture are they referring to - the culture of Nigerians or the Jewish culture, which is represented in the Old Testament? Her own response to them is that Jesus is beyond culture.

I was fortunate to be in the church where I usually worship during the 2005 celebration of Mother's Day, because Professor W. delivered the message. I quickly converted my church attendance, in part, to an observation of the interaction of the religious leader with adherents. She spoke on the theme: 'An Exemplary Mother'. She based her message on the advice of the queen mother (who was not named) to her son, Lemuel, found in Proverbs 31: 3-9. She dealt with the character of the queen mother, from whom she wanted women to take a cue. She was extremely forthright about how some mothers (and fathers), and some women have colluded with men in their corrupt practices in: institutions of learning, government circles, public places and politics. She enjoined women to speak up for the voiceless and the oppressed, and she gave examples of how, at the level of interpersonal relationship, we all get to oppress one another. She then connected this with the question of the ordination of women in the Church of Nigeria (Anglican Communion) which she regarded as discriminatory and oppressive. There were uneasy shifts on the long benches when she said that. When she was through, her audience applauded her loud and clear and she responded: 'To God Be the Glory'. Her response is significant, because although she is part of the campaign to get women ordained as priests, she also has put up a personal resistance that gives her psychological freedom. She said she tells herself, and also tells people, that God has ordained her as priest, it is now left to the Church to acknowledge this publicly through the rite of public ordination.

A Yoruba Traditional Religion – The Worship of Sango

A Female Traditional Religious Leader (FT) - Ibadan

In attendance at the interview was a male ruler (MR), who is considered the custodian of all traditions (including religion) in his domain in a section of Ibadan.

OM: What is Sango?

FT: Among all the gods (Oosa), Sango is powerful. Sango does all things. Sango does magic (*idan*), and fire comes from his mouth. At times, he helps worshippers to fill a basket with water and it won't leak. Sango controls the thunder (*ara*). Sango is helpful in several ways. Look, even persons overseas acknowledge the importance of Sango. Sango provides children, Sango heals and Sango provides relief from problematic situations. Barren women ask for children from Sango and he gives them children.[11] When people come to ask Sango about lost items, it doesn't take Sango much time to expose the perpetrator. The clouds will gather and thunderstorm will strike the thief. When Sango strikes with thunder, he doesn't like people weeping and wailing. He would rather they sing his praise. He is Alapadupe, meaning he kills and expects gratitude.

OM: Sango appears rather difficult.

FT: Yes of course he is, but he is also good, as he takes care of people. The Almighty God gave him authority among several gods. The point with Sango is that he dislikes cheating and abhors injustice (*ireje*). He kills thieves. In one instance, some men kidnapped a child. They were arrested by the police, but they kept denying that they kidnapped the child. We then went to the police station, and told the policemen that Sango will seek out the kidnappers. We called on Sango and thunderstorm came down, pulled one of the men from the police station and dumped him outside. When the same thing happened to the second man, the third man quickly confessed that he actually stole the child and handed the child over to Sango's first casuality, and that the child is still alive.

OM: What is Sango's position on women's participation in politics?

FT: Women can participate in politics. The reason is that women possess enormous powers. Their powers are comparable to that of witches. There is nothing a woman cannot do. Today, if a woman is barren and other women decide she has to be pregnant, she will become pregnant. If witches bar a woman from giving birth to a child that is due and women bring the pregnant woman to Sango, the witches will take flight, and the woman will be delivered of the baby safely.

OM: Are you saying that Sango does not consider that women are inferior to men? You know in the new religions – Christianity and Islam – they say God said women should not partake in politics, that men should be the ones to lead, take care of political matters.

FT: No! No! (*Oti ooo!*). Women are more powerful than men in all respects. If a man misbehaves or exceeds limits, a woman can seize his manhood, and if he pleads with the woman, the manhood can be returned. You don't mess up with a woman. If you do, you run into problems.

MR: As a matter of fact, *Ifa man so, o ni obinrin ni iya aiye to bi aiye. Obinrin ni iya orun to bi orun. Ta ni yio so pe ti obinrin bawo?* (Ifa, the Yoruba god of knowledge says women are the mothers of the earth, they gave birth to the earth, and they are mothers of heaven, they gave birth to heaven, who then dare questions the relevance of a woman?)

OM: If a woman approaches you for help in respect of her participation in politics, would you help her?

FT: It is Sango that will help her. But Sango will not support a dishonest person. The first step is that with the aid of bitter *Kola*, we will ask about the woman's character from Sango. If the woman is bad, Sango will alert us, and we will tell her to go to her house, and that she cannot have Sango's support.

OM: I imagine that, given the way the ones who govern us behave, many of the people who are our leaders will not dare move near Sango

FT: No. No. They don't come to Sango. They go to the white garment churches and the imams. Sango will not tolerate dishonesty. When things then get rough for them, they say it is the way God wants it. Our leaders should be made to swear by Sango when they are taking the oath of office. They swear by the Holy Books of the new religions and they know nothing will happen to them when they misbehave, and nothing happens. Let them swear by Sango and they will behave better.

OM: Are there many female Sango priestesses, supporters and worshippers?

FT: Women are the majority.

OM: Now I imagine that, given your position, men don't attempt to be rude to you, and in your work as Sango priestess, no man challenges you. But do you get the feelings that the male Sango priests and the male supporters try to put on airs of superiority over other women?

FT: No, they don't do that.

OM: What is the relationship between Sango worshippers and the adherents of other religions? Do the adherents of other religions consult Sango?

FT: I have been to Jerusalem and to Mecca. Actually, if you look at Christianity
       and Islam, some of the angels are Sango. Sango worshipping is not restricted
       to Yorubaland alone…[12]

Given the position of religious leaders on women's civic-political participation;
and the references that respondents made to religion, we thought there was a
need to find out the kinds of influences that affect and shape respondents and
their understanding of women's participation in politics. We asked respondents
to indicate the religious, ethnic, political, social and cooperative thrift and credit
groups/associations to which they belonged. Most of the women in formal
work belonged to more than one group. Most indicated that they belonged to
cooperative thrift and credit associations and religious groups. All the female
students in Lokoja indicated that they partook in the activities of religious groups
and that they were dedicated to those activities. Only six of the students indicated
that they took part in other activities like departmental associations, sporting
and Rotaract Club activities. In Ibadan, most of the students also took part in
religious activities, but they combined religious activities with a wide range of
essentially non-religious activities, such as organizing (and ushering at) social
events, and participation in the activities of press clubs, ethnic associations,
sewing and decorating, sporting, departmental association and NGO activities.

      Like women in formal work, many women in the informal economy also
typically belonged to more than one group, and they cited their religious groups
often, followed by their trade guilds and ethnic associations. Most female
apprentices said they did not belong to groups, for reasons that we had earlier
alluded to. The few who belonged to groups were members of social clubs,
religious groups, cooperative thrift and credit societies and community youth
development associations.

      In conclusion, on participation in civic-political affairs, women appeared to
be attentive to religious leaders, such as the male and female Christian leaders in
Lokoja and the female traditional religious leader in Ibadan, for even when the
female respondents set standards for prospective female leaders, their standards were different from those that the religious leaders, whose positions were
apposite to the women's or ambivalent, had laid down. Some of the reasons the
male respondents who will not vote for women who desire to occupy the topmost
civic-leadership positions gave (children will suffer; it is not the will of God;
they are better at care giving; they are fragile, etc) are in tandem with the positions of the male Muslim leaders in Lokoja, and to a lesser extent, the positions
of the female Muslim leaders in Ibadan and Lokoja (who would not want women
of child-bearing age to contest elections), and the female Christian leader in
Ibadan, who would like women to influence things from behind, like the wife of
Pontius Pilate. We have to note that concerning leadership of the religious institutions, all male Christian, and all female and male Muslim leaders, were opposed
to women taking the topmost jobs in churches and mosques.

Notes

1. When I was trying to figure out how to characterize the participation of Nigerians in governance pre-1960, I sent a text message to Dr Abubakar Momoh, who is a political scientist. After five minutes, he replied my text message with 'constitutional despotism'. Now, now, I said to myself: 'Does Abu want me to write this down?' So I called him. His position was that there was limited participation in governance by Nigerians prior to the general elections in 1951. And that even then, the Governor General had the power to sanction decisions taken by the legislative councils, and this was the case even after independence. It was when Nigeria became a Republic in 1963, that she had full independence.

2. This is true. There were restrictions on movement, especially of vehicles, on election days.

3. PDP is the People's Democratic Party.

4. In the past, mainly due to voter apathy, some state governments threatened that citizens would be asked to produce their voters' cards if they wanted to access social services and government contracts.

5. Translates to: we bring bad governance on ourselves by voting for those people.

6. We should remember that Amina is an apprentice, and she could not leave the shop to go and vote because her madam had gone to vote. Amina may not also be able to vote throughout the day if, on her madam's arrival, they have customers that they have to attend to.

7. This translates to: because I am a good person and a long standing member of the association.

8. Dr Dora Akinyuli is the Director General (DG) of the National Directorate for Food and Drugs Administration and Control (NAFDAC). She has been visible as the DG of NAFDAC and, has been widely acknowledged as effective in leading an organization that was, until her leadership, unable to curtail the menace of fake drugs and unwholesome food in the economy.

9. Translates to: A woman will introduce wickedness into whatever she decides to do.

10. It is not good for a woman to contest elections.

11. E. B. Idowu (1962:89-95) raised doubts about the positive attributes that have been ascribed to Sango, a former Oyo king, whom he described as self-willed, cruel, tyrannical and passionately devoted to carnage. Idowu indicated that somehow, Sango became associated with 'the wrath' of Olodumare – God. He pointed out that the high moral standards (which are prominent commandments in the Yoruba ethical system and) that are currently being associated with Sango originally belonged to Jakuta. He told us that Jakuta (the one who hurls stones or one who fights with stones) was actually the Yoruba way of conceptualizing 'the wrath' of Olodumare against all forms of wickedness. He then indicated that the sacred day of Jakuta is observed regularly by the priests of Sango, in connection with the worship of Sango.

12. G. Parrinder (1969:30-33) made references to the presence of storm and thunder gods in a number of West African countries.

3

The Subordinate Role of Women in the Private and Public Spheres

Given the observations in Chapter Two, one can infer that the determination of men to exclude women from politics, that Longwe (2000), and Ibrahim and Salihu (2004) had observed, is traceable to what most men (and women) assume to be the roles of women in the public and private spheres of life, opinions which they derive from their own understanding of women's nature, from their upbringing, and from religious injunctions. We recollect that Denzer, cited in Mama (1996), had observed that, 'Nigerian and British attitudes concerning female roles had much in common' (p. 14). The point that Denzer made was that colonialism, with its patriarchal nature, met unequal relations of power among men and women in Nigeria that it then worked with, and that fed into it.

The British colonialists brought their own conception of human nature and women's nature, which had roots in theories of 'human nature' and 'women's nature', particularly 17th century patriarchalism, to Nigeria. There were obviously other influences on the colonialists from within Britain and other European countries, especially the ideas of philosophers such as Plato, John Locke and Hegel (Fashina 1998). Fashina indicated that patriarchalists justified the domination of women by men through reference to a theory of human nature derived from the scriptures. John Locke, in spite of his view that human beings were born 'free' and 'equal', still took the position that the subjugation of wives to husbands had a ground in human nature. Hegel was of the view that if the state were to be ruled by women, it would be placed in jeopardy because women were guides, not by universality and reason, but by feelings and lack of abstract reason; that women were good wives, but not good public lawyers and judges. Fashina concluded that from essentialist premises, the philosophers drew conclusions validating views that women were, by nature, inferior to men. No doubt, this was the frame of reference for the British colonialists who took over our country, and who fused their attitudes with existing ones and also wrote their beliefs (which were essentially patriarchal and Christian) into laws.

Concerning the influence of Islam, although Islam was said to have been present in Hausaland in the northern part Nigeria before the jihad of Uthman Dan Fodio in 1804, Pereira observed that, 'the narrowing of women's roles to those connected with domestic life began as a consequence of the reinterpretation of Islam that followed the Shehu's jihad' (Perreira 2005:79). She noted that prior to the jihad, women in Hausaland were visible and active in the public sphere; and that although Uthman Dan Fodio's 'position was relatively liberal and supportive of women's education, his proponents interpreted Islam more narrowly than he did'. While making the case for women's education, Uthman Dan Fodio spoke to the subordination and maltreatment of women, and the need for women to know as much about business transactions and economic regulations as they did about religious rites. Fafunwa (1974) recorded Uthman Dan Fodio as having said:

> They treat their wives and daughters like household implements which are used until they are broken and then thrown on to the rubbish heap. Alas! How can they abandon their wives and daughters in the perpetual darkness of ignorance while they daily impart their knowledge to their students. This is nothing but error because they are instructing their students in this manner out of sheer egotism and hypocrisy (p. 56).

Fafunwa (1974) further recorded that Uthman Dan Fodio said:

> if anyone says that a woman is generally ignorant of these matters [for example matters relating to business transactions] my reply is that it is incumbent upon her to endeavour to know these [commercial regulations] as it is binding upon her to know about other matters pertaining to her religion like ablutions, fasting and praying (p. 56).

Forty-four years after the end of formal colonialism, with Christianity and Islam being omnipresent in the polity and competing for the souls and hearts of Nigerians, in the face of glaring economic changes that have affected many women and men, and also in the context of the existence of formal International Declarations of equality of all persons, of all races, gender, religion, etc, we asked female and male respondents, and religious leaders to talk about the roles of women, and what the roles of women ought to be, in the private and public spheres of life. Their responses are reproduced in the section that follows.

The Roles of Women in the Private Sphere

Literate women in formal work in Ibadan and Lokoja identified more than two roles for women in the private sphere of life. In the two locations, many women said the roles of women are: to be home makers (home managers/pillar of home/maintain peaceful homes); to care for and nurse children; care for the husband and, cook. Others are: to be partner to and complement husband;

support husband in all his life endeavours; assist and advise husband; be the husband's helpmate, and be role model for children. The other roles that women in Ibadan identified are: give moral support to husband; give spiritual support to the family; and, be role model in society. The additional roles that women in Lokoja identified in their words are: be a wife and mother; stay in the kitchen; bear children; be a breadwinner; be a teacher and disciplinarian; manage resources; mould God-fearing children; and, be seen and not heard. It is important to our discussion to look more closely at the exact responses of some of the women. Adetutu said, 'The roles are the same as that of the men – lead by example, cater and care for the home. I do not believe in gender discrimination'. Aanwo said, '...partner to the husband, mother to the children, co-breadwinner to the family'. Aanu said:

> Women are expected to be good home keepers, manage your home, children, even your husband properly so that the society can be better off than what we have now because the society is the reflection of the homes we have in this country.

While Ruth believed it is to 'be submissive and loving', Omolade said the role of women in the private sphere is

> supposed to be that of moulding God-fearing children who will grow as physically, socially and spiritually capable men and women, who can stand the test of time and also whose husbands will refer to as backbones in any successes they might attain.

Adedigba said: 'To cook, rear children, fetch water, keep the home clean and perform all kinds of dirty jobs at home. They are just to be seen, not to be heard and should also be breadwinning'. And Hauwa affirmed:

> In the homes, the men expect the women to do all the house chores and take care of the children and nothing more. But, as a woman, I feel she should do more than just that, by contributing to the welfare of the house.

Female students in Ibadan and Lokoja considered the following to be the roles of women in the private sphere of life, and I present them in the order in which they were frequently mentioned: care of home/family; care of children; care of husband and, cooking. Female students in Ibadan mentioned other allied roles that they thought women should attend to. They included: women should give moral support to their husbands by being their partners and mothers; women should be counsellors and role models to kids; they should be decent and transparent; teach children morals and fear of God; and, attend to the management of the home. The female students in Lokoja identified other roles too. Some said women should be submissive to their husbands. They also added roles like: entertain guests; wash; fetch firewood and water; and, advise the husband. We take some of the responses of the female students. Ademidun said: 'To accept the submissive role of the wife and perform the duties subsumed under it, i.e., cooking and taking care of the kids'. Toun submitted: 'A woman is expected to keep the home front. She is expected to be a mother to her husband and children; she is to be the soft yet strong figure in the home'. Folarin said: 'To be a good wife and a caring mother. Also, to take proper care of home and be submissive to her husband and give him due respect irrespective of her status'. Jumai said, '...the confidant and chief assistant of the breadwinner, the manager of the home'.

The roles that semi-literate women in the informal economy identified for women in the private sphere are: tidy the environment/home, clean, be neat; care for/feed the children and give moral and financial support and advice to husband and be of good behaviour. The care of children, support of husband and to care for and feed the family topped the list. Compared to women in Lokoja, more women in Ibadan emphasized care of husband. Oreoluwa's response was different from the responses of the other women: 'No difference between men and women in what to do, especially education of children and feeding the family'. Women in Lokoja identified other roles for women in the private sphere. They are: to cook; make sure the home is peaceful; be tolerant and friendly; wash clothes and respect husband and his family. Taibat said:

> The roles are many. Without a woman, a man can't do it alone. The men can only have sex with females but the bulk of the job is for the women. The woman takes care of the family, husband, look after the house. She supports the family, too, both morally and financially.

Riskat saw a woman's role in the private sphere thus: 'Take care of children, bath and feed them on time and watch their character, so they don't bring shame on us later, so that the children will not suffer the same fate as we are suffering'. As for Hassana:

> If you want to stay long in your husband's house, you will respect your husband and his family. Wake up early by about five or five-thirty. Prepare good breakfast and boil water for your husband's bath. When you know what your husband likes, do what he likes and obey him.

Morenike believed that 'to care for the home/family is the responsibility of a woman'. Nkechi said, 'Take care of the home. Woman work dey finish? Woman work no dey finish' (does a woman's work ever end? A woman's work is endless).

Agun said, 'Take care of the children, feed them irrespective of whether their father provides or not. Most especially girls, you have to keep advising them on how to live their lives'.

Female apprentices in Ibadan identified the following roles for women in the private sphere: be neat, tidy the house, see to the smooth running of the house; take care/control of the children; care for/support/encourage husband; cook; support the family; care for relations and be hardworking; and the unmarried should take care of their parents, and tidy the home. The female apprentices in Lokoja also identified care of the home, care of children, cooking and care of husband as the roles that women should play in the private domain. They added some other roles – women should plan with husband for care of home, bear children, be prayerful and, respect their husbands. Specifically, Otolorin said, 'the children's wellbeing should be a woman's priority and the house should be tidy'; while Tomiwa submitted, 'Take care of the children, tidy up the house and don't allow housemaid[1] to prepare food for your husband'. Iyanu said: 'Take care of the husband and the children and tidy up the home. The unmarried should take care of her parents and tidy up the house'. Inunkan urged women 'to take over after the man. They are supposed to control the children, cook for the children, shop, clean the house'; while Chinedu said, 'Women are more at advantage at home, take care of the home, give birth and plan with your husband on how to take care of the home'. Salamotu argued:

> If you want your husband to love you, make sure you're neat, not dirty. Take good care of the children, cook for him, so he won't take another wife. Welcome a husband well and wash his clothes.

Towoju said, 'Women who have children should take care of the children. Take care of the house; respect their husbands, cook for their husbands at the right time and they should not go home late'. And, Tinuola affirmed, 'Women should submit to their husbands. They should be responsible and women should take care of their children'.

In Ibadan and Lokoja, men who work in formal settings expect women to take charge of the private sphere, although they expressed this in different ways. In Ibadan, the men said: care for/see to the welfare of household/home; they are home-builders; take charge of domestic affairs and work for progress of family. The other roles that the men identified are: manage home/domestic economy; care for/be mothers to the children and mother to/adviser to husband and to love husband. The men in Lokoja said women should cook; they are housekeepers; give birth/procreate and bring up children as responsible citizens. While men in Ibadan couched women's roles in flattering language, although they said exactly what men in Lokoja said, the men in Lokoja did not mask the tasks. We recall that all the respondents in Ibadan had at least BA/BSc degrees and three possessed Masters degrees. In Ibadan, one man said women should play similar roles with men and in Lokoja two men said women should complement their husbands' effort/work hand-in-hand with men.

Many male students in Ibadan and Lokoja identified cooking, child-rearing, education/training of children and housekeeping/cleaning the home/care of the home as the roles that women should play in private. The other roles that both sets of students identified are: building a home together with the husband/ complementing the efforts of husband; and, assisting the husband in decision making at home. In Ibadan, a student said the woman is expected to be subordinate to the man at home, while a few said women should care for/support their husbands and manage the resources at home. One student in Lokoja said women should be there when needed; another said women should be helpmates to their husbands; and yet another grudgingly accepted that women are breadwinners. Mejabi said: 'They are home-builders, in some cases breadwinners, and their contributions to the growth of the society could sometimes be impressive'.

Summary and Discussions

Most of the female and male respondents in this study gave the traditional view of the expected roles of women in the private sphere of life – to bear children; care for the children and husband; care for the home and cook; and, manage the resources at home. A few thought women's roles should be that of being partners with men, or to complement men's roles. Two women, one each in formal work and the informal economy, were of the view that the roles of women are the same with those of men in the private sphere.

Among women in formal work and the informal economy, there were a few references to women as breadwinners or co–breadwinners, while there was just one grudging acknowledgement of women as breadwinners among male students.

Although subordination/submission to husband was not mentioned frequently by women in formal work and women in informal economy as a role that women are expected to play, it was implied in the responses that they gave. Hassana's response is a good example, and it highlights what many women strive to do.

The few surprises were the young women and men, that is, the female students, female apprentices and male students, most of whom were unmarried. Although submission to husband was not a typical response, a number of this group of respondents said women should be submissive to their husbands and, the expectations were strident, especially among female students.

The Roles of Women in the Public Sphere

Many women in formal work in Ibadan and Lokoja said women should: take their jobs seriously; be diligent dutiful, hardworking, responsible and obedient at work. Many said women should be dedicated to community development; impact positively on their communities; help the needy; and, encourage peace within their communities. They also said women should lead by good examples. Two women said women should be team players. One of them, Adetutu, had earlier indicated that women's roles at home should be the same as men's roles. The other roles that a few women in Ibadan identified are that: women should hold a job/pursue a career, which is the ultimate; care for and love all; be accountable to the electorate and listen; counsel the young ones; be more involved in governance and speak against law/legislation that is unfavourable to women. In Lokoja, some other roles that women identified are that: women should contribute their own quota to governance; interested women should participate in politics like men; women should contribute to spiritual development of society; assist in governance and support government in implementing programmes for women. Others said women should have endurance and speak boldly, no matter the circumstance. Here are examples of what the women said: Aanwo indicated that a woman should play her role 'as a taxpaying member of the community, a member of the community that could lead, mobilize and guide in all spheres – community, workplace and governance'. Omolade said of a woman's role in public:

> Expected to be a woman who will help to make the society better rather than add to its woes and evil. A woman dedicated to her job – who deserves the salary she earns and who is ready to affect others positively.

Adedigba cynically indicated women's roles in the public sphere as:

> an addendum to men and a peace-maker who is always seen as wise in communication in the community. She is to perform jobs that are not taxing but still profit making.

Esther opined that a woman's role in the public sphere should be that of 'a mother to the nation, a builder of the nation, a symbol of beauty, an example in honesty, faithfulness, hard work and in reliability to the men folk'. And Hauwa added:

> In the public place, women are always given the second position, it should not be so. Since we attend the same school, pay the same fees and do a lot of things that men do, we are expected to be given roles just like our male counterpart.

Female students in Ibadan identified the public roles of women as: to contribute own quota to the economy; be peace-makers and role models; love; possess team spirit; be dedicated, dutiful and diligent at work; vote; temper the raging dispositions of men; be fearless and, constructively critique government policies. Others are that women are to be transparent and accountable in governance; and, should be confident, not feel inferior. We take a few of the responses. Modupe averred: 'The role of a peace-maker, a builder, a temper [sic] of the raging dispositions of men, adviser (because they think more deeply than men) supporter and an inspirer'. Toun had this to say:

> In the community, a beneficial contributor. In her workplace, smart, attractive, i.e. both in words and appearance, the soft yet alluring edge in the company. In governance, a supporting future with hindsight.

Ajoke said: 'Not to be too prominent or authoritative. To take lower position like deputy and vice position', while Chigozie said women in the public sphere,

> should be able to project our image in their day-to-day activities. They should try to build the confidence in themselves that they can always handle any position in the society.

Damilola's position was that women's role in the public domain should be that of being 'career women, professionals, managers, politicians, role models'. Female students in Lokoja considered the roles of women in the public sphere as: to hold leadership positions at any level of governance; nation-builders; to vote and be candidates in elections; be vigilant to, and prevent bribery and corruption; be respectful and diligent at work; encourage good governance; support and implement programmes initiated by men; be involved in commerce; and, participate in politics. Specifically, Jumai said: 'Women are needed to support the motion[s] of men, and help in executing them'. It is worthy of note that this is consistent with her position about women's roles in the private sphere. Comfort said:

> to be involved in commercial activities, i.e., trading. To be involved in any development planning programme. To contribute meaningfully to the national wellbeing by participating in politics.

Medaiyese believed that 'women should participate in governance and should be ready to endure hardship there in. It is time for us to come out'. But Pelumi said: 'She should be respectful. She should be submissive', while Olaore argued:

> Women are great influencer[s], they mould and make a community, they provide encouragement in the workplace and make good governance.

The roles that women in the informal economy in the two locations identified as expected of women in the public sphere are: face their work/work hard; be at peace with others, be gentle, humble and care for all; women who occupy public offices should care for other women; and, women should participate in politics if they are interested, so they can move Nigeria forward. The other roles are that: women should care for and make the work environment neat; women should contribute positively wherever they are; and also, be good examples to their peers and persons who are younger than they are. Others said women should respect themselves; be modest in speech and dressing; be kind and honest; while Moji said, 'Women should support their husbands who are in power'. Other women, while stating the expected roles of women in the public domain, actually made demands on women who hold public offices that they should: give loan[s] to women for business; allow banned goods to be brought into the country; and, create jobs for the masses. Rukayat in Ibadan said women are expected to,

> take care of the work environment and be there on time so as not to lose customers. It's only men that have roles to play in the community. I don't poke my nose into the affairs of the community except I am called upon to do so. Women in governance should take care of us because we are the salt of life.

Taibat, also in Ibadan, said 'Women know what to do in governance, women can look after everybody because they are not callous like men. In the workplace, a woman should be gentle in nature to everybody. In the community, a woman should be hardworking and make some moves on how to move the community forward'. Bolaji said: '...co-discuss public issues, women should campaign, vote for people and contest elections'. Morenike in Lokoja believed women should 'perform the role of secretaries'. For Agun, 'Women should be able to advise women that are lazy, to get busy. They can help other women by providing sheds for them to display their wares and sell, so as to stop laziness'. Hassana said:

> Know how to relate with people, don't try to hurt anybody. Ask for forgiveness when you have done wrong. Care for others. Try to be nice. Not all women have the power to contest elections. If you know you can do it, go ahead. Women should vote and campaign for contestants.

The roles that female apprentices in Ibadan and Lokoja identified for and expect that women play in the public sphere are that: they should work hard and ensure that their workplace is clean and runs smoothly; they should be patient, responsible, good, truthful and should not engage in gossiping; they should love and care for all, advise others, and partake in community discussions/work/care. Others are that: women who are in Government should care for women and others, and they should not embezzle money like men. Three women thought women should not partake in politics or try to lead. The reason, according to one of them is that a woman does not have good brain. Six women were very specific that women should participate in politics/contest elections. Again, we take the exact words of a few of the women. Otolorin in Ibadan said, 'In the workplace, a woman should face her work and be truthful to her master or mistress. In governance, a woman should take care of the womenfolk and she should not embezzle money like men'. Olonade said:

> Live with love. Have the spirit of unity. If our husbands are not in and they call us we can partake in community discussions. But, of course, a woman should partake in community discussions. If men come with their experience, women come with their experiences and views too.

As for Ope,

> a woman does not have good brain so she ought to ask her husband for assistance before taking any decision. She should be able to assist the husband financially and she should support community services.

Koripamo said, 'Women are not supposed to participate in politics. Women should respect themselves, not gossiping and not prying'. Salamotu submitted, 'Be sure to be in your workplace. Participate in community activities. Shouldn't try to be governor and president and member, National Assembly'. But Elizabeth said, 'Women ought to partake in group activities, if they pool opinion, maybe the work of the country will move faster. Women should work hard, women can contest elections and can campaign'. Tinuola averred that, 'Women in Government should be able to do things that will favour women. In the workplace they should be responsible and face their work'.

Many men in formal work expected that women would display exemplary character – diligence/dedication to duty; honesty/integrity/high moral standards and, be responsible; and lead by example in the public sphere. A few thought that women should be role models in governance, and peace-makers in the community and workplace. A few also thought women should allow the 'motherly touch' to be reflected in their work, and they should be tidy, both in the community and workplace. Again, a few felt women should partake in community development projects. While one man felt women should complement men's efforts, two felt women should play supporting roles to men. One man said women should partake in politics, so as to cater for women, and another, clearly tongue-in-cheek, said women should partake in women's liberation. The man has an MA in Sociology, and had indicated somewhere in his questionnaire that he did not believe in the equality of men and women. While one man said women should be at par with men in public, another said women should play equal roles with men at the workplace. Here are a few examples of how the men presented their views. Abayomi said, 'a participant, initiator as well as contributor to community development,' and Adeoti affirmed, 'In the public sphere women should be shoulder to shoulder with men for the development of the society'. Joseph said, 'Women should be active in the community as role models. In the workplace, the motherly touch should be there while, in government, they should be active politicians so as to cater for the female gender'. According to Ogazi, 'In the public sphere, they are to be seen and not heard, often treated as second class citizens', while Haliru said, 'Women in public sphere are expected to be role models who are not corrupt'. Alonge said, 'to maintain peace, humility and tidiness in the community and workplace', while Audu thought that 'At the community level, they are expected to complement the men's efforts in community development. At the workplace and in governance, they are expected to play equal roles'.

Unlike the views of male students about women's roles in the private sphere, there was no convergence of opinion in respect of roles that they expect women to play in the public sphere. In Ibadan and Lokoja, male students said women should: take part in politics and contribute own quota to nation-building. In Ibadan, the students said: educated women should take up leadership positions at the workplace and occupy political offices, and aspire to any position compatible with their capabilities. Still in Ibadan, other students said that in the public sphere: women should be subordinate to men; they should teach younger ones to respect their husbands; they should work/govern but not to the detriment of the home; they should ensure children are of good manners; and they should be obedient to their bosses and be more flexible than men. The students in Lokoja said women should be peacemakers; be dedicated to work; assist their male counterparts at work and, do anything men can do. Again, we present the exact words of the male students. Akin said: 'In the public sphere, they are supposed to be obedient to their bosses and be more flexible than men'. Fijabi asserted: 'In public, teach younger women to respect their husbands, engage in activities and join associations for the betterment of community, seek election into offices that will allow proper blending with domestic responsibilities'. Yisa said,

> In the community, they should be seen to be playing a leading role among committee of women. In the workplace, they should be able to contribute their own quota towards the achievement of the organizational goal; and in governance, they should be encouraged to contest election, they should also be appointed as ministers, special adviser etc; their ability has never been in doubt.

For Olanipekun, 'In the public, women are expected to do anything men can do'. While Daniska said a woman is expected to 'partake in the schedule of responsibilities assigned to her in workplace and govern well, if given a chance', Sunkami believed that 'in the public sphere they are expected to perform same role as men do', while Daniel said, 'In the public sphere, their expected roles include taking part in all endeavours channelled towards development and nation-building'.

Summary and Discussions

Most of the female and male respondents appeared to take the fact of women's presence in public life for granted. They all expected women to work hard. Women in formal work, women in the informal economy and male workers expected women to display exemplary character to affect children and society positively. Women in the informal economy and men in formal work expected women to imbue performance with relationship of care – 'motherly touch', 'feelings', and 'breast will move'. However, male students expressed concern that public life should not hinder women's domestic responsibilities.

There were just a few respondents in all six categories that thought women should play equal roles with men in the public sphere. While many respondents implicitly or explicitly acknowledged that women had roles to play in the economy, the community, governance and in politics, a handful of female students, female apprentices and male students explicitly said women should play subordinate roles to men in public. Some of the male students in fact said they expected women to: be more flexible than men; teach younger ones to respect their husbands; and, be subordinate to men.

These observations are beginning to tie up with the responses in respect of women's civic-political participation. We recollect that an overwhelming majority of women would vote for women, but some with provisos. Essentially too, we note that many men would vote for women, some of them with provisos too. For both male and female respondents, the provisos were that women should possess sterling qualities. This ties up with many women and men expecting that women partake in public life either as equals with men, or better than men, in the sense of imbuing performance with care, attentiveness and responsiveness.

The calls that women play subordinate roles to men in the public sphere; that women help secure men's position (that is 'teach young ones to respect husband'); and that women do not shirk domestic responsibilities, reflect resistance to women's participation in public life, and this ties up with responses that say: women should not partake in politics.

The question now is: why do we have these responses in respect of the roles of women that have tied up, almost neatly, with responses to the participation of women in politics? The focus will be, not on the typical responses, but on the atypical ones that we have observed to be strident – the views that women should play subordinate roles to men, and the view that women should play their roles in public life fairly differently from how men have been conducting themselves in public.

Factors that Influence Women and Men's Views of the Roles of Women in the Private and Public Spheres of Life

The factors that many women in formal work in both Ibadan and Lokoja identified as influences on their views of the roles of women in the private and public spheres of life are: experience; family background/upbringing; and, personal understanding. In order of frequency of occurrence, religion came fourth on the list. Other factors are: exposure; educational background; current trend in the world; and, a combination of all the factors already listed. One woman, Banke, a lawyer, holds a typical view of the roles of women in the private sphere, but the factors that influence her views are not exactly typical. According to her:

> My educational background and Christian background. As a Christian, men and women are equal before God. What a man can do, a woman can do better. Also, my educational background, a lawyer can aspire to any level in life, whether you're a man or woman.

Noimot, the only one that advocates an activist role for women in public said, 'My experience, my view and my upbringing. Women are no longer persons to be relegated to the background and their voices should be heard'. Lanke, one of the few women who made it clear that interested women should participate in politics, identified the factor that informed her view as, 'In my personal understanding, women should participate in politics. It's a way of competing with men'. Kunbi, Theresa, Ruth and Tiwa who hold regular views of the roles of women in the private and public spheres affirmed women when they gave factors that influence their view of women's roles in both spheres. Kunbi said, 'Involvement of women in any assignment increases decency and decency increases development'. Theresa on her part said, 'They are uncompromised when they are holding a post. Women always want the best in whatever they do, they are bold, and they show men that they are capable. The religious bodies always preach truthfulness and hard work'. Ruth expressed her views thus:

> I like to work hard and also want to be recognized for my hard work. My own mother was not educated but she was very hardworking and very industrious. Women should quietly make their impact to be felt in their chosen career.

And Tiwa was of the view that:

> When a woman is given a chance and support to work, they move the nation better than their counterpart who believe in bribery and corruption. You can never corrupt or bribe a woman while performing her duty.

Only female students in Ibadan were asked to indicate the factors that influence their views of the roles of women in the private and public spheres. Many of the female students responded to the question by deepening the views they had earlier expressed. Ademidun said: 'They're laid down conventions, there's no reason for you to shirk your duties'. Modupe asserted: 'My upbringing (I'm a Christian) also my own personal understanding and opinion of a woman's role'. Toun said, 'Everything you can think of that influence the views of a person my personal understanding, my background, the society etc'.. Ajoke affirmed:

> Family, friends and society as a whole. You are scolded by relatives if you can't cook, if you are not tidy enough, and when you express view contrary to societal expectation of women, some friends both male and female respond negatively.

And, Folarin said:

> Firstly, my mother's way of life has greatly influenced my view of the expected roles of women in making the home. While in public, people like Prof. (Mrs.) … has tremendously changed my view about women's role outside the home. A woman has to be fearless, diligent, hardworking and contribute greatly to the development of her community

The name of the female Professor has been intentionally left out of Folarin's response. I had an interview with the Professor (Prof. W), and Folarin's response just confirmed the Professor's concern that female students should work hard, and make their marks, in spite of the limitations that the structure of society imposes on women. Good enough, Folarin made it clear that she got her view of women's roles in private, especially that of being submissive, from her mother.

The factors that women in the informal economy cited as most frequently influencing their views of women's roles in the private and public spheres are: experience and upbringing. Personal understanding was frequently cited by respondents in Ibadan, but rarely mentioned by those in Lokoja. The position of respondents' religion/what the religious leaders preach were not mentioned as frequently as experience and upbringing for respondents in both locations. A few other respondents in Lokoja cited at least two other factors – what they like/what their minds tell them is right; and, 'the way things are'. We give the examples of the responses of some women whose views we had earlier cited in respect of the roles of women in public and/or private, and women whose views we had not cited at all. Hassana said, 'religion and what I like'. Morenike said, 'My own personal experience is that women are more at home than men. Moreso, they are more important in the home than men', while Nkechi said, 'my upbringing and, na so e be',[2] and Agun said, 'I got all these from my own experience'. Margaret revealed, 'I come from a large family. When there is a matter for discussion; they call the women to add their voice. Women live at home, so they should add their voice. Women ought to claim their rights'. Abereoran said, 'Religion. Women should honour their husbands as head of the house,' While Caroline said, 'My upbringing. This is because I notice that in a community, women always take care of situations and put things in order'.

Most of the female apprentices cited their upbringing; personal experience/ understanding/own thinking; and, experience of others, as influencing their views of women's roles in the private and public spheres. Only six women, three each from Ibadan and Lokoja, cited religion as being responsible for the views they hold. We should remember that hard work was one of the roles that many of the women expected of women in public life. Those who specified hard work cited their upbringing, personal experience/understanding/own thinking as influencing their views. Again, we listen to the female apprentices: Olonade said, 'Where I lived in Lagos, they taught us how to live with others. Our religion says love is important, so we also abide by that'. Ope who said women do not have good brain, attributed her view to her personal understanding. Koripamo, who said women are not supposed to participate in politics also attributed her view to her upbringing and experience. Inunkan who said in public, women should go to work and can contest elections said it was about her own experience. She said: 'Own experience. If you're ready, you can be what you want, if you put your interest. There are men and women lawyers, doctors'. Chinedu said, 'In the Qu'ran, a woman is a teacher who teaches the child. This is from my personal understanding and from religious teaching'. Salamotu who said women should not try to take the top jobs added, 'When men alone discuss, it may not be taken seriously, but if women partake, it will be taken seriously. Woman cannot hold a man, because man is the head of the family. It is not allowed. If you want to follow Bible or the Qu'ran, it is not allowed for a woman to hold a man'. Salamotu apparently believes that women should take part in discussions, but should not take leadership positions. Zainab, who is of the opinion that an educated woman should work in the office and the artisan should open her shop, attributed her view to her personal understanding and stated that, 'A woman should not depend entirely on a man to get her needs'. Tinuola, who believes that in the private arena, women should submit to their husbands and that women in government should do things that favour other women, attributed her views to her upbringing and personal experience.

When men in formal work were asked to state what factors influenced their views of the roles of women in the private and public spheres, they used the opportunity to deepen their views on the roles of women in both spheres. They identified factors such as: normal life expectations; religion; tradition; social experiences/societal expectations; personal philosophy of life; the nature of women; and, the constitution. Others were: age of respondent; and, the fact that respondent is married/is a family man/has observed or interacted with women over time. Some respondents did not give factor(s) but just deepened their earlier responses with their belief that: what men can do, women can do better, and that there ought to be equal rights granted to all. We again take specific examples of the opinions of the men. Ola, married, legal practitioner, and whose age range is between 40 and 50 said:

> I see women as having more important roles to play at home than in public. As the custodian of the home where future generations are raised, that stable is more important for the society or community than their contributions to public affairs.

Okanlawon, single, aged between 30 and 40, and a Masters degree holder said, 'I believe everybody, no matter the gender, should access equal right cum equal avenue to exercise their ability/ies'. Adeoti, also single and aged between 30 and 40 said, 'Women's nature is very warm and caring. Therefore they can nurture home. For a woman to be relevant in the community, workplace or in governance, she must have had qualitative education'. We recall that Adeoti was the one who said women should be at par with men in the development of the community. Koyejo said, 'Being a married man, I can see them performing these functions at home'. Ogazi said, 'The ratio of women holding positions considered important to that of the men is embarrassingly low. This becomes glaring if we dare take a statistics of this ratio'. We note that even Ogazi, who is clearly critical of the treatment of women in public, appeared to have conceded to societal expectations of the role of women in the private arena. Oyeyipo indicated that, 'At my age and my experience, I know what women are supposed to do, and the roles they ought to play in the society'. Audu, a Masters degree holder and above 50 submitted:

traditionally, women are expected to complement the efforts of men in day-to-day activities. However, with the advent of modern education, women have come to play dominant roles both at family, community and governmental levels, depending upon their educational background and exposure

The factors that male students in Ibadan and Lokoja cited as responsible for their views on the roles of women in the public and private spheres include: their experiences/homes/families; their own thinking and observation of society; religion and what they read in and or hear from the media and other publications. The students in Ibadan cited additional influences such as: formal education; cultural heritage; careful observation of (married) women; societal values and the emotional/biological/psychological make-up of women. Students in Lokoja also cited the nature of women and their own personal beliefs about women's roles as being responsible for their views of women's roles in the public and private spheres. Again, we take some examples. For Akin, 'It is as a result of their emotional, biological and psychological make-up (not as "hard" as men)'. Fijabi argued:

> I believe that women, apart from having a responsibility in home building, should have the privilege of extending such quality of leadership into the larger society. Since the success of families, put together, is invariably the success of the larger society/nation.

Yisa said: 'As said earlier, women's ability has never been in doubt because of their cool headedness. This is seen in the leadership role they play, e.g. NAFDAC Director General'. Olanipekun believed that 'because man has no time for any domestic work, all that responsibility is left for a woman. But in public, there is no work that men are doing that women cannot do'. But for Daniska, it was that, 'from the scripture, I learnt that God exalted women to serve as supporting tools to men and from then it has been, and so shall be forever'. Sunkanmi said, 'To shoulder responsibility takes only desire, assistance, talent and zeal, not by sex. And also one's capability is responsible sometime'. And, finally, Daniel submitted:

> I have always had the impression that every human being (irrespective of sex) has equal potentials. Hence, I believe that the role of women should not be just cooking and cleaning but also participation in all spheres of life.

In the next section, we examine the views of religious leaders on the roles of women in the private and public domains.

Religious Leaders on Roles of Women in the Private and Public Spheres of Life

Islam

Male Muslim Leader - Lokoja

Male Muslim Leader (MML): Women, as Islam puts it, are potential assets. Women, according to Islam are highly respected and accorded opportunities to excel in any field of human endeavour. During a war, Al Salmiah, the first nurse on earth (not Nightingale as some people are claiming), was at the war front with the Muslims fighting to defend and protect their faith, the life of their followers as well as non-Muslims who may be in their midst, as well as their properties. This woman organized a mobile clinic where the wounded were taken and given first aid treatment before going into any major health centre.

Women have their roles to play in their own right as prescribed for them by Almighty Allah and exemplified by the Holy Prophet Mohammed. Women have been given two roles in any given society. One is domestic and one is outward bound. The domestic, like the Prophet has said, is that the woman is the queen of the house, the husband is her guest. The prophet explains further about how she is the queen of the house. He said she stays at home to take care of the children, take care of the properties of the man or of the family while the man is out to go and fend for that family. The woman is also a potential social worker as Islam sees her before we even go to the other extreme. A social worker in the sense that the woman has to produce a lot of things that will be of benefit to the society. She will be in the house, prepare/produce things such as woven materials and food and then take them outside. Food is essential, for there are bachelors here and there; those who cannot afford to marry. For Islam said if you cannot marry, then go afasting.

Feminine responsibility is there, and masculine responsibility is there, and that is why Allah is telling you, you are the queen of the house, stay there and take care of the domestic home, go out and fetch me water, go out and carry the wood, go and do this, so that you are not tired.

Olutoyin Mejiuni (OM): Hypothetically, if war suddenly breaks out in Lokoja...

MML: May Allah forbid it.

OM: And there are many women around. Women who are confident, strong and you have drafted all the men to war, and three quarters of them are gone, and you can still draft the women to war ...

MML: To go and take care of the wounded.

OM: Would you say we can be defeated, you women just stay back?

MML: Okay, I will tell you one instance. The issue of courage, the issue of boldness, was exemplified during the war of the Tartars when the Turkish people, in their war with the Mongols because of the Turkish deviation from the path of the Almighty Allah. Allah now reduced their power, so the Mongols attacked them. But there was a lady who was standing, she courageously went and confronted the soldiers, but that was out of Allah's infinite assistance, grace. With that, she was able to defeat those people. That was exceptional.

OM: We could have more women like that.

MML: But that is exceptional, fundamentally that is not their job except if, by circumstance, they have been compelled, they have been forced to go into it.

OM: That is why people are saying the circumstances are pretty different now.

MML: Yes, okay look at what is happening now to our female soldiers. How many of them are going to the war front?

OM: I think the point you're making is that women have their roles, let them stick by them. I think you also believe that women can complement the efforts of men

MML: Yes, that is what we are saying.

OM: But I think also there is the belief that women are too weak for some of the things that we are calling them to do.

MML: Yes, and which is outside their divine job.

OM: Some contradict this position by saying the job of fetching water, the job of giving birth to a child, the job of taking care of the house, going up and down, is such a big job that women exert energy, much more than men do. It is said that what men do is just sit around for people to nurse them more or less; and when men go to war, they don't go and fight with their hands anymore. They use guns. And if you teach anybody to use a gun and strategize, she will be effective.

MML: Madam, what I want you to understand is, if you look at the nature of a woman primarily she should take care of her kids at home. They give birth and bring them up and because this is lacking in our society now; that is why we have this widespread immorality throughout the world. Because women are now taking up the job of the men and this is a major reason why God, in his infinite mercy, has assigned to the women their primary assignment. They can complement the men in certain aspects of life. Likewise the masculine gender, too, can do the same to the feminine; but one thing is, it is the man's responsibility to go out and fend for what will take care of the family.

OM: Are you suggesting that a woman should hang around the house and not go out to work?

MML: Even if they work, they are not responsible for taking care of the family. They can work.

OM: They can work but should not contribute to the financial upkeep of the family?

MML: If they do, that is their own wish. That is out of volition. They are not compelled to do so. It is compulsory for the men to take care of the house in totality.

OM: If I may ask, what kind of feedback do you get from Muslims when you talk in terms of keeping the home the way you have just said it. I imagine, for example, in Nigeria of today where a man earns a salary that is not enough for him to pay rent and pay school fees, that you're saying a woman should only out of volition contribute to upkeep. I thought it should be normal for a husband and wife to just complement one another's efforts, and for a man to accept and appreciate the fact that the wife is doing something.

MML: They appreciate, but it is not compulsory for her.

OM: So, a woman can just sit back and say since Allah says the man should make all the provisions, then I shouldn't bother.

MML: She can do it if she will be contented with whatever I bring.

OM: I was going to say I hope the frustration that comes from the burden of providing or trying to provide everything for the family doesn't get manifested in other ways.

MML: If I may come in here, Madam, there is one thing that is very much obvious – taste and choice. They are very important and what Islam says is that the husband and wife should live in accordance with the means of the husband, so that where, for example, I am on grade level 4 and my wife happens to be on level 15, you know there is salary variation, I will try to spend money on my responsibilities. That is why I have said often in this country that the so-called minimum wage is nonsense. However, Islam put in place a minimum wage which will be enough for a family, for the relation and for miscellaneous expenses, and have enough to keep for any eventuality, that is what the Prophet called the minimum wage, not the small money that they are giving out.

A woman can complement my effort willingly and I will appreciate it, in addition to the great reward that awaits her in keeping the family. Because it is not her responsibility, that is why she gets double reward. Because she has taken it up to assist her husband and build the home, Allah in his mercy will now bless that family. The Prophet says if your wife takes a pair of trouser to wash, Allah reduces some of her minor things. Even when she is cooking for you to eat there is rewarding, but it is not compulsory for her to do it. I have been told that I should provide.

OM: What would being wife to a husband mean if she does not have to cook and wash his clothing ...?

MML: Islamically?

OM: Yes.

MML: The primary objective of marriage is to legalize the cohabitation between the two. It is the duty of the husband to now take up the responsibility of feeding the wife. They also say a wife should obey the husband. If she does that, she gains virtuous rewards. The wife is a garment to the husband and the husband is also a garment to the wife, to give comfort to one another, this is the way Islam looks at marriage.

Female Muslim Leader – Lokoja

Female Muslim Leader (FML): Women should be role models at home and outside. They have to be helpful to others. If you're at home and you don't go out to work, then you do all the household chores. If you go out to work, and therefore share in providing for the home, then the man should help with some of the chores. Actually they do. Not all of them ignore women and look on as women do all the work in the home – take care of children, cook. Usually, also, there are others at home with you, apart from the husband, who help.

This is where gender equity comes in. Culture says man is breadwinner, women are caregivers. Can't a man be a caregiver and a woman breadwinner as women actually are? We have designed certain roles to please ourselves. Abu plays ball because he is a boy while Amina does all the household chores – cooks, sweeps, washes plates, fetches water and firewood – because she's a girl. You know when two hands wash each other, they wash better. We need to push whatever is bad in our culture aside, so we can move.

Of course, a woman should be submissive to the husband if she wants to be blessed and have a happy home. Even, the issue of a man cooking depends on how you as a wife behaves in the home. If you please your man, and you have treated him the way he should be treated, you don't even need to tell him to help you, before he does it, and before you break down. I know of a well-respected medical doctor whose wife is a pharmacist. I visited them once, and the man was cooking while the wife was caring for the baby in the sitting room. On another occasion, the man was washing the nappies. They told me that when neighbours pass by and see the man doing household chores, they call the man 'women wrapper'. But you see they are living happily, and that should be our focus. Let's forget about our negative cultural practices and stop interpreting the Holy Book into culture. We should live the life that will make both men and women happy, and make their children happy too. By so doing, the children will also learn about how to live well from us and they will be happy.

Female Muslim Leader – Ibadan

Female Muslim Leader (FML): At home, women should be honest with their partners, ensure peace in their homes. They should take care of husbands, children and extended members of the family. She's minister of internal affairs. They should know the dos and don'ts of their husbands, bring up children in the fear of the Almighty God, children that will serve their Creator, useful to parents, and that will be of assistance to fellow human beings. Men should be above the women in terms of who heads the house.

Olotoyin Mejiuni (OM): How do you reconcile sex role socialization with the Qur'anic injunction that says women don't have to do household chores, although if they do, they will receive Allah's blessings?

FML: Ours is not a purely Islamic state. Culture interchanges with Qur'anic injunctions. The purpose of the injunction was to allow women concentrate on care of children, children who will fear their Creator and not become miscreants. Women who are housewives work. It is just that they don't go out to offices. They have always worked. Men are to provide every comfort so that women's minds can be focused on how to raise children. When children come back from school, they come back into the warm hands of their mothers who will feed them and go through their assignments. In addition, the woman will be ready to receive the husband back from work. She will ask about his joys, the setbacks/troubles and share with him. It is only when a man is able to provide all the needs – clothings, housing, feeding – that he is to marry. In Islam, the message is clearly spelt out. But because our culture is in conflict with the injunctions, problems arise.

It is not that the woman would sit down and fold her arms. She sits at the table with the husband when he returns from work and talks to him. Qur'an says before your husband comes from work, go to the bathroom, wash yourself and put on a sweet smelling perfume and be ready to receive him. So, if the man finds beauty in you, he wouldn't look elsewhere. The man should do everything for you – provide accommodation for you, buy your clothing, be able to feed you, but you also have a duty to perform. You should ensure he takes his meals regularly. Seek out his dirty clothing for a laundry man. Mend his loose buttons. Since raising children is enough work, if the economy can take it…

Christianity

Female Christian Leader – Lokoja

Female Christian Leader (FCL): As a woman clergy, I tell women that they have to show exemplary character where they are in terms of their outlook, what they say, the way they behave and dress. They are to dress neatly and moderately, although individuals have different ideas about how to dress. I preach decency, neatness, hard work and I encourage my women to be diligent. Diligent in the sense that although the book of Proverbs 22 vs 29 refers to diligent man, it is not talking to men alone. It is talking to men and women. If you have a duty to perform, you must prove yourself to be a hardworking person, and must be seen to be a hardworking person. Do your work at the right time, and don't go late to work. If you are in the private sector, open your business on time and let people who work with you learn good deeds from you. If you operate a restaurant or you plait hair or you are a dressmaker, do it well. I have seen women who have built bungalows from plaiting hair. What some highly-placed government officials earn is meagre compared with what some of the women in the informal sector make. I am a deputy director in the Ministry of Education, but I don't make as much money as my dressmaker per day. She told me the other day that their association had decided to charge 500 naira per *iro* and *buba* and I shouted. For those artisans, what they earn also depend on how diligent they are.

I preach to my people, to women, to love. They need to love. Love originated from Jesus Christ. John 3 vs 16 says: 'For God so loved the world that he gave his only son, which is Jesus Christ to the world, to die for their sins'. When we preach love and a hungry person comes to you, and you tell the person the Lord will feed you, that is not sufficient. You have to support love with your good works, actions. Jesus volunteered to die, so we should love our neighbours as our-selves. Even in terms of counselling, we should counsel our children and our husbands. If you want your husband to live long, you have to be friendly. If you see him moody after returning from work, ask him what the problem is, cheer him up, pray with him and advise him. That is showing our husband love by our deeds. I also tell husbands to love their wives because it is not good for these things to be one-sided.

Olutoyin Mejiuni (OM): Should women bear the burden of housework and again give in to sexual overtures at night?

FCL: As I tell my people, it was in those days that you say the duty of a woman is to stay at home and take care of children. Women need to work, to support the family, and it is then the husband's mind will be at rest, and he will be happy and loving too. It is the duty of the woman actually to get up early in the morning, bathe the children and take them to school. But a loving husband will prefer to take the children to school so the wife can cater for herself, shop for the food that they need in the family. Some husbands don't even like house helps cooking for them. At a seminar, women asked the question of what will happen when after a day of hard work, they are tired, and the man is demanding for sex. It is our duty as wives to submit in totality. We have to submit in all aspects. A loving husband will know when the wife needs rest, and a loving wife too will know this is the time the husband is aroused for sex, and would want to satisfy the husband, otherwise something else will happen. Even if you're tired. God gives life and strength, and because he has said we should be submissive, you have to give in. Ephesians 4 vs 22 says wives should be submissive. Because if you resist, some men will not argue with you, they will just use that as an excuse to move out, and that is another problem. He can move out and contact gonorrhea or AIDS, which is the problem we are battling with now. At times too, the woman is aroused. That is why we should give and take. If a woman is sick or tired, the husband should understand, although there are some who will not just understand. In fact, some men know they have the HIV/AIDS and they still go on having sex with their wives so that the source of the disease is not obvious.

In a matter of life and death, however, we teach women to dodge sex if it will cause them death. I am a member of the State Action Committee on AIDS. A woman who knows that her husband goes around with women got in touch with me about her health problems. I took her to the hospital to have her take the HIV/AIDS test. She was uncomfortable until the results came out and they were negative. We asked that the man should come around for the same tests but he refused. At some point, he told the wife that he would go for the test in an area where he is not well known. We told the woman to dodge sex until he takes the test and until it is no longer possible to continue to dodge. God said a woman should be submissive, but did not say a woman should die through her husband's deeds. In the churches, we preach submission, obedience, and faithfulness. That is the role that the Church can play.

Male Christian Leader – Ibadan

Male Christian Leader (MCL): Without women, there can be no marriage. One of God's institutions is the institution of marriage. A woman forms marriage partnership with a man and a family is born. When you talk about things relating to family, marriage and how to take care of their husband and their children, you're influencing them through those teachings to know how to conduct themselves at home, in their work places and the society. You talk to women about things that relate to their assignment. Life is all about responsibilities. Women have their responsibilities in life, and a man has too. Even in marriage, there is the responsibility of the man and the responsibility of the woman. For example, the Bible says husband, love your wife. That is responsibility. The wife, submit to your husband. That is the woman's responsibility. So a woman has roles to play. Even in churches, there is the role of women.

OM: Are there specific roles prescribed by the Bible?

MCL: You will not say prescribed by the Bible; but by the make-up of women, there are things that they are fit to do. For example, a woman will do well in taking care, in decorating the house of God. A man cannot be good in doing that. Women do the decoration of the church. There are men too but you can't see many men getting involved. You know women by their make-up have flair for certain things. That is the way God made them. So, there is the way God has made man too. When it comes to decorating and sweeping, a woman will fare better. When it comes to cooking, although some men compete with women now, but indeed, there is no way you can compare a woman's cooking with a man's. A man can try. Maybe some men because of where they were brought up they are exposed to it; but naturally, a man can't be good in doing domestic work.

OM: You have just alluded to where some men were brought up, so maybe the point is about where people were brought up, it is not actually natural.

MCL: It is not natural, some people were brought in an environment where they have to do something.

OM: So they cook.

MCL: A ha, they cook.

OM: Can we extend this to many aspects of women's lives that, perhaps because we have brought women up to sweep, so they are better sweepers, better decorators of the church, they are ... because we have brought them up to do so. Which means in societies where men are brought up to sweep...

MCL: No, not necessarily. It is their make-up, the way God has created them. So they can easily ... you see women have the flair for doing some things. It is God that made both man and woman, so there is the aspect of capability and ability. That is what a man has capacity for, a woman does not have capacity for the same. For example, the kind of weight a man can carry, a woman cannot carry the same. I cannot watch my wife carrying some load because I know she does not have the stamina for it.

But the man, by the way God has created man, they are built with energy to do certain things. So if a woman wants to compete with a man, that woman will just be suffering. These days they say what a man can do, a woman can do. Not all. It is not scriptural. God did not make them to be competing. God said 'I will make him an helpmate'. A woman plays the role of an helpmate. By the time a woman is competing with a man, she will not be playing the roles God has created her for. He said I will make him an helpmate. A woman plays a supportive role.

OM: I think your position is pretty clear about women's roles in the home, what about their roles in the public?

MCL: There are many things. There are openings for women now in educational circles. Women are knowledgeable, so they can play the roles that men can play in the society because they are trained for it. There are trained doctors, nurses, lawyers. It doesn't mean the brain of a woman is inferior to that of a man. It is the same brain cells. God is the one that created it. A woman can be trained intellectually to know how to handle some things, so in the society she can play some prominent roles. She can vie for positions as long as she knows that she is competent.

OM: So, what this means is that if a female member of your Church tells you that she is vying for the position of Governor of this State, you will tell her to kneel down, so you can pray for her.

MCL: I will not discourage her, but I will want her to be sure that she is led, she is convinced. Whatever a person wants to do, it is good to seek God's clearance. I will ask her to find out whether it is the will of God. If she has cleared this, she will not get there and start misbehaving. She will not join them and become corrupt. Whatever position you are in, you're to use it for the well-being of people, not for self aggrandizement. It should not be what you can get out of it, but what you can give.

As far as spiritual things are concerned, there is no feminine gender. There is no female holy spirit, and no male holy spirit. It is the same Holy Spirit. If someone seeks the assistance of God, the Holy Spirit can help. The only thing is we don't announce on the pulpit. We don't use the pulpit for that kind of a thing. It is a personal decision, and if the person comes for counselling, I owe the person the duty to counsel her, so as to be sure she will try not to compromise her stance, and then, it should not affect her family. That is why some marriages are scattered because some people don't plan. What you will do that will scatter your home, you better don't engage in it. What you will do that will make you not to be committed to serve God, you better don't commit yourself to it.

OM: You have said that in spiritual matters there is no feminine gender. Does it mean that you have female pastors in Winners' Chapel?

MCL: There are some who are ordained, who have visions and have ministries of their own.

OM: Within or outside the Church?

MCL: They are part of the Church, but maybe they just felt that God want them to do certain assignments and they want to be ordained. But we do not have a female pastor over a Church. Not because it is wrong, but in our set-up here a person may have problems. In advanced countries this may be acceptable. When you're talking about religion, you have to consider our culture too. If not, one would have problems. There are some things that are not acceptable culturally. If you want to reach out to people, you may not be accepted. That is why Paul said, 'I become like the Jews in order to win the Jews'. If you want to win people, you have to become like them.

OM: What you are saying is that patriarchy still persists.

MCL: Yes it does. If you then give female pastors to people who believe strongly that men should be the ones in charge, people may have problems with them. They will have problems because their perspective affect their reasoning and vice versa, and so they may not submit willingly to the woman as leader.

OM: I know that one church in Ilorin and another in Lokoja have female leaders. I have interviewed the woman in Lokoja and she does not appear to have any problem leading the church.

MCL: Yes, it varies from place to place. There are some who may accept it. Someone has to be wise. Like Paul said, 'I became weak so that I will win the weak'. It is not that we are compromising; it is just wisdom to reach out to people. There is nothing wrong with women leading the church, but one has to study the environment first and be sure this person is acceptable. Even here, some of the pastors' wives preach on invitation. For example, a woman who is a pastor's wife, and who is ordained too, will be good in speaking to other pastors' wives, and will be good in speaking to children, depending on the role they want to play. It is not that women don't feature in our services. They feature, but what we are saying is that when you now say a woman should be the overall head of the church, there may be problems in some places. Over the years, some people have become matured and people respect and accept them as individuals.

Female Christian Leader – Ibadan

Female Christian Leader (FCL): A woman is a builder, and a pillar. When we are talking about the structure of the home, a woman has to be there. If you look at some of the people that we have out there, armed robbers and

419, all sorts, they are traceable to the homes, to broken homes. That is why I tell women that even if they are not going to do anything else, they should stay with their husbands because of their children. A woman does not die. So women should know that they are in a family to make an impact. When a mother tells the child that she believes in the child and that the child is the best, that is how the child will turn out – the best. You see, so many women, because of career, because of competition with men, they neglect their families. Look, women are too much to be competing with men.

Every man knows he can't do without a woman. Competing with a man is lack of sense and inability to know your worth. A woman who is going to impact on society and the people around must believe in herself. The problem we have as women is that tradition, religions and even women fight women. If you have a female boss, it's a problem. So there are so many things that make women feel very inadequate. One of the reasons I run the school of ministries is to put dignity in womanhood, to let women know that we are not an accident that is about to happen. If you look at the scriptures very well, God did not ask Adam before he created the woman. He looked at the man and thought he should make somebody that will add colour to his life. A woman is like the icing sugar on the cake. Women should assure their children that they believe in them, but they must believe in themselves first because it is what you have that you can give.

Olutoyin Mejiuni (OM): When you say tradition and culture fights us, what do you mean?

FCL: In some cultures, it is a woman that works, the man sits at home. In some cultures, the woman must not talk and they refer to Paul. The reason Paul told the Corinthian women not to talk was because they did not have manners. They were not reliable. They were not responsible. But when you see a woman that is in her place, and is submissive; surely, she has a place in destiny.

OM: I can see you're placing some of the injunctions in the Bible in context…

FCL: In fact, Paul was not biased against women. Jesus was not biased against women. As a matter of fact, Jesus gave the first woman who met him after his resurrection three solid ministries – the Prophetic, the Preaching and the Apostolic Ministries. Look at Jesus' Ministry very well. There was nowhere in the scriptures where he refused a woman. Jesus' message to us is that he has come to restore dignity to womanhood. It is important that women know this because, you see, many women think the beauty of their womanhood is to usurp the man. No. The beauty of a woman is actually in submission. When a woman is submissive, her beauty comes out, even if the man is not seeing it as submission, so long as the heavens see that you're submissive. Female achievers usually forget that the beauty of their achievement is having a cover over their heads, and the cover is their husbands. The beauty of a woman is in submitting to the authority of a husband even if the authority is a dummy. I am talking from a biblical angle. Someone who is talking from a secular perspective may not say what I am saying. But the Bible is a standard; there is nothing you can do against the truth.

OM: Let me ask you, the Bible says women submit to men and also, men love your wives, I've been wondering, of whom does the Bible require the biggest sacrifice?

FCL: That is in first Peter. As a matter of fact, love is stronger than submission, because Jesus loved us and died for us, and there is no woman that you love that will not submit. When we realize Jesus' love, we do not have a choice but to submit. When a man truly shows love to his wife, submission becomes very easy. Culture and tradition are factors here, even religion. In some churches, you see men have to sit somewhere and women in another place. You see, people turn the scriptures upside down.

In public, we shouldn't usurp authority. Look at Pilate's wife. She was in charge but she didn't have to come out so everybody will know that she is in charge. It was Pilate's wife that told him, come, be careful, I had a dream. Why is it that God went through the woman and not to the man directly? Because of that, Pilate washed his hands clean of the blood of the innocent man. The woman took her place in the society without really making noise.

OM: What about women vying for political offices...

FCL: Let me quickly say something. Some people say that when the Bible says a woman should submit, that means that she should not preach. You are only to submit to your husband. I can't be submissive to every man. As a woman, you can still be the head of the Church. For instance, by the Grace of God, I am a woman of God; I run a ministry and some men work for me. That is my privileged position. I have authority over the men around me. That does not reduce the fact that in their various homes they are husbands and their wives still have to submit to them, and I submit to my husband. If a woman is going to maximize her potentials and bring the best out of herself, she must learn submission. You must learn to stay under authority. The woman should be contented with her position as a woman and be able to influence things.

OM: I think I understand what you're saying, but I think there are contradictions here about women and dignity and about submission.

FCL: There are no contradictions. Look at Mary and Joseph. They were in courtship. They were to get married, and, the angel told Mary she was going to be pregnant. If the woman did not feel secured, she would have thought she is losing everything because Joseph would not marry her again. But she celebrated. She was excited. She said from this day henceforth, all generations will call me blessed. She believed in herself. A woman is ugly if she is not submissive. Submission, not to everybody, but to your man. Know your worth, believe in yourself. You can be humble, but you don't have to be stupid.

A Yoruba Traditional Religion – The Worship of Sango

A Female Traditional Religious Leader – Ibadan

Female Traditional Religious Leader (FTRL): In public and private, Sango wants women to be respected. He wants our children to be useful. If the children go to school, he would want that they indeed acquire knowledge. He would like that they are sound mentally. When the children are not doing well, Sango can be asked to give guidance.

Discussions

It is interesting that the positions of most of the respondents in this study tally with the position of the religious leaders on the roles of women in the home and in public affairs. It is therefore possible to conclude that many of the respondents in this study take cues from their religious leaders, both consciously and unconsciously. Almost all the respondents cited their experiences, upbringing, religion and what they think as influences on their views about the roles of women in the public and private spheres. Female students, women in the informal economy and female apprentices also alluded to 'the way things are'. A handful of literate respondents referred to culture, tradition and socialization.

What many women in formal work did in this section was essentially to affirm women, and the affirmations were in favour of women's participation in politics. Interestingly, they had tacitly accepted the roles ascribed to women in the private sphere. The only literate woman, Adetutu, who said the roles of women are the same with those of men in the private sphere said of the influences on her view:

I come from a family with three brothers and no sisters – each child has always been treated as an individual, given choices and allowed to fly or falter, based on his/her choices, so I see people as individuals, and not as male or female.

In the section of the questionnaire where respondents were asked to comment freely on the issues that were raised in the questionnaire, Adetutu provided more insight into her background, and clearly, it had shaped her perspective on women's roles. Hear her:

> I have the impression that this questionnaire sees the male as different "specie" from the female. I could not possibly disagree more with this, as may have been seen from my responses, ingrained by my mother, who happens to be her mother's only daughter, and was even about 70 years ago, treated no differently from her brothers, some of whom she trained – one is a professor, one a lawyer and a third excelled so much, he obtained a masters degree outside Nigeria. She, however, also insists that I should enjoy cooking and housework, just like my brothers, two of whom cook very well!

Adetutu also urged me to form a relationship with Christ if I do not have it yet. We recall that I had mentioned that Adetutu takes her religion seriously, and one has to acknowledge that religion does not appear to have disempowered her. Adetutu's testimony is particularly interesting and instructive because while many female respondents cited their upbringing, a handful of the male respondents said they came to conclusions about the roles of women from 'careful observation of married women' and 'observation and interaction with married women over time'. We note that upbringing is socialization/informal learning while '(careful) observation' and 'interaction ... over time' are some of the ways in which informal learning takes place. At least two male students said they came to the conclusions from what they read in books, and what the media disseminate. In this respect, Oloruntimehin (1998) had observed that the family, religion, schools and the mass media teach children and adults to learn and accept their expected and 'proper' roles in society. And, whenever men, women and children behave contrary to their expected roles, they are treated as deviants and punished.

Ajoke, a female student, supported Oloruntimehin's position. In her response in relation to the roles women should play in the public sphere, she said, it is: 'Not to be too prominent or authoritative. To take lower position like deputy and vice position'. When we asked her what influenced her belief, she said one is scolded for not learning particular skills (cooking and cleaning) and invites negative responses for expressing views that deviate from societal expectations of women's roles.

So, while Adetutu did not experience sex-role socialization and sexual division of labour, Ajoke did, and she is aware of the punishment that results from deviation from the norm. Suffice it to say, Adetutu's experience is not the norm, at least not with the responses in this study. And, it is not the typical experience of growing up for many Nigerian women.

Notes

1. Housemaid is household help.
2. 'Na so e bi' translates to: that is the way it is.

4

Who am I? Prescribing Women's Identities

The discourse of identity has focused on characteristics that all human beings share in common with certain other human beings, and the way in which individuals are unique (Kluckhohn and Murray, cited in Mennel 1994), leading to discussions on personal and collective identities. The three traditions that are represented in the discourse of identity – essentialism, social constructionism and decons-tructionism – have their strengths and weaknesses, and they make an attempt to define personal and collective identities difficult. Even then, defining collective identity is easier than defining personal identity. Mennel (1994) refers to collective identity as:

> a higher level conscious awareness by members of a group, some degree of reflection and articulation, some positive or negative emotional feelings towards the characteristics {which Wiley (1994) refers to as "long term abiding qualities, which, despite their importance, may not be part of human nature as such" (p. 130)} which members of a group perceive themselves as sharing and in which they perceive themselves as differing from other groups (p. 177).

With respect to personal identity, the position that is becoming widespread, noted by Mejiuni (2005), is that although self-definition and assertion of individuality are essential to empowerment, the self here, is, self in relation, and so the masculinist psychological model of selfhood is rejected. It is therefore thought that it may be worthwhile to avoid a sharp split between personal identity and collective identity.

Calhoun (1994) had indicated that a useful framework for the understanding of identity, and that is less problematic for theory and practice, is to draw from both essentialist and social constructionist approaches, and to the dualism, add the deconstruction and claiming of identities for persons and groups.

Also essential to the discourse of identity are the questions of the multiplicity of identities and the pressure that individuals face about favouring particular identities, and the negotiation/renegotiation and transformation of identities.

Identities become political and problematic when certain characteristics are attributed socially and institutionally to individuals and groups, and such define their rights and duties, and affect their quality of life (Wiley 1994). Once identity becomes political, subjectivity (the self-conscious perspective of the person or subject or the 'I') is possible only through the individual's agency. Calhoun (1994) made the point when he said, 'it is not just that others fail to see us for who we are sure we really are, or repress us because of who they think we are', we are constantly confronted with discussions of 'who it is possible or appropriate or valuable to be' (p. 20). This inevitably affects the way individuals see themselves, with the attendant doubts and tensions.

In reckoning women's identities and the implications of the identities for empowering and disempowering women, we return to the question of the self, that is, self-definition, self-recognition and recognition or non-recognition by others. Rogers (1998) had indicated that feminist theories 'postulate a dialectical selfhood, comprising close connections with other people as well as strong senses of who one is, what one needs and values and where one wants to apply her energy and devote her attention (p. 366)'.

This position of feminist theories, presented by Rogers, is an appropriate response to the problem that Calhoun (1994) had observed and raised as follows: 'there are too many challenges to the efforts of persons to attain stable self recognition or coherent subjectivity' (p. 20).

Also, given women's positioning in different social contexts and within different matrices of domination at different points in their lives, in reality, women have an identity that is a set of identities, and as such comprise inconsistencies and paradoxes that can result in resistances and creativity (Rogers 1998). Clearly, also, women do not retain an identity (or set of identities) throughout their lives, and so when they are confronted with new experiences and new realities, they may 'do a rethink of the principles they hold dear, they may transform their thinking and perhaps turn it into action; they may form new alliances, and they may not take an either/or position. They may look for a third space, where they may at times feel confused, or feel comfortable and thrive, or they may feel challenged' (Mejiuni 2005:296).

Realistically, then, in our analyses and discussions of women's identities in this work, we need to return to Calhoun's suggestion about drawing from the traditions that are represented in the discourse of identity, and then add to them, the deconstruction and claiming of identities. As we do this, we need to keep Rogers' (1998) position in view. She said:

> selfhood and identity invite us, in sum, to demonstrate the possibilities buried under what culture has deemed impossible or inconceivable... To secure ourselves and enact our identities in liberated ways requires bringing to the cultural surface what lies buried beneath its institutionalized sedimentations... In lieu of seizing those challenges, we can remain queued up in the lines of society's matrix of domination. We can remain what culture has named us rather than what we name ourselves (p. 374).

Self-Definition

The four groups of female respondents in this study defined themselves in at least fifteen different ways (we can see Table 4.1 for details), and many defined themselves in more than one way. In other words, many inhabit multiple identities. Here are some examples of the ways women defined themselves, beginning with women in formal work settings.

Rebecca said of herself: 'I am a woman endowed with unique and rare qualities, full of virtues that will change my environment for the best. A lovely mother and, full of joy always'. Odunola described herself as, 'A woman, easygoing, industrious Lawyer. Married with children, Okun by tribe from Kogi State', while Esther said, 'I am a simple, intelligent, hardworking, committed and visionary woman who loves God and committed to his service' and Omolade said: 'I am a serious-minded, plain, God-fearing young mother of four who believes that I am to account for whatever I do and say to affect others around me'.

The female students included Banke who said: 'I am a woman. Created because there is a man out there that would not be fulfilled except he has me. I have a mission to accomplish, I am just the best for it'. Then there was Abosede who said:

> I am a girl who believes in equality and that whatever a man can do, a woman can do, not better or anything but simply can do. I am a, should I say, a woman and proud to be one and treated like one, not according to societal standards of inferior and second class citizen, but simply a woman.

Ruth had this to say: 'I am a gentle lady but do not tolerate nonsense. I love good things and I always maintain peace with others and help others. I love and respect others and in return wants to be loved and respected'.

Women in the informal economy included Noimot who said: 'I am a good person, hardworking and I love doing business and, above all, I am trustworthy'; Feyi who described herself as, 'Outspoken, bold and I have confidence in myself'; Esther who told of her personality as follows: 'Just a human being, ordinary girl, gentle, simple, if anybody is in pain, I will help. I like my job, and I'm blessed with it. I will get married'; and Ruth who confided: 'I am a human being. I am a very jovial person and I am not troublesome'.

Female apprentices also told us who they were, beginning with Abike who said: 'I am a woman and I'm pretty'; Tanwa who was concise with: 'A woman, God-fearing, hardworking and a mother too'; Ireti who told us in Pidgin English: 'Quiet, I don't look for trouble but if you look for my trouble... mmm... I no go take am easy ooo';[1] and Mariam who said: 'I'm a Muslim, I'm a good person, I don't do bad things'.

The responses from literate women and semi-literate women appear to show that women identify more with their gender identity or their identity as women

Tabe 4.1: The Subjective I

	Literate Women In Formal Work Settings	Percentage	Female Students	Percentage	Semi-Literate Women in Informal Economy	Percentage	Semi-Literate Female Apprentices	Percentage
Ethnic	4	3.9	2	1.7	3	2.9	1	1.9
Religious	13	12.6	12	10.1	11	10.5	3	5.6
Gender	21	20.4	26	21.8	25	23.8	16	29.6
Character	18	17.5	23	19.3	38	36.2	25	46.3
Physical	2	1.9	13	10.9	5	4.8	4	7.4
Professional/ Vocational	9	8.7	13	10.9	3	2.9	0	0
"Feminine"	7	6.8	16	13.5	7	6.7	2	3.7
"Masculine"	2	1.9	1	0.8	0	0	0	0
Marital	8	7.8	2	1.7	4	3.8	0	0
Deconstructed Identities	5	4.9	3	2.5	0	0	0	0
Age	3	2.9	3	2.5	1	0.95	0	0
Mother/Natal	9	8.7	0	0	3	2.9	1	1.9
Activist	2	1.9	1	0.8	0	0	0	0
Co – curricular/ Other Interests	0	0	1	0.8	0	0	0	0
Human/Person	0	0	0	0	5	4.8	2	3.7
Total	103		119		105		54	

Source: Data generated from the open-ended questionnaires completed by (or for) all four categories of female respondents who provided information during fieldwork.

and their individual characters. Interestingly, if one ranked which identity came first and second for the two broad groups of women, literates and semi-literates, an interesting picture emerges. For literate women, gender identity ranked first (was most frequently mentioned), and character ranked second, while for semi-literate women, character came first, and gender came second. What this means is that the two groups of women, particularly semi-literate women, defined themselves mainly in terms of their character and gender, or gender and character.

However, women in formal work and female students defined themselves in more ways and self-identified with a whole load of interests than the semi-literate women. Female apprentices were the ones who defined themselves through the least number of interests, that is, eight out of fifteen that have been identified by the female respondents in this study. The interests/identities are: ethnic; religious; gender; character; physical; professional/vocational; 'feminine'; 'masculine'; marital; identities that are deconstructions of feminine or masculine identities; age; maternal (natal); activist; co-curricular/other interests and human being/person.

It is helpful that we note how women defined themselves through identities other than gender and character. For women in formal work, after gender and character, they identified with religion, while their profession and their identities as mothers, followed immediately after religion. After gender and character, female students identified with their femininity, while their physical attributes and their professional identity (in this case, course of study) both followed identification as feminine. Religious identity then follows. For women in the informal economy, after character and gender, come religious identity, and their femininity. Female apprentices described themselves in terms of their character and gender and, to a lesser extent, their physical attributes. We ought to note that for both women in the formal economy and women in the informal economy, identification with religion came immediately after identification with character and gender or gender and character.

At a general level, women have described themselves, and shown/portrayed themselves to be confident persons who: are comfortable with themselves as women; are comfortable with their characters; draw lessons that are inspirational and so empowering (and the not so inspiring and disempowering lessons) from religion, and are also comfortable with being feminine. In addition, women in the formal economy appear comfortable with their identities as: professionals, married women and mothers.

One fact that has emerged from women's perception of who they are is that apart from the obvious fact of their being women by virtue of physiology and social construction, women have defined themselves from the point of view of their character. It is therefore important that one takes a close look at the specific character by which women have defined themselves.

Women have defined themselves as bold, aggressive, humble, gentle, patient, brooking no nonsense, hating cheating, and not feeling inferior to anybody, intelligent and so on. We note that one literate woman described herself as *flexible*. We can take a cursory look at the details of the characters of the different groups of women in this study in Appendix II. This is how women view themselves; and so, in this study, we assume that their self-definition is a reflection of who they think they are, irrespective of whether or not they had factored into their definitions the point about who others think it is valuable to be. One wanted to know how women saw themselves in relation to men and one also thought that it would be better that one finds out what characteristics men thought they share with women. That is, we attempted to find out what women and men thought they share and how they thought they differ from one another.

Women are Similar to Men

Some women in formal work felt they were similar to men in terms of characteristics that are traditionally, socially, and in contemporary times associated with maleness/masculinity – aggression, courage, boldness, independent-mindedness, being pushy, daring and achieving. Other women thought they shared with men matters relating to their character, especially at work – diligence, discharge of duties and hard work. The women therefore saw themselves as performing well at work. Although one may be tempted to assume that because women in formal work, like men in formal work, earn a living and support the family, many women would cite earning a living as a point of similarity with men. However, only two women said: 'I earn a living' and 'I fend for the family', roles that are so often associated with men and which, to a large extent, are thought to be the reason men are leaders at home – that they solely provide for the material needs of the family. A few women identified their educational attainment/academic qualifications and the fact that they were human and thinking beings as points of sameness with men, while others indicated that they were similar to men because they were both created by a higher being (God). On the whole, most literate women in formal work alluded to equality with men in: their character; their work ethics and performance; their educational attainments; their source of existence (created by God); and, in their hopes for the future. Only two alluded to material provision for their families.

Female students, like literate women in formal work, also thought they were similar to men in the sense that they had character traits that were deemed masculine such as: strong-willed; courageous; aggressive and independent; strong-hearted; brave; and steel-minded. Not surprisingly, many female students identified: thinking, reading and reflecting; the same education; reading the same courses; and their intelligence as grounds of commonality with men. The students identified a few other characteristics that they share with men (leadership abilities and male features), but also spoke on their hopes for: impacting on their community, achieving greatness, and realizing their goals and dreams.

The obvious differences in the similarities that women in formal work and female students identified with men is that women in formal work understandably spoke to their characters at work and the fact that they earned a living/supported family, because they worked, while female students did not do regular jobs as yet. Also, while women in formal work identified the source of their being and men's as God, female students did not touch the subject. Among female students, their statements of hope and possibilities as a point of similarity with men are clearer and more direct than women in formal work.

Most of the points of similarities with men that semi-literate women in the informal economy identified centred on material provisions for the family, work ethics and performance: I support/feed the family; I shoulder responsibilities that they shoulder; I work hard like they do. The semi-literate women identified other points of similarity with men – boldness, strictness, driving; and one woman said she went to the stadium to watch football and other male-oriented sports.

As for semi-literate female apprentices, many felt there were no points of similarities with men. The few that identified similarities put their fingers on hard work, and the fact that women are human beings like men. One woman indicated that she supported her family, while another said she worked like men and also repaired electronic equipment in the house.

While literate women attempted to deconstruct maleness by insisting that they also had attributes that were ascribed to men, which was a good way to proceed, semi-literate women were deconstructing male superiority by claiming and valuing the specific role (material provisions for the family) that supposedly makes men more important than women in present-day Nigeria, and which gives them the authority to claim superiority and leadership in the home.

Clearly, in our society, it is not just material provisions for the family that make men claim superiority over women. Patriarchy, made worse by our colonial experience, has established that. Patriarchy affects the ability of women to access resources – education and land, as some women have pointed out in this study – and so dictates the material condition of women, who are poorer than men in terms of material well-being. However, given capitalism, men and women have had to work outside the home and both are now breadwinners. In addition to breadwinning, society has ensured that women retain their ascribed roles of care-giving. The basis on which men can then continue to claim superiority (and insist on leading women) in their homes and the larger society is patriarchy, and ecently, religion. That is, religion apprehended, not as liberating, but as an opium which powerful groups (in this case, men, supported by women) have successfully fused with culture, or long-held, institutionalized and conventional beliefs (patriarchy) to determine women's interests, their roles and their identities.

We also note that while many semi-literate women acknowledged themselves as breadwinners or co-breadwinners in clear and unambiguous language; and were, through that, deconstructing maleness, literate women did not strongly identify material provision as grounds for challenging male superiority. Also, more than the semi-literate women, literate women flaunted their marital and maternal identities. Clearly, most semi-literate women in this study were married, and had children whom they cared for, but they did not define themselves through their husbands and through their children like the literate women did. In her response to the question of similarities between men and women, Fehintola, a trader said, 'I support the head of the family. There are no husbands again, but father of children'. This is a refrain that has become entrenched among illiterate and semi-literate Yoruba women. Among these women, when a man is not a sole breadwinner, in the sense of picking the bills, he becomes – 'Baba omo' – father of a child. This is more so if he does not pick the bills or is unable to pick the bills because he is married to other women or has informal liaisons that he funds. Whether or not men are breadwinners, however, today, among a lot of illiterate and semi-literate Yoruba women, there are many allusions to a man being 'Baba Omo' once he pays attention to more than one woman, and or maltreats his wife. He becomes truly, not a husband but one who has fathered the children in the sense of providing the sperms for conception, not in terms of fatherhood. This way, this group of women distance themselves from the husbands, especially at a psychological level, and so they are not quick to define themselves through their relationships with the husbands.

The male respondents in this study used direct language of equality to describe similarities between women and men; and some also supported their views with religion in a manner that was potentially empowering. However, the similarities that literate men in formal work and students identified between women and men differed from the similarities that literate and semi-literate women pointed out. While literate women in formal work and students identified themselves as possessing characteristics that are traditionally and socially ascribed to men, such as aggression, boldness, being independent-minded, and pushy; and very few literate and many semi-literate women indicated they were breadwinners and co-breadwinners, men did not identify women as similar to them in these respects (we can see Appendix III for details). This is telling because apart from the male reproductive organs, one of the roles ascribed to men – the provision of material needs for the family – is what makes men the male gender.

Women are Different from Men

In articulating the differences between women and men, literate women and semi-literate women stated the facts of how they differed from men, not just as they perceived it, or as it applied to them personally, but also realistically, even though at times, the realities have become real only through social constructions.

In addition, at times, women communicate their own beliefs and what they have learned (both positive and negative) as the truth/fact about how they differ from men. Some women in formal work said, for example, that women and men are physically and psychologically different. This is true. A woman said men and women have been ordained by God for different things. In this case, the woman is passing on her belief as what is. Another woman said: 'I exhibit the normal hormone of caring that every woman has'. Clearly, this woman cares, but she assumes that because women are thought and taught to be nurturing, then caring is normal for every woman and, perhaps, caring is not normal for all men?

Female students appear to court less controversies in their engagement with differences between men and women than literate women in formal work and, much of the time, they spoke to facts as they saw them. They stated for example that: they have breast and they can get pregnant; they differ from men by physical features; men have XY chromosomes and they have XX chromosomes and that they do domestic work which men do not do. One female student said the difference is in each person's individuality, not maleness or femaleness. Another said she has a womb and motherly affection, and yet another said the experiences of women differ from those of men. This is a statement of fact, corroborated by a male respondent who said women carry pregnancy and are vulnerable to humiliation, discrimination and attack.

While some semi-literate women believed they were not just similar to men at all, some said they were just women, and yet others could not see how they differed from men .There were statements of fact such as: 'I manage the home front, they don't'; 'I give birth, he can't'; 'men are seen as head of the family' and, 'they will be able to get up and talk in some places, while I will not be able to'. There was a denigrating remark, obviously a lie that one woman had imbibed: 'women's brains are smaller than men's'. This is unfortunate, coming from a woman, because only a few male respondents in this study did not believe that women and men are similar in intelligence and ability to think rationally. Clearly, we ought not to lose sight of the fact that semi-literate men were not respondents in this study, so we may not have a clear enough picture of how (all) men assess women's intellectual capability. Another semi-literate woman said if she were to trade places with men, she wouldn't maltreat them the way they maltreat women.

From among semi-literate female apprentices came the view that men are more intelligent than women. The common factor between the two groups of women (women in informal economy and female apprentices) is that their educational attainments are low or at times non-existent and they both work in the informal economy. The semi-literate women in the informal economy are the teachers of the female apprentices. If an instructor holds the view that a woman's brain is small, she would most probably pass this on to the learner. None of the literate respondents gave an indication that they thought men were more intelligent. In fact, as has been earlier observed, intelligence was one of the grounds in which literate women claimed equality (sameness) with men, even if at times, they did not say so in many words.

On the part of literate male respondents, their responses to what differentiates them from women can be categorized into the following: statements that are true; statements that are true as a result of social constructions; statements that apply to a few, but are then generalized to all, because that is what men would rather be; make-believe and self delusion, and unfortunately too, outright lies(we can glean these in Appendix IV).

We take the view that men are assigned the presidential role in their families and the macro-society. This is true, although it is so as a result of the construction of men's roles and women's roles. The views that: men are emotionally stable; have ability to withstand pressure more than women; are more mentally stable; and are better leaders, are make-believe and self-serving. A lot of men in this study, in responding to questions about political participation, have actually acknowledged that women are better managers of resources; more suited to discharging official functions; will not be partial in taking decisions; organize people better; are meticulous; and are responsive and attentive, etc. What attributes do men who say men are better leaders require of a leader which women do not already have?

In addition, there is already a response from literate women and semi-literate women to the assertion that men are less flexible than women. Women had said: 'when a woman is in an office, her yes would be yes, and her no would be no' and 'will not condone nonchalant attitudes to duties and indiscipline'. This indicates firmness, definitely not flexibility, in the sense in which the men in this study would like us to believe. As a matter of fact, Daniska had indicated that he would not vote for a female as President/Governor because according to him, 'if given a chance and probably win the election, men are in trouble, they would whip the arse of all men and oppress men and their fellow women'. A female respondent who is a school teacher, and whose principal is female had said she would not vote for a female President/Governor because, according to her, women are too harsh. In this study, only one literate woman characterized herself as 'flexible'. Clearly, expectations that women be flexible can be deduced from the ways some men have characterized women. One male respondent explicitly stated that women in public should be obedient to their bosses and be more flexible than men.

The point, actually, is that men would rather have women believe women are flexible, because that accords with femininity – being unable to make up one's mind, pliable, indecisive, etc. Given the way socialization, nurturing and social construction of identities of persons work, when men continuously tell women that they are flexible, women begin to believe they are, and they begin to act flexible, especially if they get 'rewarded' for being flexible. When one stands by ones words, especially in the socio-economic and political context of our country today, one gets sanctioned for not being pliable. One of the sanctions for a woman is to be denied the opportunity to be voted into office (Ibrahim and Salihu 2004). So, she is taught what is valuable to be, which is, being flexible.

One other interesting difference that some literate men pointed out between women and men is that men provide, and women are caregivers. Semi-literate women in the informal economy had, in their responses to women's similarities with men, faulted this positin; and they had deconstructed the view that only men are breadwinners. Perhaps at some point in our history, in the era of colonialism, this was the case. To hold on to this view today is not only fruitless, but the height of self-delusion. If we were to take a survey, we are likely to find out that many of the men in this study, who are lawyers, journalists and civil servants, and many of the men in higher institutions got or get most of their material needs for their education from their mothers, not their fathers. It appears men have to continue to hang on to the view that they are the sole breadwinners in order to claim leadership at home, and in the larger society.

Given, then, the identities of women that have emerged from this study, which are that women are persons who: bother about their character and how they relate to other people in public and private; can be aggressive, bold, pushy and independent-minded; care – have feelings, are nurturing and loving; are breadwinners and co-breadwinners, and bother about work ethic and performance and so are effective managers with plenty of organizational and social skills, what women do, in both the private and public spheres of life is that they humanize leadership and they humanize their actions, and thus they are not flexible.

How Men See Women

An individual's perception of who she is, is often shaped by who others think she is, and who others have taught her that it is valuable to be. It is difficult for individuals to achieve objectivity in a situation where they are constantly told who they ought to be, and are constantly shown the benefits that will accrue to them for sticking to identities that others would rather have them favour. Given the identities of the women in this study, we tried to find out how far their knowledge and understanding of who others think they are have influenced their self-definition, or their identities that have emerged from this study.

It is interesting that there are a lot of points of convergence between the differences between men and women that men pointed out, and the way women thought men perceived women. To a large extent, all women do not think that all men see women the same way. Given this, women used phrases such as 'some see', 'some think', 'others think' and 'it depends on'. Similarly, all men do not view the differences between men and women in the negative. Some pointed out, for example, that women are patient, careful, more sensitive and not dubious.

However, most of the differences that men believe exist between men and women were stated in the language of superiority. It is therefore not surprising that many women understand men as believing that women are: senseless, inferior beings, chicken-hearted, housemaids and men's subordinates. Although women were at times contemptuous of, or condemned some of the behaviours of men, they did not claim superiority over men. They stated facts as they saw them. Perhaps they are unable to claim superiority over men because they are indeed in an inferior social position to men. We note, however, that when women responded to questions of civic-political participation, they did not only claim equality with men; they sometimes insisted that they were superior to men. Apparently, those responses were aimed at challenging men's claims to superiority over women and, by extension, men's claim to sole leadership, especially in the public sphere. Interestingly, men who believe that women should aspire to political offices, including the highest in the land, also used the language of superiority of women over men to articulate their position. Some of the responses of women in respect of how they thought men view women are contained in Box 4.1.

We note the responses of Abebi, Toun, Ibukun, Rukayat, Amina, Labake and Abike in Box 4.1. They are the ones who are of the opinion that how men see women depend on how women portray/project themselves or behave. Whereas their position could be understood as a call to women to exercise their active agency, one is aware that some women feel that other women elicit bad behaviour from men by the way they behave. Much later in this work, the flaw in this kind of thinking will become evident. The respondents appear unaware that if a man has taken a position that women are inferior to him, he is not likely to change his view because she 'behaves well' or 'comports herself'. The man will probably not behave badly to a woman only if she behaves well or comports herself according to his own understanding of good behaviour and comportment at a particular time, on specific issues.

Again, as always, we take a look at the negative views because they matter, especially in the way they shape behaviours, actions and people's identities. Women (and men) come to conclusions about themselves and one another through: day-to-day interactions, experiences, myths, lies and educative influences. In the following paragraphs, we take some of the experiences of women, which have definitely led some of them to believe that men hold negative views of women. Precisely, that men think they are superior to women.

Women and Feelings of Inferiority

As we had indicated above, in the process of pointing out differences, men made: true statements; statements that are true as a result of social constructions; statements that apply to a few, but are then generalized to all, because that is

Box 4.1: How Men See Women

Women in Formal Work

'Not all men are the same. Some men think women are inferior, because they don't understand why God made women or they have their own deep-seated psychological problem' – Banke

'Most men have a chip on their shoulders, and think that the female gender is somehow inferior' – Adetutu

'They see women as a set of inferior beings whose ability to think proper is affected. I have met with men who had no single regard for women. I am blessed with a husband who knows the value of women. These crude men will not get to the limelight of their potential because there is a role a woman has to play in their lives' – Esther

'I think men generally see women as second rated group. Inferior, fragile and a set of beings who have come to compete with them. Though they have to come to agree that we are important, they still believe that we are a necessary evil' – Omolade

Female Students

'They believe women are the weaker sex and don't really have a mind of their own and those that do would be "Margaret Thatcher" in their respective homes, and thus, avoid them.' – Enitan

'If it had been in the past, I'd say men think women are fickle and only fit to be relegated to the background (having nothing to contribute); but now, I think men think highly of women (especially educated women) and are more careful of the way they treat and address them' – Modupe

'I think it depends on the way we put ourselves to them. If we put ourselves to them as responsible and someone that needs to be respected, they would take us as such; and if it is otherwise, the reverse too would be the case. So, it depends on the individual' – Abebi

'Men generally see women as the softer side of them. But then, there are different views about women. What then determine the view is the women themselves. As a woman, what you project gives men what to think about you' – Toun

'Men see women as people you woo, fell, get them and then you can treat them anyhow. No matter how much a man says he respects a woman, there is always that dictatorial tendency in his relationship with her, and the belief that she is the one that should give way and that men's ideas are always better than women's' – Ajoke

'If you respect yourself, they respect you; and if you flaunt yourself, they might end up abusing you' – Ibukun

'Men see women as their helpmate. They (men) believe women should be restricted to domestic work, odd jobs and not challenge their views or probe into matters they have concluded on. The women are believed to be back benchers' – Chinyere

'Some of them see women as factory producing children, human beings without a right of their own but dependent on men, cooks and househelp. Only a few see them as soul mate, and or source of inspiration' – Rolake

Women in the Informal Economy

'It is the way a woman behaves that the man will see her; so it depends, because we have different types of women' – Rukayat

'Indecent dressing has made men not to see us as good vessels, men look at us as tattered rags i.e. we don't mean anything to them anymore unlike the olden days' – Lanre

'They don't really have any regard for a woman; in fact they don't normally like giving birth to female children though the females are achieving much more than men' – Fadeke

'Men see women as the weaker vessel that cannot do without them. But I don't believe in this because women are turning up as the breadwinner in houses nowadays' – Ebunola

'Men are good, women are good too. Even when they don't like women, they say they do. They deceive women' – Wunmi

'As men see women, na im make dem dey spoil their life'[2] – Amina

'Women are slaves to them and that is not so' – Margaret

Female Apprentices

'As the weaker sex and as their mothers. They are afraid of women o' – Tomiwa

'It all depends; if you comport yourself very well a man will see you as important but if not, then he will see you as worthless' – Labake

'Some see women as rags to be used and dumped and some see women as good beings; but to me it also depends on the way you the woman behaves' – Abike

what men prefer and are comfortable with; there were make-believe and self-delusions and, sadly too, outright lies. Unfortunately, all the differences that men pointed out are reflections of what men believe about women, and these get reflected in men's behaviour towards women. All the women that took part in this study were asked to indicate whether or not they had at any time felt inferior to men, and whether or not men had tried to make them feel inferior. Their responses are contained in Table 4.2; while some of their voices, and/ or the examples they cited are in Box 4.2.

In the following paragraphs, we take a look at women's experiences of discrimination, sexism and violence in different spheres of life – in the home/family circle; in educational institutions; in workplaces, and in public places – and how their experiences have challenged, subdued, irritated and, perhaps, affected them positively and negatively.

One could categorize the responses of some of the women who said they had no reason to feel inferior to men into two. The first are literate and semi-literate women who feel equal to men, for they have excelled at work, they occupy or had occupied positions of leadership at work, in governance and in civic groups and they think they do what men are supposed to do. Given this, they just do not feel inferior to men. Esther and Ruth among women in formal work, and Rukayat and Oreoluwa among women in informal work represent this category. The second category is women who feel comfortable with patriarchy and the way things are, especially in terms of accessing resources like education and land. We interpret this as indicating that such women are comfortable with their subordinate position to men. Anike, Caroline, Alaba and Idowu's responses put them in this category. Interestingly, they sometimes justify their position by appealing to religion in a way that can only be deemed fatalistic. They display what Friere (1973) referred to as 'magic consciousness'. We should examine, once again, the responses of Anike, a semi-literate woman in informal economy and Idowu, a female apprentice.

We note that although both literate and semi-literate women said they did not feel inferior to men, apparently because they feel equal to men, only semi-literate women did not actually feel inferior to men because they were comfortable or appeared comfortable with the way things are. The semi-literate women, whose opinions are represented above, felt comfortable with the experiences of sexism and discrimination because they thought: that is the way things are, or, that is the way God wants it. The only literate woman who did not indicate that she does not feel inferior to men because she feels equal to them still expressed her irritation with the demands that social engagements place on women's time (Mejiuni and Obilade 2006).

It would appear that women in formal work do not or did not have a lot of experiences of discrimination or sexism; so, only two of them said they ever had a feeling of inferiority, while two said not all the time. It may also be that the literate women do not just feel inferior to men, or that they have decided to be silent about it. I think the former is the case, for when they were then asked whether men had tried to make them feel inferior, at least one-third of the women said yes. The women in formal work cited their experiences of discrimination while in school, and at work. Debo and Jumai who were female students cited their experiences of rejection in school politics. They are from Ibadan and Lokoja respectively. Arinola and Tundun cited what appeared to be discomfort with their own level of performance, relative to their male counterparts.

Table 4.2: Women and Feelings of Inferiority

| | Have you ever had a reason to feel inferior to men? | | | | | | Do men attempt to make you feel inferior? | | | |
| | Yes | | Not at all time | | No | | Yes | | No | |
	Frequency	Percentage	Frequency	Percentage	Frequency	Percentage	Frequency	Percentage	Frequency	Percentage
Literate Women In Formal Work (42)	2	4.8	2	4.8	37	88.1	16	38.1	23	54.8
Female Students (46)	10	21.7			31	67.4	16	34.7	27	58.7
Semi-Literate Women In Informal Economy (56)	18	32.1			38	68.0	18	32.1	27	48.2
Semi-Literate Female Apprentices (39)	15	38.5			24	62.0	14	36.0	17	44.0

Source: Data generated from the open-ended questionnaires completed by (or for) all four categories of female respondents who provided information during fieldwork.

Box 4. 2: Have You Ever Had a Reason to Feel Inferior to Men?

No Reason to Feel Inferior

Literate women in formal work

'No except for societal demands that limit a lady to certain social engagements and time' – **Grace**

'Not at all, after all, I am heading a school where several men had failed and God has given me the enablement to do well' – **Esther**

'Throughout my school days I have performed better than majority of men. I have performed well as a sole administrator/caretaker chairman and in the office I am very competent and dedicated in my duties' – **Ruth**

Semi-literate women in Informal Work

'No. No man can do that to me because I am bold and strong, In fact I've been the Chairperson of Tailors'Association for the past six years'- **Rukayat**

'I don't mind because I think it is what God wants me to be' – **Anike**

'No. as a woman, I do what a man is supposed to do so no regret' – **Oreoluwa**

'Women bi human beings, but boys get leg for im parents house pass girl. Dem no go any where. Boys bi owner for im papa house and im no dey go anywhere and he go help everybody when he dey work, but the woman husband go take am away. For education, if crises dey, I go ask the girl make im stop. If she sabi pass the boy, I go ask am to continue' [3] - **Alaba**

'Men are better than women. In the next world, I'll be a man' - **Wunmi**

'In my place in Anambra state women don't inherit land or property and I am comfortable with it. This is because you are married to somebody else' – **Caroline**

Female Apprentices

'I can't say that because I have to accept the way The Lord has created me as a female, if I say I'm inferior or that I don't like it that means am blaming God' – **Idowu**

No Reason to Feel Inferior

Literate Women in Formal Work

'When it comes to the matter that woman cannot handle' – Theresa

'In primary school, men's names were first called on the register before women. They were also given their meals before us. Men were always in the class while most of us went to cook or perform domestic chores for our teachers' – Adedigba

There are Reasons to Feel Inferior

Literate Women in Formal Work

'As a worker, discrimination at my place of work, when my boss doubts my capability and prefers that a male handles certain schedule of duties' – Itunu

Female Students

'When I have to rely on them for some solutions in terms of relationships, I just had that inkling that he/they had the upper hand/ say in the matter being discussed' – Enitan

'I wanted to contest for the post of president in my department and I was rejected' – Debo

'That was when I was admitted in my former school into the Dept of Elec/Elec. Eng, I felt every guy knew most things about the course except me' – Arinola

'In my department a boy called … is the one leading. Any time he is talking pertaining to our field I look at myself and feel inferior to him' – Tundun

'During the last Association election when I was informed that no woman qualified to be the President of NAPAS' – Jumai

Women in Informal Work

'Men tend to shout one down even when you want to advise them on certain issues. They see women as not having a good sense' – Fehintola

'When men see you as not possessing a type of brain that can equal theirs e.g. when trying to suggest a way out of a family problem, they don't buy your idea instead they see it as an affront "I am talking you are talking"' – Adunola

'A woman cannot be as powerful as a man, so men tend to take one for a ride sometimes; and since am not as powerful as they are, I can't beat them' – Asake

'An example is that of my younger brother and I before we got married. While we were still young, my younger brother can bring his girlfriends home without my parents raising an eyebrow but I did not have the audacity to do such. If I ever tried it, hell will be let loose even though I am older than my younger brother by many years' – Alake

'An example is my father. He refused to send us girls to school while we were young. His argument was that girls are not serious and that we will get ourselves pregnant by unseriousness, thus putting a stop to our education, and wasting his money. So he didn't see any reason why he should send us to school' – Toun

'My father refused to train me in school, because I am not a man. He instead wanted me to get married, so I ran away from home' – Yime

'The way my husband treats me especially when we quarrel makes me wish that I am a man. He even behaves as if he is my father' – Nkechi

'I once had a misunderstanding with my husband, even though he is the one that was at fault, I was told to go and apologize because I am a woman' – Chioma

'In my village, as a woman, I can't follow masquerade like boys my age. Then, my step brother who is older than I am beat my mother and I when our father was sick, and told me to shut up that I am a woman' – Nwanneka

'When my husband doesn't take care of me and I am experiencing bad market, I wish I were a man because they don't go through it' – Omoregbe

Female Apprentices

'The boys carry girls but we cannot' – Farinde

'My parents did not deem it fit to send me to school because I am a girl. Though there was no money then, they looked for money to send the boys to school; so, I ended up being an apprentice' – Toluhi

'My former boyfriend impregnated me and denied; so, I had to abort the pregnancy and I left him alone' – Rosaline

'Because I was overpowered by a boy and he beat me up though he was at fault' – Chinedu

'I once lost a close friend and was not allowed to see him immediately until about two hours later because I'm a woman. Also this idea that women can't be president' – Stella

'My four elder brothers go to school. Two are in the Polytechnic and two in Secondary School. But I am not because my parents felt it was waste of money since I always ran home from school while I was in primary school. So when I wanted to go to sec. school, they refused' – Olaitan

'When they make advances and you refuse, or they have taken you to bed, when in a group, they talk rough and bad about the person' – Koripamo

'I don't like the way they took our property especially land after my mother died. If I were a man, I would have reacted. But because I bi woman, I no get order, say make dem leave' [4] – Temi

'Because some boys feel proud and they don't do a lot of house work like girls at home' – Iyadunni

'Because I once witnessed a man beating his wife and I thought to myself that I wished I were a man' – Feyisara

Women in informal work and female apprentices, who are the semi-literate category of this study, cited experiences of discrimination, sexism and violence: in relationships with husbands and boyfriends; in family life and this includes domestic work; in public places, and in accessing resources – land and education. The women appeared really irritated when they spoke about their relationships with husbands/boyfriends, and the way they were denied access to education. The women said their spouses thought they were senseless, and Chioma said she was asked to beg her husband after a quarrel, even though he was at fault. Women's inability to access education while they were young because of patriarchy is also a sore point. In addition, one female apprentice, Koripamo, spoke to the condescending behaviour of men towards women because they deem women to be objects of desire. So whether or not women have gone to bed with them, they throw disparaging remarks at women. It appears like a no-win situation.

Within the experiences cited, we note outright discrimination, sexism and violence that left women feeling inferior to men. However, we also note that there were women who played into the hands of patriarchy and, so, men took advantage of their errors. Examples are Olaitan who played deviant while she was in primary school, and gave her father an excuse not to send her to secondary school, and Rosaline who was impregnated. There were women who felt inferior not exactly as a result of (overt) discrimination or sexism, but because of the feeling (and the fact) that they fell below the achievements of the men who were their counterparts. Two female students, Arinola and Tundun fell into this category.

There were those who were both victims of economic depression and patriarchy. Persons close to them resolved what appeared like economic dilemma with patriarchal norms. We know that many girls who have had problems accessing education have actually been affected by the problems of poverty and patriarchy.

We also note the experiences of Alake and Farinde. Their experiences are similar to those of many young women, and the thinking among older persons is that they frown at girls receiving male friends at home to protect their daughter from abuse and also protect the integrity of the family. However, the same groups of parents allow girls to pay visits to their male children. Perhaps this ought to be interpreted to mean that they are not worried about their boys abusing other people's girls, and that when boys receive female guests does not mar the integrity of the family, since the boy will marry a girl, and would have to, at least symbolically, bring the wife to his father's home. At any rate, women have pointed this out as a privilege that men enjoy that they do not enjoy.

Finally, we note the responses of Wunmi who said she had never felt inferior to men but that she would come to the world the next time around as a man, and Feyisara, who had a reason to feel inferior to men. Feyisara said she felt that way after watching a man batter his wife. These two women would like to trade places with men; and Feyisara is presently, obviously, uncomfortable with women's position relative to that of men. Wunmi appears comfortable with the way things are, for she does not feel inferior. However, the fact that she would like to trade places with men may be an indication that she is actually uncomfortable with the way things are. It may as well be that she appears comfortable with patriarchy because to challenge an obviously oppressive structure, such as the one she is comfortable with, is to have painful confrontations with a structure too huge for her to take on (Hooks 1998; Cranton 1994).

How Men Have Attempted to Make Women Feel Inferior

The paragraphs below represent women's responses to the question that asked that they cite instances of how men have attempted to make them feel inferior, while the preceding paragraphs sought to know whether women have indeed felt inferior as a result of their experiences. To some extent, for the purpose of argument, and also in reality, the responses in Box 4.3 represent part of the processes of construction of women's identities, while the preceding paragraphs indicate how successful the processes of construction of identities have been. In considering the experiences of women that ought to have, and that have, shaped women's views of who they are and what they (should) believe, we should remember how men understood the differences between themselves and women, and women's apprehension of who men think they are. In Box 4.3, we cite some of the experiences of women who are of the view that men have tried to make them feel inferior, and also cite the responses of those who said they have never had that kind of experience.

Religious Leaders on Women's Identities

Islam

Female Muslim Leader (FML) Ibadan: Women are creatures of the Almighty
Allah, created to coexist with menfolk, to be their wives, helper, confidant,
mothers of their children and daughters of their own parents. Women
should be dedicated to their creator and obey God in totality.

Christianity

Female Christian Leader (FCL) Lokoja: Women are the female sex. Biblically,
the first woman was created as a helpmate to her husband. We are helpers
to our husbands, helpers to our relations, helpers everywhere. If you
look at Genesis 2:18, it says and the Lord God said it is not good that a
man should be alone, I will make him a helpmate.

Women have various interests. Generally, women like to look beautiful.
They love to be neat. Women care about their appearance. Women like
to have a home. Any reasonable woman, religiously, will like to have
somebody as her husband. Somebody that people can call her by, whether
or not she is a doctor or a professor. She would like to be called Professor
(Mrs) or Dr (Mrs) so and so, as a shield, an umbrella, so as to give her
protection wherever she is, so that she looks responsible. Women don't
want to be idle. They are caring, loving, and because they care for others,
they want to be cared for. They want somebody to support them and
they like to have people around them. They want to share ideas and
feelings with others and would also like others to share with them. They
like to share experiences with other women.

There are those who have other interests. Some like to put their thoughts
into writing. Some like to go for excursions, dance, listen to music, and
some like to read the Bible. They want their children to attain higher
heights in future, so they want to commit the lives of their children into
the hands of the Lord. Some have had visions of schools, and they have
established the schools. There are two women like that in Lokoja here,
and they have standard institutions.

Male Christian Leader (MCL) Ibadan: Biblically, women are equally created
by God. The Bible makes us to understand that when God created man
in Gen. 1 vs 24, he said male and female did he create them. So women,
just like men, were created by God.

Olutoyin Mejiuni (OM): Did he create them equally?

Box 4.3: Women's Experiences of Discrimination, Sexism and Violence

No Experience of Discrimination, Sexism and Violence

Literate Women in Formal Work

'I actually attended an all girls school and while in the university, my class was more of female students than male students' – Banke

'I went to a mixed school, where the standards were high and the female child was treated exactly like the male child' – Adetutu

Semi-Literate Women

'No. Men do respect me a lot, maybe because I am big and bold; and they call me Iron Lady. I've never been messed up, except for a policeman that harassed me, but he later came back to beg me' – Modinat

'I don't care about what they say or do' – Alake

'Normally, I don't go out of my way to engage men in anything; at least, my work does not relate to men' – Olaiya

'No! because the Bible says men are the head. Sometimes my husband jokes about hair dressers being prostitutes' – Morenike

'Since I have married, my husband has not maltreated me. If he did, I would have been having such experiences' – Caroline

'I ignore them' – Tanimola

Some Experiences of Discrimination, Sexism and Violence

Literate Women in Formal Work

'When my step brother told me that I do not have a say in the family matter; that I am just a woman and should not talk when they, the men, are talking' – Tiwa

'One good example was the election of our Union president. The men folk said it was only men that were capable of being a Union president' – Medupin

'An example was when I was made a fee collector and coordinator in my former school. Our male counterparts felt it was an all men affair and they thought they could do it better' – Idiat

'Because my GPA is always above their own, they will now turn to use of abusive words' – Atolagbe

'While in school, there was this boy who always felt I had done more to get my high grades' – Aanwo

'If a captain were to be chosen, they prefer a male student' – Temitope

'When I was in primary school, some of the boys in my class would come around and threaten that it was no longer possible for a girl to lead them in examination. Some would go and barb their hair and come to show me that if I didn't understand, they had taken the position from me. Most of the time I would just smile. Sometimes they would tamper with my books or seize an exercise book. Well, I led them always, except in the final exam in primary school, I was beaten to the second position'

– Esther

'When I was in school, boys always felt there were positions meant for boys and not for girls' – Theresa

'When they don't care to know 'bout the level of your intelligence and by the constant phrase that what does a woman know and that our role is in the kitchen'

– Itunu

'In the front seat of a bus, men would rather seat at the edge and not women as one told me one day to come down from the edge for him to seat there' – Rebecca

Female Students

'Yes! those who are close to you i.e. husband or boyfriend act and speak in a domineering manner at times' – Segun

'Male colleagues say what do you think you can do after school rather than become a full housewife. They do not see women as aspiring further than the first degree certificate qualification.' – Teniola

'One of my classmates is big and tall, he thinks whatever he says in the class is the final, he is so domineering. His voice is so loud and he does this at times when we have to do assignments, he likes intimidating everyone' – Kehinde

'One particular lecturer seems to think we girls are in school simply to distract men from their studies and we make them unserious human beings e.g. a girl and a boy were talking in class, it was the guy he caught talking, he sent him out and asked the girl after a moment if she was the one distracting him even though it was the boy he caught. He sees all girls as dressing naked' – Ajoke

'My maths lecturer walked up to me on this day (I went to a vigil the night before, so I was stressed up) and said "You, you will fail this course, why are you frowning, can't you pretend?" (I know he's a womanizer)' – Debo

'In my practical group, I'm the only female among four guys, they hardly allow me to participate in the practical, they have the feeling that they will be more accurate in taking readings than me' – Chigozie

'For instance, some male students believe that they are better than you are and if you score more than them, they thought you are being given extra marks' – Folarin

'During our last field trip, the males in my group protected the ladies from excavating when the trench was going deeper. The males excavated while the ladies sieved and sort out finds' – Aramide

'For example, all the department in school, it is only male student that are been voted for as the President. We can contest for any position, if not that they are claiming superiority' – Tundun

'Several times, my course mates (male) say women can't compete with them academically. As the best student in my class, they make me assume it will end in the kitchen, I never gave in.' – Rolake

'When you perform better than them, they look at you with contempt as if you have used your body, not your brain' – Ngozi

'In the area of choosing or electing the class captain, they feel that women or ladies are not competent enough to oversee the affairs of the whole class.' – Olaore

Women in the Informal Economy

'I felt like that with my brother, because he took my land that I had already put blocks on. He said that if I talk, I will see what he would do to me. Why should he take what belongs to me, when it is not family land? I was given the land while I was young, then he took it and sold it off. If I were a man, I would have gone to any length to retrieve the land back' – Hassana

'When I first got to Lokoja, I thought I needed to get close to a man. After we went to bed, he gave me N200. I got thinking, and I wept, because I thought I had just sold my body' – Niniola

'Yes, as we dey so, e hard make woman be governor, e hard make woman be president. If a woman contest, people will not vote for her because she's a woman. I pray that a woman gets there'[5] – Nkechi

'If I were a man, no man would have forced me to cook for him and at the same time abuse me when the food is late.' – Chioma

'My father told me and my sister that we could not inherit any part of his house because we are girls.' – Nwanneka

Female Apprentices

'Sometimes they just talk to ladies anyhow' – Bimpe

'My younger ones are boys; they don't behave like a lady. They play football and I'm busy working, helping with the cooking, washing plates and fetching water. They wash plates at times, but they don't cook and fetch water' – Farinde

'Some men throw banters at women when they are passing by, you know that they can't do that to a male like themselves so it always makes me feel inferior.' – Rosaline

'Since men believe they are the head, They do things that suit them.' – Beyeruka

'Especially when boys talk to girls and they refuse their proposal, they will sit together and talk about it and make uncomplimentary statements.' Chinedu

'When my father refused to send me to school, I knew that if I were a man, he would have still sent me to school even if I did not want to' – Olaitan

'My father loves my two brothers more than we the girls. Whenever they request for anything he gives them without complaining but the reverse is the case for us girls.'
                                                                                          – Ireti

'Like the case of a quarrel that got to court and the woman withdrew the case because she did not have the money to continue with the case.' – Temi

'There is usually family meeting in my family but we ladies do not attend because they say we are women and not strong.' – Mary

MCL: It depends on the way you look at it. He made a woman out of a man. The Bible makes us to understand that the man had a deep sleep and God took out of his ribs, and then created a woman. The man then acknowledged that the woman was taken from his ribs and he called her a woman. A woman is a man with womb. So when you ask whether they were created equally, a woman is a man too. A man is created without a womb. You still see man in every woman. There is manhood in every woman.

Female Christian Leader (FCL) Ibadan: I have passion for women. I believe the hand that rocks the cradle rules the world. Without women, there is no humanity and womanhood is mysterious. If you check the problems we are having in the world today, of course a lot of people said it was caused by a woman. But thank God that everything was restored also by a woman, because I am talking from a religious perspective. If you look through the Bible, women raised generations and impacted on their communities. No one can afford to underestimate the power of womanhood. A man can be head but the spirit of the woman rules the home, rules the world. For instance, at the conception of Jesus, Mary said 'Waoh! from now henceforth, all generations will celebrate me' Although God was not happy with what Adam did, he used a woman to bring salvation back to humanity.

OM: How then are women different from men?

FCL: If you look at the scriptures very well, women are not different from men. I say women are better than men. Look at the scriptures very well, God made the man to sleep, made the woman from the rib of the man, and when the man saw the woman, I believe the atmospheric condition of Eden changed, and the man said this is a man with a womb. That is, a woman is a man with a womb. So, there is no difference between a man and a woman. The Bible said it was in the image of God that he created them, that is, both male and female. It was the man who actually called the woman a woman. God actually called her a help. What was lost in the man, God put in the woman – the breast and the womb. A woman is awesome. If I have to come back to life again, I will still come back as a woman.

In spite of the confusing signals from the female Christian leader in Ibadan, in respect of women's civic-political participation and roles of women in the private and public spheres, she appeared very clear about the question of the identity of women. In one of her sermons, recorded on video tape, she said: 'if the devil wants to oppress, he will oppress you with your identity … know who you are. You're not a foolish girl because you're married to an unbeliever who tells you you are worthless'. She insists that tradition and relationships oppress women, but that women who are 'born again' should not continue to struggle with identity, for, according to her, 'when your maker picks you up, your value increases'. She cited the example of Mary the Mother of Jesus to buttress the point. She urged women to straighten up, tell themselves they are gems and are uncommon. She says it is not about pride; it is just about celebrating oneself. When I put it to her that her views about women's identities do not seem different from those of feminists on the issue of women's identity, she said it is just that she has found liberation in Jesus. She makes it clear that she is biased in favour of women, and she would not have held the interview with me at the time she did, if I were a man.

Yoruba Traditional Religion – The Worship of Sango

Female Traditional Religious Leader (FTRL) Ibadan: Sango loves women. Oya, Sango's last wife, is the goddess of windstorm. When Sango wants to act, his wife (through windstorm) precedes him, and then he acts through thunder. Given this, Sango loves women. There is just one category of women that he is unable to tolerate – the witches. Don't also forget women plait their hair. Of course Sango plaits his hair too.

Overview

The identities of women that have emerged from this study can be summarized as follows: first, is the individual character of women that influences, and is influenced by, their relationships with other people, their work ethic and performance at work. Second, is claiming and valuing those qualities and ascriptions that make men the male gender – some of their character and their roles as breadwinners. Third, is the acceptance of the socially constructed female, one that is subordinate to and inferior to men. The last is the acceptance of what is deemed feminine – care, feeling, nurturing – but which has the potential for being put to productive use.

Christian and Muslim leaders acknowledged women as creatures of the Almighty, created to coexist with men as helpers. The female and male Christian leaders in Ibadan said a woman is a man with a womb and the female leader argued that this makes women superior to men. They all seem to want us to assume that they believe that women are indeed equals of men. Women had apparently taken and rejected cues from the position of religious leaders on women's roles in the private and public spheres. So, in spite of seemingly positive lessons from religious leaders about women's identities, most women's perception of who they are reflected in their acceptance of some of the teachings of religious leaders about their roles in the private and public spheres of life; that they are care-givers, and are subordinate to men. Some women rejected these lessons. They asserted that they are breadwinners/co-breadwinners; bold, courageous and aggressive.

Notes

1. Translates to: I don't look for trouble, but if you step on my toes, I will not take it lightly.
2. Translates to: men ruin the lives of women because of their understanding of who women are.
3. Translates to: women are human beings, but boys are more influential in their parents' house than girls. Boys don't go anywhere and they own their father's house/or they would inherit their father's house, and they will help everybody when they start work/earn a living. Whereas a girl's husband will take her to his house.
4. Translates to: because I am a woman, I do not have the power to make them leave.
5. Translates to: Yes, the way things are now, it is difficult for a woman to become Governor or President ...

5

The Violence of Power: Power Relations and Women's Experience of Violence

Violence against women involves the physical and verbal (both subtle and overt) coercion of women of all age groups, ethnic/racial backgrounds, religious persuasions, and socio-economic background. Violence against women is the profane treatment of women and total disrespect for them. It is a reflection of the inferior social position of women and the outrage that men feel towards them. Physical and verbal coercion of women have adverse implications on women's physical, psychological, emotional and economic well-being. It affects women's reproductive rights, their progress (both at work and in institutions of learning) and their ability to function fully as citizens. Although many well-meaning scholars, activists and religious leaders are comfortable with the psychological model of explanation of the abuse of women, violence against women is actually an inevitable consequence of the unequal relations of power between men and women in many societies.

Freire (1993), Foucault (1980) and Hooks (1984) offer illuminating views of the relationship between power and violence. Hooks (1984) captured the relationship between power and violence as follows:

> The Western philosophical notion of hierarchical rule and coercive authority is ... the root cause of violence against women, of adult violence against children, of all violence between those who dominate and those who are dominated' (p. 118).

Foucault compels us to take a deep and broad view of power. Mejiuni and Obilade (2004) observed that Foucault alerts us to the fact that individuals see power in terms of apparatus of state alone; and so, they think an analysis of power that does not focus on economic issues is unimportant, and individuals also believe that 'they' do not exercise power, 'others' do. Foucault believed that power is 'present in the smallest, apparently most inconsequential human interactions' (Brookfield 2001:7), and it is exercised through the body, sexuality, family, kinship, knowledge, technology and so on.

Violence against women is therefore both a means by which men preserve their power, and a habit. In this respect, Hooks stated that whatever group is in power would likely use coercive authority to maintain that power if it is challenged or threatened. It is therefore not surprising that when women put up resistance to their oppression and domination by men, men visit violence on them to maintain their authority and their dominant position. Freire (1993), also stated that 'violence is initiated by those who oppress, exploit, fail to recognize others as persons – not by those who are oppressed, exploited and unrecognized' (p. 55). It is for the reason of maintaining dominance over others that victims of violence who have, through their own oppression, imbibed the view that the powerful need to maintain their authority over the powerless through coercion, also mete out violence to others less powerful than they are.

Violence becomes a habit when the powerless do not resist violence in a productive way because of a variety of reasons. And although macabre, the powerful then enjoy meting out violence to the powerless, especially where the environment is conducive – for instance, where the culture of silence and the culture of impunity are pervasive. This explains why men hit, rape, sexually harass and exploit women who are 'gentle', 'meek', 'good' and 'feminine', and also socially, economically, culturally and politically less powerful than they are. This is also the reason why men mete out violence to babies, children and mentally retarded persons who trust them and or who do not have the capacity to object to their violation. Foucault (1980) hypothesized that resistance to power is to be found at the point where power relations are exercised. He said:

> There are no relations of power without resistances; the latter are all the more real and effective because they are formed right at the point where relations of power are exercised: resistance to power does not have to come from elsewhere to be real, nor is it inexorably frustrated through being the compatriot of power. It exists all the more by being in the same place as power; hence, like power, resistance is multiple and can be integrated in global strategies (p. 142).

Unfortunately, violence against women as a means of preserving men's power and as a habit continues to thrive in the context of a distorted view of God and God's will, and an unfair and inequitable insistence on adherence to what we have been told are God's injunctions. According to Freire (1993:61), 'under the sway of magic and myth, the oppressed see their suffering as the will of God' (because they are often told that it is the will of God), and Freire added 'as if God were the creator of this "organised disorder"'.

In the analysis of data that follows, most of the observations that have been made in the preceding paragraphs would come alive.

Women's Personal Experience of Violence, and or Knowledge of Others' Experience of Violence

Women were asked to indicate whether they or someone known to them had been a victim of violence. About a quarter, that is, twenty-three out of eighty-six literate women in formal work and female students, and about half, that is forty out of ninety-three semi-literate women in the informal economy and female apprentices indicated that they had been victims of violence (rape, battery and sexual harassment) or they knew somebody who had experienced violence. From the information in Table 5.1, more women in Lokoja than in Ibadan indicated that they had been victims of violence, or knew someone who had been a victim. Female students in Ibadan and Lokoja appear to be the group that had limited experience of violence, and limited knowledge of other's experience of violence.

Female respondents reported violence as follows: battery by husbands; battery by strangers; battery by a soldier and a mob. Rape by: armed robbers; gang of boys led by a boyfriend; and the driver of the victim's father. The women did not indicate the perpetrators of sexual harassment. The women reported consequences such as: ridicule; hatred of everybody by victim; relocation by victim because of shame; injuries; loss of pregnancy; death; attempted suicide; and perpetuation of further violence which took the form of retaliation by women in the community who beat the husband of a woman who died as a result of battery to pulp and burnt his property.

The Reaction of Victims of Violence to their Experience

According to some literate respondents, the rape victims reported to the police, and in one case, the assailant paid compensation to the victim. Another victim told her parents who reported to the police and got the assailants arrested. Five literate women indicated that the women kept quiet and were resigned to fate. Two of this category of women also reported that the victims relocated. One female student said the victim hated people, felt sorry for herself, although she later forgave all, and thought her experience was a lesson she had to learn. Two semi-literate women said a girl attempted suicide, while a ten-year-old victim of rape died.

A lot of the women, both literate and semi-literate indicated that they/the victims of battery by husbands/ partners reported to their parents/family, and the matter was settled. A number of women did nothing, and these included two literate women, while some women hit the men back, or fought them. Two women left their husbands, while a number of women moved out temporarily (and at times threatened divorce) and then the matter was settled. One semi-literate woman reported that a woman runs out of her home crying out for help when the husband hits her, while another reported that the woman simply cries when the husband hits her. Some of the semi-literate respondents indicated that

Table 5.1: Women's Personal Experience of Violence and or Knowledge of Others' Experience of Violence

	Yes				No				Total No. that Responded to the Question	Total No Sampled
	Ibadan		Lokoja		Ibadan		Lokoja			
	Frequency	Per centage	Frequency	Per centage	Frequency	Per centage	Frequency	Per centage		
Literate Women In Formal Work	5	11.9	10	23.8	14	33.3	13	31.0	42	42
Female Students	3	6.8	5	11.4	19	43.2	17	38.6	44	46
Semi-literate Women In Informal Economy	10	17.9	14	25.0	14	25.0	18	32.1	56	56
Semi-literate Female Apprentices	4	10.8	12	32.4	17	46.0	4	10.8	37	39
Total	22	12.3	41	22.9	64	35.8	52	29.0	179	183

Key: Yes – means yes, I have been a victim of violence, and or, I know someone who had experienced violence.

No – means no, I have not been a victim of violence, and or, I do not know someone who had been a victim.

Source: Data generated from the open-ended questionnaires completed by (or for) all four categories of female respondents who provided information during fieldwork.

the men begged them, or other people begged them and they made up. One woman would usually refuse to open the door to let the husband in when he was drunk, because once he got inside, he would beat her. An apprentice said she begged her boyfriend after he had hit her because she knew she had offended him.

As for women who had experienced violence perpetrated by persons who were not related to them, one woman reported that her mother hit back at the man who had hit her. A student reported to the authority of the institution and the offenders were punished. One woman did not do anything: she simply walked away from the place where she was assaulted; and yet another forgave the soldier who assaulted her after intervention by mediators.

The two literate women who reported that they had experienced sexual harassment said they did not do anything. One said it appeared normal that she was harassed and the other said she was told it was part of growing up.

Reactions of Others to Victims' Experience

Concerning rape, literate women reported that: some people were sympathetic, and encouraged victims to pull themselves together; the matter was kept within friends; and in some cases, some people threw peculiar looks at the victim and the accused. One semi-literate respondent said people cursed the man that raped a ten-year-old; another said a victim was ridiculed, and yet another said the girl's parents took her to the hospital. However, people asked the girl who was raped by her father's driver what she had gone to do in the man's room.

Concerning battery by husband/partner, literate women (in formal work settings alone) reported that: there was much bitterness directed at a husband; in another case there was apathy; and in yet another case it appeared normal. People supported the woman who moved from the husband who had been battering her; and some women were told that battery is part of marital secret. In some cases, women were said to have narrated their own experiences and then told victims to endure and be prayerful. In cases of assault by non-relations, the woman who hit back at a man got support from on-lookers, while people pleaded on behalf of the soldier who had assaulted a woman.

Semi-literate women indicated that whenever they reported to the families/parents of their husbands that their husbands had hit them, they would usually intervene and settle the problem. A particular respondent said she almost fought a husband who had beaten his wife, and another woman said in the case she had cited, the woman was stubborn. One woman said while some people advised her to leave the man, others told her to endure. Another indicated that although her father had told her to go back to her husband, she did not go until the husband came to beg her and her family. Other women reported that people: begged the husband and advised the wife; separated them during the altercation and advised them, especially the woman; advised the woman to submit to the husband as ordained by the Bible; begged the man because the woman is always at fault; and, advised the woman to run away whenever the man is feeling provoked. In the case of battery by husband that resulted in death, the women in the community beat and almost killed the perpetrator, the husband, and they burnt his property. Three women reported that: 'people advised that I should not go back to him'; 'they felt bad and begged me' and, 'they do not like the way he beats me'.

Semi-literate apprentices reported that people: encouraged the woman to fight the man; felt pity for the woman, but were wary because whenever they offered her some advice, she would usually tell the man once they have reconciled; people looked on; and in another case, the talk was that she ought not to have married when she did, and that at any rate, the man is not right for her. In one case, the woman's neighbours actually advised that she should not open the door for the husband whenever he comes home drunk. Three women reported that: 'they thought he behaved badly'; 'I was unable to intervene because they are older than I am, although my parents intervened' and, 'no one knew he had hit me'.

In Box 5.1, we take details of some of the responses of literate and semi-literate women to their experiences and or knowledge of others' experience of violence; how women responded to their ordeals; how others responded to the women's experience; and, respondents' own explanations for the reasons others reacted the way they did.

Box 5. 1: Women Cite their Personal Experience of Violence, Others' Experience of Violence, Reactions to those Experiences and the Explanations that were Proffered

---

Literate Women Said

She reported the incident to her parents and the crisis was settled although she spent three days in the hospital after her husband beat her. People were raining abuses on the husband. They all reacted bitterly but since what God has joined together, they can not put asunder ... – Abosede

I have been beaten, and I know several women who have experienced all stated above. I did not do anything. People's response was that of apathy. They believed it was normal for a stubborn woman to be beaten by her husband or boyfriend, and a victim of rape and sexual harassment asked for it by the way she dressed, spoke or behaved – Aanwo

Yes, I've been beaten and sexually harassed. I braced up to the challenge. I strengthened my resolve that I am an individual with equal rights and that I would not be a weakling. For other people, it was like it is the usual thing to be beaten or

I have not been subjected to the experience but I know a mature girl who was raped by armed robbers. She was hospitalized for two days. After she left the hospital, she requested that she should be allowed to leave the town for another place. She was just not comfortable around her environment again. She cried so much because she said she had experienced horror. People comforted her. She was a Christian and so she had Christian friends around her. The attitude of other people was positive because she was not mocked and nobody exaggerated the situation. They just encouraged her – Esther

Yes, I know a lot of women whose husbands have turned them to their boxing partners. Well, women are not angels, they have their shortcomings too, but that does not mean men should beat them. Most people narrate their own experiences and advice the women to endure and be prayerful. They give the advice, perhaps because they have had similar experiences – Theresa

Yes, I've been sexually harassed. I could not report to anyone because it was a shame telling anyone, even your mother. The blame will always be that of the woman. Others were not happy, but they said it was part of growing up. The society does not attach much importance to sexual harassment. They see it as normal, provided you didn't yield – Adedigba

Semi-literate Women Said

I've have been beaten before. I have heard of a rape victim before too. When my husband raised his fist and it pained me, I retaliated even though I was not as powerful as he was. When members of his family were trying to settle the problem, it was clear from their utterances that they were reacting negatively to me – Rukayat

One of our classmates was raped while we were young. My neighbor's husband hit her. We settled the problem between the husband and his wife. The cause was sex. Because the woman was not well cared for, she did not allow the husband to have sex with her and thus fighting ensued. I almost went as far as fighting the man. It was because I believed that women are much more important in the house, and they don't deserve to be beaten – Modinat

My apprentice was raped in Lagos. My husband beat me twice because I was stubborn. I went against his wish. I proved too stubborn thereby getting my husband angry to the extent that he slapped me. I therefore believe that some women deserve beating because of their behavior. I went to my father after the beating to report him but my father said that I should go back there. I went to stay with my friend in her house and after some days he came to beg me and my family; and so, I went back to him. Others' attitude to my husband was negative because they believed that it's not good to beat a woman and he was advised against it. They even went to the extent of telling him that there are effective ways of dealing with a woman which would not involve raising an arm –Toun

Yes, my sister's husband used to beat her regularly. She eventually moved out and even lost a child during the process of beating. People felt pity for her, because he kept inflicting wounds on her and she was suffering. And it wasn't as if she was at fault – Morenike

My husband used to beat me. I would run away, and he would come and beg me and then I go back. People advised me not to go back to him, but I went back because of my children – Adama

My neighbor's husband beats her. We usually beg the man and advice the woman because she is always at fault. She cries whenever he beats her. We don't make friends with her, because she is very troublesome. As her character be, na im no make us like am [1] – Nkechi

I know of a woman who was beaten to death by her husband and a young girl of less than 10 years that was raped. All the women in the community beat the man up to the point of death and destroyed his property. In cases like these, people keep to themselves because you will be seen as influencing the woman, if you offer pieces of advice – Caroline

Yes, my friend always beat the husband back when he beats her. I also know of a ten year old girl that was raped. The 10 year old girl died. She was raped by her cousin three times before it was discovered. She started emaciating, had protruding stomach, she had wounds on her private part, and was taken to the hospital, but she died. People swore for her cousin. They said "may it never be well with him" – Nwanneka.

Advice on Violence

In the paragraphs that follow, we will find the advice that women and men gave or would give to female victims of violence, irrespective of (for the women) whether they had themselves experienced violence or they knew someone who had experienced violence. The forms of violence against women that were specifically identified in this study are: rape, battery and sexual harassment. Two literate women in formal work advised that women who experience beating by persons other than their partners should: 'fight back in a decent and result-oriented way' and 'assess whether you are at fault, then organize retaliation'. On sexual harassment, two literate women said: 'women should not dress half-naked to avoid sexual harassment'; 'if decently dressed, rebuff the advance'; and two female students said: 'Pray that God should keep their eyes off you'; and 'seek legal attention'. Still on sexual harassment, a semi-literate woman said, 'a woman should not walk around in the dark, and should take care of herself'.

Some of the respondents were quite detailed and careful about their responses, and so they separated battery by husband from battery by other persons, and many gave more than an advice. A few gave several.

The responses vary, so were the reasons proffered for the advice given. The responses have therefore been categorized into ten different themes. In pulling the responses into the different categories, consideration was given, not only to the advice proffered by the respondent, but also to the reasons the respondent gave for offering that particular advice. The reasons given usually throw some light on the perspective/framework from which the respondent is reacting to the issue, and giving advice. By way of example, Abayomi, a male lawyer advised that a woman check herself if she is beaten. That appears ambiguous. He however added that she should contact a lawyer if raped or sexually harassed, but must be properly dressed to avoid rape and sexual harassment. The second part of his advice clarified his position, which is that improper dressing results in sexual abuse and violence. Although this is a contested position, someone else may take the same position as Abayomi, and consider that it is not just a correct position, but that it is important to give tips that will help girls prevent the abuses. A problem however arises if s/he then adds, as Abayomi did, that 'a properly dressed woman cannot be harassed or raped...' To the ambiguous statement that a woman should check herself if beaten, he clarified his position, when he said: 'women should not be beaten unjustly. Therefore parents, husband or mediator would determine and advise properly on the cause of being beaten'. So, while one would have been tempted to categorize his advice on rape as a critical comment, the reason he gave for the position he took shows that he was being judgemental, not critical. At any rate, objective questioning is not undertaken in isolation of the individual's values, prejudices and beliefs, and the normative ideologies of her/his context (McDonald, Cervero and Courtenay 1999).

Another example is appropriate here. Abimbola, a semi-literate woman said: 'I will preach to such person and advise her to pray for the person that beat her so that he can embrace Christ. I will do the same for a rape victim.' This appears like a very practical advice to give to a believer. However, when Abimbola gave the reasons she would offer the advice, her actual position became clear. She said: 'Because if the person is born again then she won't be living the type of life that got her to be raped. Because the way of life of a lady can contribute to her being raped or beaten though it's not like that in some cases'. Clearly, much of the time, while Abimbola is advising that a female victim of violence should pray, she would also be saying to herself – she's a bad person anyway, so she should just pray. On the surface, at least until one looked at the reasons she gave, her advice did not in any way show that she thought the woman brought the problem on herself. As a matter of fact, one got the impression she thought the assailant was wrong, and required prayers. This woman's response, rather than be categorized as practical, is judgemental.

The responses that we have put into the first category, Category A, represent advice that appears practical in cases of rape and battery by husband. For rape, medical checkup; proper/Christian counselling; psychological help; see qualified medical doctor; take precautions to avoid further abuse; watch the people you move with on campus and report/talk to mother/relations/trusted friend, were the advice offered. Others are: report to organizations that protect human/ women's rights; defend self physically, spiritually and intellectually; watch inte- ractions with non-relations; report to social workers. In cases of battery, the advice was to: dialogue, then report to the police; have a means of livelihood; report to own/his family; move away from hot arguments; run, and give him a wide berth; and, do not marry through match-making.

In Category B are responses that show outrage, but still seek to offer practical advice, usually corresponding with the level of outrage felt by the respondent. They are: report to law enforcement agents/the appropriate authority; seek legal action/go to court; apprehend and send him to jail, and lock him up forever.

In Category C are responses that appear like they are practical advice but are, in reality, judgemental. Behind them lie the assumption (they are offered from the premise) that the woman caused or brought the problem on herself, then follows automatically, injunctions such as: accept what has come your way, and live by it; see Bible-believing man of God for deliverance and spiritual therapy, and report to pastor.

In Category D are responses that indicate/signify apathy, lethargy; fear and powerlessness: Keep mute/keep quiet; take it as part of life; forgive assailants and forget; keep it to yourself; see it as a learning experience; comfort yourself and change abode and be patient because of the children.

In Category E are responses that appeared critical but were, in fact, judgemental? Underlining a critical view or advice by some respondents is the thinking, for example, that a woman who has done wrong deserves to be beaten. Some of the responses are: Ask her what she did wrong; careful the way you dress; know what led to the abuse; turn a new leaf; cultivate decent and polite social relationship; dress normally like a good lady; should have comported herself better; must have been walking at night; it may be an affair gone sour and, 'did you arouse the sexual desire of a male by dressing wildly?'; she should take it like that if she deserves beating; woman should have good manners and should be of good behaviour; and, she must have wronged him.

In Category F, we find responses that seek to deconstruct talks about stigmatization and silence. Examples are: speak out and, women should not be embarrassed reporting to security agencies.

Category G contains responses that appear like they are practical tips for, especially, believers. In reality, however, such advice promotes magic consciousness; it is a form of escapism and may become fatalistic. Daniska, a male student, advised that women who have been beaten by their husbands should seek spiritual guidance from God to make the men change. He went further, 'because whatever situation one finds himself or herself, God placed him or her in that situation, and it is only God that can change things permanently'.

In Category H, we find reactions of respondents who are just enraged by the problem of violence. Examples of the responses are: do not agree if he begs; retaliate; fight back; and,organize retaliation.

In Category I are responses that indicate that women should kowtow: be submissive to avoid being hurt; watch your bad attitude to men and be submissive; don't be stubborn; and, beg him.

In Category J are responses that urge women to end abusive relationships: leave him; move out; if battery is incessant, leave him, and divorce him.

In Category K are responses of persons who urged women to hang around abusive partners once there is mediation.

It is important to note that a few respondents gave advice that cut across some of the categories that have been highlighted above. Note the advice from Seun, a semi-literate woman:

> Whatever he says, she should take it and beg him. A woman should have her work so that she does not have to ask a man for money. On rape, I will tell her sorry, and advise that she should take care of herself and go to the hospital and tell the doctor. They may tell her to go for test, so it won't result in pregnancy. I don't mind her aborting that kind of pregnancy. My view stem from my upbringing and my conviction on how to live well.

One is tempted to categorize Seun's first sentence as kowtowing. However, she follows up with a practical advice. We refer, once again, to Abayomi's response. Hence again to Abayomi's response, he recommends that she gets in touch with a lawyer, but must be properly dressed. Under the above categorization, we could place his responses under those that feel outrage but offer practical advice, and those that are critical and judgemental.

Five literate men advised that a woman who has been assaulted by persons other than her husband should: 'watch her behaviour'; 'check the cause' and, 'report to the police'. On sexual harassment, seven men advised that women should report to the police or the appropriate authority; for, according to them, it is a crime. Note that the reaction of literate men to sexual harassment is unanimous, and distinctly different from the reaction of literate women. Take these two responses by male students: 'There is every need for her to exercise her legal right over the embarrassment (harassment) so that the man reaps the punishment for his offence. Sexual harassment is a crime and, if not properly treated, it will then become a "trait" which will be inherited by some other men and become their everyday practice' and,

> in such a case, it is difficult for such a female to share her experience with sympathizers. However, I advise that such female should pull herself together and take appropriate actions, such as reporting to the police or sharing with others that could assist.

Sexually harassing a female or beating, as the case may be, implies an abuse of right and an implication that she is inferior. My reason is solely based on the fact that her right has been abused, hence the need for her to take action.

What Possibilities/Potentials Does this Advice Have for Improving Women's Social Status?

We considered that it is important that we focus on advice that a woman receives after experiencing violence because it is part of her reality, or part of the construction of her reality. The ten categories of responses or advice indicated above were thus pulled into three views of how women should handle violence. I arrived at the three views by taking a look at the totality of the gains/results that an adherence to the advice will produce for: the individual woman who is the victim; the generality of women, all of whom are potential victims; the entire society, and the hope (possibility) that it holds for improving women's social status.

The first group comprises the category of responses that hold high probability of yielding gains for women. Those in this group are: A – Practical advice; B – Outraged but offers practical advice; F –Deconstructs talk about stigmatization and silence, and J – End abusive relationships. Some of the reasons that respondents gave for the advice are instructive, as they point to the gains that can accrue to women and society if their advice is followed. See Box 5.2 for some of the advice and the reasons the respondents gave for offering the advice. This set of advice, which holds high probability of yielding gains for women, liberating and empowering as it appears, is clearly not so straightforward and without problems. The advice that cases should go to the Police/Court and the appropriate authority assumes that: the Nigeria Police, the Judiciary and most male-headed institutions are efficient and not corrupt; the laws on rape and battery are straightforward and favour women (WARSHE 2004); and, that the Police, Magistrates/Judges and men in positions of authority in institutions do not hold views that consider that women are inferior to men, women are objects of desire, they cannot make up their minds and those that 'offend' their husbands should be 'corrected' by bullying.

Clearly also, when women speak openly about rape, they demystify the subject, and at some point in time, our society will have to accept that rapists should be the ones to hide their faces, not the victims, and concrete steps would be taken to make rapists hide their face. Just the same way, when wife batterers lose their wives through separation and divorce, many men will have to do a rethink about hitting their wives. However, given the way our society is presently configured, and the prevailing attitudes (many of which are reflected in some of the advice given to victims of violence in this study) women who speak openly about their experience of rape and those who leave/divorce abusive partners will still face the stigma of being 'rape victim' and 'divorcee'. In the case of a divorced woman, she would probably also have to bear the burden of being sole breadwinner, given her new status. However, on balance, this view still appears to be the position/advice that can empower women to improve their social position in the long run.

The second group comprises the categories of responses that appear to give practical tips to believers, but can also promote magic consciousness (G); that show that respondents are enraged (H); and, those that urge women to hang around abusive relationships if there is mediation (K). We will find some of the details in Box 5.3. These sets of advice may or may not empower women in the long run depending on their usage. By way of example, the view that women should pray when they have been battered and that neighbours should preach to husband and wife who have been exchanging fisticuffs, can be used either to perpetuate violence or halt violence. This view can empower women, and can be used to further abuse women. Interestingly, two distinct usages of religion appeared to have emerged from the responses of women, especially semi-literate women and literate men. From the advice that some semi-literate women gave on violence, they appear to be encouraging the use of religion to perpetuate the status quo. Whereas, many men gave liberating views of religion, when they supported their views with religion, one is not sure that all the men who attributed their views to religion will never beat their wives/rape a woman. Many 'religious' leaders are known to be wife batterers and there have been reports of religious leaders that have raped women and children who trust them. It is also possible that women who advised other women to pray when they have experienced battery or rape will have difficulties abiding by the same injunction if they were the victims.

The advice that literate women who felt outraged by the problem of violence on women proffered, which is that women should respond to violence with violence, will probably give a few women immediate satisfaction and may also serve as deterrence to bullies in the short term, but it is not likely to enhance the social status of women in general in the long term because it may set off a cycle of violence. If one person organizes retaliation on a rapist or a person who committed assault or a wife batterer, she cannot be sure he would not try to organize bigger retaliation. Clearly, wife battery, assault and rape thrive in our society because of the culture of impunity, and in the context of patriarchy/sexism, classism (Weissman 2007) and seniority. There is no evidence to show that if we organize retaliation, that is, take the laws into our hands, sexism and patriarchy will cease to exist. We cannot then confidently say that we can empower women through retaliation when women have been sexually harassed, raped, assaulted, and battered either by their husbands/boyfriends or unknown persons.

Of course, women have to resist violence in an effective and productive way, but resistance cannot be through one method alone. Resistance can be getting: women and (men) to take a fresh look at religious injunctions; mothers

Box 5.2: Advice on Violence; Group A – Advice that Should Empower Women

Literate Women in Formal Work

'Leave the partner who is abusing her if he cannot be counseled to stop; because more often than not, abused women become murder victims' – Adeola

'They should speak out and report it as soon as they possibly can. Rape carries a penalty of life imprisonment and the more people are aware of this the better. The more ladies speak of their experiences, the more the issue of rape/sexual abuse will be demystified – Adetutu

'Run for their lives and seek spiritual and medical cleansing. Never report to the Police as this would lead to more degradation and harassment. If a man hits a woman, then he can kill her one day; so, the best solution is to give him a wide berth. Reporting to the Police would only mean opening up wounds that may have healed since most times the sympathy is with the accused not the victim'

– Aanwo

'They should fight back in as much a decent and result oriented way as possible. They should not keep quiet or else, more will come their way. Keeping quiet over such issues or not acting is rather a sign of weakness which encourage more even worse of such actions from those doing it to you and even other onlookers'

– Omolade

Female Students

'They should go first and seek medical attention. They should not be afraid or embarrassed to seek redress from appropriate institution (legal). Being a traumatic experience, victims need immediate medical attention (physical and emotional). More often than not, women, instead of inciting abuse are mere victims and therefore must be protected by law' – Modupe

Semi-literate Women

'As woman no get power reach man, I go say make the woman run' – Talatu

Semi-literate Female Apprentice

'She should seek legal action and divorce the man. A rape victim should treat her self and seek legal action too. Because beating and rape is ridiculous and bad. A rapist can kill' – Tosan

Literate Men in Formal Work Settings

'She should first make a report of the incident to the law enforcement agents and thereafter seek medical attention (in case she's been beaten or raped). This will allow the law enforcement agents to deal with the culprit(s) and so serve as deterrence to others that might want to repeat such a dastardly act. Medical help will allow for proper and comprehensive medical check up and subsequent treatment' – Tubosun

'Any woman who has been beaten, raped or sexually harassed should report to the police for criminal prosecution or to the court for civil action. To beat a woman or rape a woman is against morality, it is therefore a criminal offence and justiceable'

– Jacob

'She should confide in a close friend or adult immediately it happens. Such a person is expected to encourage her to take up the matter with the law enforcement agents. The society tends to stigmatize rape victims, for instance, making them appear as guilty as the culprit. It would then take efforts as well as some encouragement to make such victims come out to confront their assailants' – Adamu

Male Students

'She should report at the police station and also seek counseling to avoid the after-effects of shock and embarrassment. This is because raping or beating a woman is a brutal behaviour that should be totally discouraged in any society' – Gafar

'She should report the case to the appropriate authority or her parents and ultimately to law enforcement agents, and finally seek redress at the court of law. Keeping it secret will be like waging a psychological war against herself. Informing the law enforcement agents would bring about justice and prevent the culprit from future attempts' – Taiwo

'She should seek redress in court. She should not be ashamed as Africans are shy seeking redress for such claims. The society does not see rape and battery of a woman as dehumanizing. But the lady could be my sister, friend, mother and anybody' – Ayodele

'She should report to the school authority and the case should be taken to court. This is because it is religiously wrong to rape a woman and it is a criminal offence'

– Zubairu

to speak up more for their daughters who have been raped and who are in abusive relationships, both privately and publicly;[2] and getting women in a certain location/community to ostracize men who have raped girls/women and men who have battered their wives.

The advice that women hang around if there is mediation may or may not empower women, depending on the framework from which the mediators intervene. Mediators who hold strongly to the view that women be subject to men are likely to blame a woman for the problems between herself and her husband, or blame a woman who has been raped. Mediators who have a sense of fairness, kindness and who are honest, and or who take a liberating view of religion may be able to empower women through mediation.

The third group is composed of categories of responses that are comfortable positions/easy arguments that hold the least probability of empowering women, and enhancing women's social position. We can glean them in Box 5.4. They are: advice that appeared practical, but were actually judgmental (C); advice that depicted apathy, lethargy, fear and powerlessness (D); advice that appeared critical but were in fact judgmental (E); and advice that implored women to kowtow (I). Clearly, these sets of advice have their own uses, especially for those who hold traditional views of women's roles in the private and public spheres of life. Given data from this study, most women and men hold such views, in spite of the objections that they have to violence against women. It is because many people hold the traditional view of the roles of women in the public and private spheres that some are unable to object seriously to violence against women, especially battery. They are therefore unable to offer advice that could be deemed bold/radical steps by our society. Women who hold on to this comfortable position usually get by, in spite of pains of violence; they stay within a meaning perspective (that is, the lens through which each of them filters, engages, and interpretes the world {Merriam and Cafarella 1999}) that they are used to, and in which they feel safe. For some of the people who hold this view, objecting seriously to violence may mean questioning long-held values and assumptions, and this may rupture their meaning perspectives (Cranton 1994), make them insecure, and take them through pains that they might consider unnecessary.

In addition, in cases of battery, the advice that women should kowtow, if adhered to, holds possibilities of giving women immediate relief from abortions, broken jaws and bruises that result from battery. In the long term, however, the implications are many. In the case of a wife batterer, he would keep up the abuse of his wife; for, he would presume that she is a mule that needs to be beaten to shape or that she is a fool, a pushover. It would also strengthen him to expand the scope of his abuse beyond 'his domain' (his home/family) to the public, and then he would begin to demand that all women do not only do as he demands, but also offer him whatever he wants on their knees. Although the following example, given by one of the respondents in this study is not about

Box 5.3: Advice on Violence; Group B – Advice that May or May not Empower Women

Literate Women in Formal Work

'First assess whether you are at fault in the situation. If beaten and you don't deserve it, be bold and organize a retaliation, if sexually harassed and you were decently dressed, rebuff the advance and prove your worth in a decent manner. It is my personal view and I oppose the view that women should be treated unjustly because of their sex! ' – Itunu

Semi-literate Women in the Informal Economy

'If she is raped, she should leave everything to God to judge and be prayerful. If she is beaten, she should change her way and be more prayerful. The rape victim is stigmatized; she may not be able to get a man to marry in the neighborhood because of the rumors; so she should be prayerful' – Moji

'My advice is that she should change her ways if she is at fault and she should be prayerful so as to keep her home intact. My religion is against divorce' – Alake

'Leave everything to God; she can't take the fight upon herself. Because it will cause her more pains and it won't help the situation' – Yime

'Some women are stubborn. Men are the head of the family, she should submit herself and pray. Beating her will not solve the problem though. God can do all'

– Margaret

Semi-literate Female Apprentices

'She should be prayerful and be patient with the man if he is her husband. Because we are made to believe that the man is the head of the family' – Tolu

Male Students

'She should take everything to God in prayers.; and seek help from professional counselors (psychologists) to work on her emotion. This will take the form of therapy. She should try and find out why that incident happened to her. We all believe in one thing or the other; therefore, seeking spiritual solution is number one. Though the spiritual is guided by faith and therefore there is need to seek human advice because both operate on the same level (physical)' – Odedele

'If any woman is beaten, probably by her husband, I implore her to seek spiritual guide from God to make him change his ways. Whatever situation one finds himself or herself, God placed him or her in that situation and it is only God that can change things permanently' – Daniska

battery, it is the case of men believing that all women are inferior to them. Rebecca, a lawyer said in response to whether men have ever tried to make her feel inferior: 'In the front seat of a bus, men would rather sit at the edge and not women, as one told me one day to come down from the edge so he can sit there'. To the likes of the man Rebecca encountered, Rebecca is just another woman, and he must have quickly reminded himself that he has her type, whom he orders around, as wife at home. Submitting to a rapist so one does not get hurt, as one of the respondents advised, would strengthen the rapist to pick up more preys, and he would convince himself that the woman wanted to be raped, and that it was actually a good thing he chose to rape her! If a woman begs the rapist, he would say to himself that her begging was rather feeble, and that she just wanted to be pushed a lot further.

Finally, there is no reason to believe that respondents in this study can give the same advice in all circumstances of violence, or that they can abide by their own injunctions when faced with the experience of violence. They may, for example, move from being totally submissive to challenging the basis of violence and insisting that women's humanity be acknowledged, and they may move from organizing retaliation to praying.

In Tables 5.2 and 5.3, I present the percentages of responses that fell under the three groups/types of advice that women who had experienced violence have been given, or the types of advice that those who would experience violence will receive. The advice ranges from that with the highest probability of enhancing women's social position to that with the least possibility of enhancing women's social status.

Concerning advice on rape, we observe in Table 5.2 that literate men gave the highest percentage (88.09%) of advice that should empower women, while literate women followed with 72.3 per cent and semi-literate women trailed behind with 59.3 per cent of their responses grouped as capable of empowering women. However, both literate and semi-literate women gave almost the same percentage of advice that has been categorized as holding the least possibility of empowering women (22.8% and 22.03% respectively) as against 10.71 per cent of the advice given by men.

On the advice that respondents gave in respect of battery by husband, although more semi-literate women than the literate women and men responded to this question, a higher percentage of advice offered by the very few literate women (55.6%) who responded was considered to be capable of empowering women, compared with 37.5 per cent by literate men and 27.7 per cent by semi-literate women. Literate men and semi-literate women gave almost equal percentages of advice that was considered to hold the least possibility of empowering women, that is 50 per cent and 50.6 per cent respectively.

Box 5.4: Advice on Violence; Group C — Advice that Reflect the Comfortable Position and Hold the Least Possibility of Empowering Women

Literate Women

'Watch their attitudes towards men; and try all possible means to be submissive. Women should dress properly to avoid sexual harassment and know the type of friends they keep. Women may be beaten by men due to their bad attitude. Most of the women who are harassed are those that dress half naked' – Omolola

'They should accept it as part of life; feel free and normal in the society' – Odunola

Female Students

'I would advice that women who experience either of or some of these abuses should go to the hospital for medical treatment and try to forget what has happened and start a new life with a good character. They should go to the hospital in order to prevent incurable diseases and unwanted pregnancy' – Foyeke

Semi-literate Women in Informal Economy

'A woman should be humble and submissive to her husband and a lady should be responsible in dressing and comportment so as not to be raped. This is my belief' – Bolanle

'She should be patient because she has children' – Bolaji

'She should pray and stay with the husband so as not to leave the children in the hand of an unknown woman. Because where ever she goes, she will be a stranger there and the devil you know is better than a new sweet angel' – Memuna

'If she knows what can cause quarrel between her and the husband, she should not do it and if she has made any mistake she should try and rectify it. Even if she has to beg the husband, let her do so. Since the husband is the head of the house, she has to submit herself' – Tade

Semi-literate Apprentices

'For beating, may be she doesn't obey, so he beats her. She must have been doing something and provoking the man, so he beats in annoyance. Perhaps she's jealous and disgraces him in public. For rape, she must have been walking late hours; make im sidon for house. She should treat herself' – Salamotu

'Women should be patient, since they are married and have nowhere to go again. If it's a boyfriend, I will leave him, for if we get married, he will be beating me. I don't know of rape. If a woman is patient, the husband will do a rethink, and may realize that what he is doing is not right' – Towoju

'A woman should be submissive, so I will tell her to rectify her faults and live in peace with her husband. Women are weak so we should not engage ourselves in fisticuffs with men' – Tomiwa

Literate Men in Formal Work Settings

'She should try as much as possible to be submissive in order to avoid being seriously injured; but after the incident, she should report the matter to the law enforcement agents and go for medical examination. The only option left for a woman under such a situation is submission; otherwise, she may sustain serious bodily injuries that could result in an unforeseen disaster' – Audu

'If a woman is beaten, she should take heart. It is one of those things' – Kalio

Male Students

'She should tell her mother and behave maturely. She should not expose herself to the public so that she can avoid stigmatization. It will take extra efforts to associate oneself with anyone who has been raped' – Nosa

'She should check if she has aroused the sexual desire of the male counterpart or did something wrong to have warranted her being beaten, and then forgive herself. Some ladies dress wildly, thus arousing a strong sexual feeling' – Fijabi

'If a lady or woman is raped or has been sexually harassed, she should keep it to herself, and then go to the hospital to explain to her doctor and probably go for pregnancy and HIV tests. If she exposes it, it may affect her social life and the stigma may take a long time to disappear. Again, a case of rape is not easy to prove in a law court' – Yisa

Table 5.2: Advice on Rape by Category of Respondents

	From Among 86 Literate Women Came 123 Pieces of Advice	Per centage of Total Advice that:	From Among 93 Semi-literate Women Came 59 Pieces of Advice	Per centage of Total Advice that:	From Among 61 Literate Men Came 84 Pieces of Advice	Per centage of Total Advice that:
Should Empower Women (ABFJ)	89	72.3	35	59.3	74	88.09
May or May Not Empower Women (GHK)	6	4.9	11	18.6	1	1.19
Least Possibility Of Empowering Women (CDEI)	28	22.8	13	22.03	9	10.71

Key:

A: Practical Advice **B**: Outraged but offers practical advice **C**: Seemingly practical but actually judgmental advice **D**: Apathy, lethargy, fear and powerlessness

E: Critical and Judgmental **F**: Deconstruction of Myths and Social Constructions

G: Practical tips for believers? **H**: Just Enraged **I**: Kowtow **J**: End relationship

K: Hang around if there is mediation

Source: Data generated from the open-ended questionnaires completed by (or for) all categories of female and male respondents who provided information during fieldwork.

Table 5.3: Advice on Battery by Husband

	From Among 86 Literate Women Came 9 Pieces of Advice	Per centage of Total Advice that:	From Among 93 Semi-literate Women Came 83 Pieces of Advice	Per centage of Total Advice that:	From Among 61 Literate Men Came 8 Pieces of Advice	Per centage of Total Advice that:
Should Empower Women (ABFG)	5	55.6	23	27.7	3	37.5
May or May Not Empower Women (GHK)	3	33.3	18	21.7	1	12.5
Least Possibility Of Empowering Women (CDEI)	1	11.1	42	50.6	4	50

Key:

A: Practical Advice **B:** Outraged but offers practical advice **C:** Seemingly practical but actually judgmental advice **D:** Apathy, lethargy, fear and powerlessness

E: Critical and Judgmental **F:** Deconstruction of Myths and Social Constructions

G: Practical tips for believers? **H:** Just Enraged **I:** Kowtow **J:** End relationship

K: Hang around if there is mediation

Source: Data generated from the open-ended questionnaires completed by (or for) all categories of female and male respondents who provided information during fieldwork.

On aggregate, the advice that literate women gave to women on rape and battery by husband was mainly advice that should empower women; although on the matter of rape, more of the advice that men gave was considered to be capable of empowering women. The reason was that on the matter of rape, although many literate and semi-literate women rejected rape of women, a number of women accepted the easy and lazy arguments that women who have been raped brought it on themselves because: of their bad attitude to men; they were dressed half-nakedly; they have been walking around at night; and, have been keeping the company of bad girls. They therefore accepted the myths and arguments that allow rape to flourish, and that hinder attempts to stem the tide of this type of violence on women. The women who imbibe and proffer these arguments do not know that they, their mothers and their daughters are potential victims of this kind of violence. They fail to take cognizance of some of the witnessing that some women in this study have given concerning how: a ten-year-old was raped; how armed robbers raped a young woman; and how a gang of boys, led by a boyfriend raped a girl. Neither did they take cognizance of the actual and potential consequences of the incidents on the victims, their families and the society at large.

The fact that more literate and semi-literate women than men took this position, a position that holds the least possibility of empowering women, is particularly unfortunate because when women are raped, those are the voices that they hear, and the views that the voices articulate condition their reactions and those of their families to their ordeal. Those views result in informal learning. This is part of the process of construction of who those women become. It is also part of the process of constructing the identity of other women who have heard the negative comments about victims of rape.

Equally unfortunate is the advice that semi-literate women who are mothers and potential mothers, who take active part (and will take active part) in the construction of the identities of female and male children, gave to victims of battery by husband. Fifty point six per cent (50.6%) of their advice had been categorized as holding the least possibility of empowering women. This is because they took the position that women who have been abused by their husbands: were stubborn; were not submissive; should have begged their husbands; lacked character; and, must have provoked the man. Although not many men offered advice on battery by husband, 50 per cent of the advice offered, very much like the advice that the semi-literate women gave, assumed that, women who are stubborn; who behave badly to men; who challenge men's authority; who are not submissive; and who are confrontational, deserve to be beaten.

In Table 5.4, we compare the advice that literate and semi-literate women who have had close encounters with violence have given (or would give) on how victims of rape and battery should handle their experience.

On balance, from the examples of the responses of literate and semi-literate women that are represented in Table 5.4, there is no clear-cut difference in the positions of literate and semi-literate women (who have had close encounters with violence) on how victims of rape and battery should handle their experience.

We recall that literate men gave more of the advice on rape that were considered capable of empowering women than did literate women, and both literate and semi-literate women gave almost equal percentages (22.8% and 22.03% respectively) of advice that was considered to hold the least possibility of empowering women. And, more literate and semi-literate women took positions that were considered to hold the least probability of empowering women than did literate men.

These results underscore the position earlier articulated in this work that women do not benefit from education in the same way that men do. Although literate women and men have had the same formal school training and work on the same kinds of schedule in their work places, the differences in the positions taken by literate women and men in this study are traceable to the educative influences/experiences (socialization achieved through day-to-day interactions in schools and outside the schools and religion) that women have, that men do not have, and that women and men teach women or compel women to learn through a system of rewards and punishment. These educative influences that have become knowledge, will account for why 22.8 per cent of responses from literate women were comfortable positions that would not challenge the superior social position of men.

We need to recall what Aanwo, Itunu and Adedigba – three literate victims of violence – did when they experienced violence. They did not do anything. Listen to them: 'They', people she means, 'believed it was normal for a stubborn woman to be beaten by her husband or boyfriend, and that a victim of rape or sexual harassment asked for it by the way she dressed, spoke or behaved'; 'It was like it is the usual thing to be beaten or sexually harassed and that there's nothing you can do about it'.

> I could not report to anyone because it was a shame telling anyone, even your mother. The blame will always be that of the woman. Others were not happy but they said it was part of growing up. The society does not attach much importance to sexual harassment. They see it as normal, provided you didn't yield.

All these statements reflect women's knowledge of reactions of some members of society to violence against women.

Even though we had categorized reportage to the police/appropriate authority as a position that depicts outrage and practicality, and capable of empowering women, and many of the male respondents gave this type of advice, Aanwo, a victim of violence said: 'Never report to the Police as this would lead to more degradation and harassment'. Although we may say a negative interpretation of

Table 5.4: Advice Offered by Women who have had Close Encounter with Violence

Literate Women	The Experience	What she Did	Advice On Violence	Further/Other Comments
Aanwo	I have been beaten, and I know several women who have experienced all stated above.	I did not do anything	Run for their lives and seek spiritual and medical cleansing. Never report to the police as this would lead to more degradation and harassment	If a man hits a woman, then he can kill her one day, so the best solution is to give him a wide berth. Reporting to the police would only mean opening up wounds that may have healed, since most times the sympathy is with the accused not the victim
Itunu	Yes, I've been beaten and sexually harassed	I braced up to the challenge. I strengthened my resolve that I am an individual with equal rights and that I would not be a weakling	First assess whether you are at fault in the situation. If beaten and you don't deserve it, be bold and organize a retaliation, if sexually harassed and you were decently dressed rebuff the advance and prove your worth in a decent manner	It is my personal view and I oppose the view that women should be treated unjustly because of their sex!
Omolade	Yes, I know women who have been beaten – my mother and a young church member	My mother (a widow then) slapped the man back. Surprised and caught unawares, he turned away as others jeered. The lady ran to take solace in my house as it was becoming too much – she had wounds. We later counseled them and she returned home.	They should fight back in as much a decent and result oriented way as possible. They should not keep quiet or else, more will come their way. Keeping quiet over such issues or not acting is rather a sign of weakness which can encourage more or even worse of such actions from those doing it to you and other onlookers	Well, a woman should not be treated as a nonentity and the earlier men/people realize that, the better
Adedigba	Yes, I've been sexually harassed	I could not report to anyone because it was a shame telling anyone even your mother. The blame will always be that of the woman.	Report to the police. It is a new world since the situation has changed	
Semi-literate Women				
Rukayat	I've been beaten before. I've heard of a rape victim before too	When my husband raised his fist and it pained me, I retaliated even though I was not as powerful as he was.	Concerning beating, women should be patient because of their children As for rape, I can't take it, in fact I will tell the victim to report to the authority immediately	This is because the rape Victim will not be able to face the world because of the stigma
Toun	My apprentice was raped in Lagos. My husband beat me twice because I was stubborn. I went against his wish. I proved too stubborn thereby getting my husband angry to the extent that he slapped me. I therefore believe that some	I went to my father after the beating to report him but my father said that I should go back there but I went to stay with my friend in her house and after some days he came	I would advice a woman that has been beaten to meet the man's family and tell them to warn him against beating her and also tell him what can result from such beating.	I can not tell the woman to move out of her husband's house I would rather tell her to be patient

Table 5.4: (continued)

Toun	My apprentice was raped in Lagos. My husband beat me twice because I was stubborn. I went against his wish. I proved too stubborn thereby getting my husband angry to the extent that he slapped me. I therefore believe that some women deserve beating because of their behavior.	I went to my father after the beating to report him but my father said that I should go back there but I went to stay with my friend in her house and after some days he came to beg me and my family and this made me to go back to him	I would advice a woman that has been beaten to meet the man's family and tell them to warn him against beating her and also tell him what can result from such beating.	I can not tell the woman to move out of her husband's house I would rather tell her to be patient
Morenike	Yes, my sister's husband used to beat her regularly	She eventually moved out and even lost a child during the process of beating.	A woman who has experienced continuous beating should move out of the house. If raped, she should go to the hospital and report to the police	A woman may lose her life in the process. A rape victim can become pregnant so she should treat herself and report to the police for justice. Otherwise, the rapist would have cheated her.
Adama	My husband used to beat me	I would run away, and he would come and beg me and then I will go back	I tell them to stay in their husband's place and settle the quarrel because of their children	

life experience (Merriam, Mott and Lee 1996) had taught her to take a position that is apposite to an empowering position, that is her own reality, and it will require some efforts and real changes to convince her that reportage to the police/appropriate authority stand to benefit women. In spite of her experiences, Itunu still retained the meaning perspectives that considered that victims of rape and battery are at least partly responsible for their ordeal. From this framework, she advises that a woman should take decisive actions against her assailants when she knows that she has fulfilled societal expectations about how a woman should conduct herself and her affairs. On how she reacted to her abuse, she said: 'I braced up to the challenge. I strengthened my resolve that I am an individual with equal rights and that I would not be a weakling'. This response is indicative of the fact that she dealt with the situation by tapping on her inner strength, her active agency.

On her part, Adedigba, who could not report her experience of sexual harassment, advised that women should report to the Police, for, according to her, the world has changed. Given Adedigba's responses to many of the questions in this study, her meaning perspectives too has changed. She, for instance, took a cynical view of the roles of women in the private sphere of life when she said their expected roles are: 'To cook, rear children, fetch water, keep the home clean and perform all kinds of dirty jobs at home. They are just to be seen not to be heard and should also be breadwinning'. We recall that Adedigba had told us about how she had to do household chores for her teachers as a primary school pupil, because she is a female.

In the paragraphs that follow, we hear what literate men have to say about their capacity to hit women.

Literate Men's Capacity to Exhibit Violence

Three quarters (45 of 61) of highly literate respondents in Ibadan and Lokoja indicated that they cannot beat/hit a woman, while the rest (1/4) said they can beat a woman or would probably beat a woman. Those who said no responded this way: 'No, God forbid'; 'No, I cannot beat a woman', and 'No, why should I?'

The reasons they gave ranged from: it is indecent; morally and religiously wrong; it's ungentlemanly; women are weak in nature; that is lack of self-control and being irresponsible; and, my religion forbids it, to: not polite; it's the exit of love between the couple and, it will misguide the children; they are flexible in nature; she's a human being like myself; and, I'm used to their temperament. Details of the reasons that some of the men gave for their position can be found in Box 5.5. Those who said they can beat a woman said they would do so for the following reasons: 'if extremely provoked and that is an acceptable defense in law'; '5 per cent of the time because of the presidential role of man in the house and to check her excesses, but it will be light beating'; 'yes if the

Box 5.5: Why Many Literate Men Will Not Hit Women

Literate Men in Formal Work Settings

'It is inhuman treatment to beat a woman you call your wife, the mother of your children. Such beatings can result in serious injuries and cause problems for the whole family' – Jacob

'Women are weaker vessels as enjoined by the scripture and more so, women are not strong like men to deserve beating rather they deserve pity' – Zaki

'Women are fragile and if beaten they can easily collapse. I hit a young lady when I was in secondary school who fainted, thereafter; I swore never to do so' – Haliru

'I would rather end a relationship if we are not compatible than endure until it becomes unbearable and frustrating. Women on the other hand can be easily swayed. Dialogue works magic' – Adamu

Male Students

'I can't beat a woman because women are special gift to us by God and also my upbringing and religion does not permit such acts. In fact, I love women because one is my mother, two are my sisters, and one day I will have one who will be called my wife and I would also have daughters' – Odedele

'Actually, ladies should be respected; if not for anything, they should be respected for bearing children' – Samuel

'It is not scriptural. It does not show the manly character in me' – Oyesiji

'Their physical constitution, they are a highly emotional gender, and because I respect their cultural role in homebuilding, child bearing and childrearing' – Fijabi

'I have a mother! Beating a woman might mean that I have no respect for my mother. In addition, I do not see women as weaker sex who should only be corrected by bullying. Therefore, I can never beat a woman' – Daniel

situation demands it, no if she happens to be my wife'; 'if extremely provoked'; 'this will create fear in her to avoid confrontation'; 'it all depends on the attitude or behaviour of the woman'; 'there are nagging women and the only language that they understand is being beaten'; 'if a woman attacks me first', and 'if she misbehaves like being involved in extra-marital affairs'.

We thought it might be interesting to know the type of advice that men who can, or would probably, beat a woman gave to women who had experienced violence. Details are contained in Table 5.6

Table 5.6 shows that men who can hit women had no doubts about how they expected women to handle rape cases. They thought women should seek redress in court, or report to an appropriate authority. Only one of the four, Oyeyipo,

Table 5.5: Literate Men on Violence Against Women

	Yes				Probably				No				Total
	Ibadan		Lokoja		Ibadan		Lokoja		Ibadan		Lokoja		
	Frequency	Per centage	Frequency	Per centage	Frequency	Per centage	Frequency	Per centage	Frequency	Per centage	Frequency	Per centage	
Men in Formal Work Settings	0	-	3	10.3	4	13.8	3	10.3	9	31.0	10	34.5	29
Male Students	1	3.1	3	9.4	2	6.25	0	-	13	40.6	13	40.6	32
Total	1	1.6	6	9.8	6	9.8	3	4.9	22	36.1	23	38.0	61

Key: **Yes** – Means yes I can hit a woman.

Probably – Means I would probably hit a woman if …

No – Means I cannot hit a woman.

Source: Data generated from the open-ended questionnaires completed by the two categories   of male respondents who provided information during fieldwork.

Table 5.6: Advice on Violence by Men who can Hit Women

Literate Men in Formal Work settings	Why I Can Beat a Woman	Advice on Violence	Reasons for Proffering the Advice
Oyeyipo	If extremely provoked. This will create fear in her to avoid confrontation	If a woman is beaten, she should try to avoid what brought the conflict. If raped, she should seek redress in Court for the abuse	This is because her consent has to be sought in sex related matters
Alade	It all depends on the attitude or bahaviour of the woman. There are nagging women and the only language that they understand is being beaten	She should either seek redress in the law court or get the family to settle with the person involved	This is to ensure that such an act does not occur in future.
Duro	Under very serious pressure but not my wife	Report to the Police and seek counselling	Women's rights should not be violated
Male Students			
Zubairu	If she misbehaves, like getting involved in extra marital affairs	She should report to the school authority. The case should be taken to court.	Because it is religiously wrong to rape a woman. Because it is a criminal offence

came clear about how a battered woman should proceed, and his position was that the woman should avoid what brought the conflict. This is a presumption that the other party, the man, could not have caused the conflict.

Religious Leaders on Violence against Women

Islam

Male Muslim Leaders

Male Muslim Leader (MML): Do not approach fornication or adultery (reading from the Qur'an). It says do not approach, not do not commit. It says don't go close to – like caressing, touching, romancing, kissing all those ones that are not legally married to you. It is forbidden, talk more of going to commit... That is, don't go near anything that will take you close to committing fornication. And the Prophet is saying there is fornication of the eyes, hand; it is in the Hadith that gazing, that is looking at a woman lustfully, is fornication and that is why it is said in the Qur'an – lower your gaze. Let the living men and the living women lower their gaze. If you look at Chapter 24 vs. 30, it says that you should lower your gaze and safeguard your chastity.

Olutoyin Mejiuni (OM): When Allah says lower your gaze and says that to everybody, men and women, and then men complain that women are dressing in a particular way; shouldn't we be asking them whether they have been looking at the women?

MML: You know our society is a place for all people and you do not expect me to close my eyes when you are passing by. But what we are saying is that you try as much as possible to discipline yourself, and even if somebody is going and you see the person, take away your eyes, do not keep on looking. The Prophet says first look lawful, second look unlawful. For instance, I have seen you like this, I am supposed to take away my face. You see, if it is not because of the programme that brought you people, after seeing you, I will turn away my face even if you're talking, I will just be backing you; okay. This is because the Prophet says he sees Satan run round our body as blood runs round our body. Before you know it, Satan don already jam you people; and before you know it, the deed is done. That is why Islam wants this thing to be prevented. The Prophet says even scent, the man's scent has a sharp smell but that of a woman is coloured and mild. Secondly, the prophet says you should not wear bangles and be shaking it when you're passing in order to call attention. The Prophet says that you should not wear shoes that will call attention to you when you're passing by. Immediately you attain the age of puberty, you cover all the parts of your body that men will want to look at to hide away your beauty. Chapter 24 vs. 30-31 will give you all these.

So when you talk about rape, definitely there is no way you can even approach it if actually you follow all the tenets that have already been laid down. Why would you even want to rape? You've gotten your own wife based on some conditions, okay? And the condition here is righteousness and piety and if you see that this woman is nothing but blessing/garment to you, then why rape? Why go and pick somebody to rape? How will punching and beating come in? There is no room for beating, when this is a gender that you must respect. Even between husband and wife, the Prophet said you should not jump on your wife like an animal. In fact, Islam provides for much romance. That is, you play with your wife very well. In fact, he says do not go to your wife as if you are going to a log of wood. In fact, you have to have some prerequisites to lovemaking, like kissing, caressing, romancing, you're playing until the two are moved to go into it before they do it. Like the Prophet said, if you have actually done it and released do not stand up like that. You will remain there until the two of you have actually enjoyed what you have done. That is what the Prophet says.

OM: Do we preach this?

MML: Yes, we do. There is a section in the Qur'an that says when there are differences between you and your wife, admonish her; that is the first stage. If she does not change, then the second stage is distance yourself from her, show her that you have a grudge. After that, you can frown. Some people say you can beat, but scholars say you frown. Frown here does not mean beating; rather, it is that you can rebuke her, talk to her in a harsh manner. Let her know that you're really annoyed. If you have done this and she does not change, now it is time to call on the elders, the parents, and they will settle things. This is the process to frown the face.

Female Muslim Leaders – Lokoja

Female Muslim Leader (FML): We organize workshops/seminars and group discussions on salient issues in our society, including violence, and in most cases, we bring people within and outside to talk to adherents. We discovered there has not been any serious report of violence, all because of the stigma that is associated with it when it is heard. And so, people keep these things to themselves, dying in silence. But we keep talking and counselling on what they should do if such a thing happens, and what they should do to avoid such occurrences. We have discovered that street hawking that results in rape, for example, has an added problem of poverty because if you're rich, you will not want to expose your child to the hazards on the streets. This is why government should look at programmes on poverty reduction. Why should the privileged ones continue to benefit from programmes aimed at alleviating poverty among poor people? And the masses, especially women, are not happy because when you talk of poverty, it carries the woman's face. Until the economic power of women improves, the issue of street hawking will continue to pose a problem.

OM: Highly educated women and women with some economic power experience violence too, why is it so?

FML: Stigma and protection of marriage do not allow highly educated women to enforce their rights when they have been abused by husband and others. In other words, the possession of formal education does not prevent violence on women in some cases. Some are fighting it though, but they are few because of the fear of losing the family. The problem here though is not religion. It is culture. Even when you run to your parents, they tell you 'my daughter; go back to your husband's because of your children'. It is better that you urinate in a place than scatter the urine about. Stay there and bear all the children for a man. Islam does not encourage divorce. That is why there is a council of elders. If there is any problem you believe you cannot chew, report to the elders.

Female Muslim Leaders – Ibadan

Female Muslim Leader (FML): The Prophet says, 'the best among you men is the best to his wife'. A wife should be a wife, companion and confidant. Women are told to respect their husbands. Where conflict arises is when some of us acquire Western education and by stroke of luck rise above your husband by grade/salary, then you begin to raise the eyebrow to the husband. An example in the Holy Qur'an is that the first wife of the Holy Prophet Mohammed, Hadijat was his boss. The Prophet was one of the attendants in her workplace. The Prophet was wenty-five while the woman was forty. She saw his honesty and dedication to work. When she lost her husband, she approached the younger man. He said he would think about it, so he made supplications to the Almighty Allah and told her he would marry her. The woman called all the workers and told them this is my husband, from today onwards, myself and all the things I have will submit to him. So with all her wealth, she still submitted. But if she had let all those things get into her head, the man would want to say no, I have my own personality to keep. So if you rise above your husband in all ways, you should still be his wife, not his boss. Let him be the head of whatever you have. It is when you do that that you will enjoy his cooperation. A man will not want his wife to belittle him anywhere, and I think that is one of the things that bring conflict. Where women are wealthier than their husbands and they are submissive, you will see that there is always peace in the house. The Qur'an admonishes women to be submissive, no matter their status.

OM: What about drunken husbands?

FML: Well, if adherents follow the Qur'an, there will be no drunks, for it is one of the reasons Islam forbids drinking. Before the message came, people in the Arabian world drank and drank and committed all kinds of atrocities, such that even when they were to worship Allah, they forgot to, and so Almighty Allah had to send the message that banned people from drinking. Muslims are not supposed to drink, sell or handle alcoholic drinks. Battery will not arise if Muslim men adhere to the injunctions that they should not drink

OM: We have been told that the Qur'an says when your wife offends you, the third stage in getting her to do a turnaround is to frown your face, and some men interpret frown your face to mean beat your wife.

FML: Frowning is not the same thing as beating. If a wife does a wrong, and the husband follows all the guidelines as stipulated and she does not change, even when you sleep on the same bed, you turn your back to her, and that will send a message that something is wrong. Even according to Sharia, if you're to beat, you should put something under your armpit and hold the stick, and what you have under your armpit should not fall off while you're beating. This means you can't even raise your hands above your shoulders to beat. It has to be gentle.

Christianity

Male Christian Leader – Lokoja

Male Christian Leader (MCL): The first thing is to modernize our culture so as to see our women as our mate as it were. In the Bible, they use the word that indicates somebody with whom you do something side by side as it were, and some people even say that is why God created women from the ribs not from the head or feet, so she can be side by side with you, your partner. Because if we respect them, we remove all those things in our culture that are against the rights of women, and withhold and indeed develop things that are positive to women in our culture, then we can remove things that arise as a result of negative usage of our culture. So when you talk of rape, I look at the totality of it. I was listening to the BBC this morning and they were talking about rape in Darfur. A lady, speaking in her language said they gathered round her and pointed guns at her. Now, how can somebody who respects a woman or sees a woman as partner, his wife as partner, just stumble on a woman you have not met before, how can you even have the arousement, you know, to have sex with her? You can only do that if you are an animal. That is, your instinct is not human in that sense. Even dogs still circle themselves and do all sorts of things before they then penetrate. But here you just see somebody you've not met before, you tear her cloth and then you come erect and you... I do not understand. But it is because you don't think of that lady as she should be seen. You have so downgraded her that you just went to an animal, and then you descend to that level too and do it.

It is the same thing with battery of women. I used to say it when I am preaching the sermon on marriage. The Bible says that when you quarrel with your wife, and that includes battery, you're called a murderer. And I used to tell them: I say some of you men that have just gotten married now, and you're sitting together now, if you want your prayers to be answered as individuals and collectively, and the prayers are not answered, you are battering your wives, quarrelling, etc. I also tell them that Jesus says don't allow the sun to set on your anger. So when prayers are not being answered or you're having difficulties, you must look inwards because your wife is supposed to be part of you. By marriage you have become one, so it will be foolish or stupid for an individual to decide to bash himself, for that is how God sees it. If you beat your wife, you are beating yourself. If you know whom you are, and you think your wife is part of you, then you wouldn't beat her.

The problem is a lot of us don't practice our religion. We say we are Christians, yes we are Christians; but as situations arise, we behave unlike a Christian, and people are watching. They ask, ha ha, why should you behave like this when Jesus said love your enemy, pray for him, so why are you now chasing your enemy and beating him? They will say no o... that was in those days, I cannot turn another cheek, and I don't have another cheek to turn, you know, which is unfortunate. You have to be a Christian all the time. If you bash your wife, you inhibit your progress and everything you stand for. That is what it is. That is the way I see it, and that is what I tell them.

So one must see his wife as an extension of himself. Once one is able to do that, then you will respect your wife, and she too will, and should do the same. We were discussing this some days ago. Some tribes, I won't mention their names, their women naturally want to be independent even when they are married. This is as opposed to, I think, women in Calabar area where by the time you go to the fattening room, you are taught how to look after a man[3]. I remember when I was going to be transferred to Calabar, I was told I would be finished if I go there, for I will just marry one of the women because of the way they will treat you – pet you. You know men are like little boys. Once you pet him and give him what he wants, that's it. So it was said that unlike women from Calabar, the other group of women try to be independent and even compete with their husbands. Inevitably, the one that pets the husband will bond with him better than the one that tries to be independent. So women have to respect their husbands too, and cooperate so that they can work together for the good of the family, for the good of each other and for the good of the nation, because the family means the nation.

OM: From all of these, I conclude that you don't think the pursuit of women's rights is against Biblical injunctions.

MC: No, no; after all, they brought out a woman caught in adultery and they said the law says they should stone her and Jesus said no problem, among all of you, the one that has no sin should cast the first stone. Legend says Jesus started writing on the ground. Apparently, he was writing their names according to the gravity of their sins. They saw what he was doing. By the time he got up, it was the woman alone that was standing there, and he said go and sin no more. So if you deprive anybody of his fundamental human right, you are not doing anything good at all. And the main problem we have is man's inhumanity to man arising from the greed to selfishly acquire and acquire power, authority. In acquiring power, you suppress other people, even when you are in the home.

Female Christian Leader – Lokoja

FC: I frown so much against rape. I also preach against adultery and fornication. Rape is a result of lack of discipline. Any disciplined man, no matter how aroused, will look for somebody that is willing to offer sex. After all, it is on that ground that enjoyment can be found. The Bible frowns at having sex with just anybody. It says be faithful. Once you're married, you're only allowed to have sex with your partner. Bible does not support that you have concubines, not to talk of raping other people. If a man keeps beating his wife, the wife should at least report to the pastor.

OM: If a Church member comes and says her daughter has been raped and she knows the person, what would you say?

FC: The Bible says we should not take ourselves to court – we can report to religious leaders. I would not blame anybody who takes such a case to court, but I would rather advise that having taken it to court, it should be withdrawn, so that some elders can be called to wade in. The elders will call the parties involved, find out how and why it happened. Because when it comes to forgiveness of sins, Matthew 18:22 taught us that we should forgive 70 times 7 times. That is to say whatever type of offence anybody commits, we should be able to forgive. That is after making sure that the one that committed the act is ready to admit his fault. Having done that, we should be able to forgive. If the person who did the act refuses to own up, then he should be taught a lesson so that others can learn from that. A part of the Bible says we should punish the offender so that that will help others learn their lessons. We can also commit a rapist who has refused to own up to his misdeeds to the hands of Satan and what will Satan do to him? He will destroy him. That is why it is better that the person own up and confess and stop the act. He needs to go into prayer and fasting, to ask God for forgiveness. For there is no sin that God is unable forgive.

Male Christian Leader – Ibadan

Male Christian Leader (MCL): You find different types of people in the Church. When we preach about these issues, we address the situation, we don't focus on the individual. Addressing a person will not solve the problem. We let them know what the word of God says, and the consequences of disobedience. Sin is sin; there is no small or big sin. All disobedience, the Bible says, is sin. You address the spirit of adherents. What makes a person do a bad thing is inside. When the inside can be purged, the outside will be affected positively. There is no one who has the spirit of God who will be involved in these things.

Olutoyin Mejiuni (OM): Including beating? Some say the Bible recommends a little bit of spanking for women, for a wife.

MCL: No. It is not scriptural. The Bible says there is no one who will not cherish his body. If like the Bible said, the wife is the body of the man, now when a person beats himself, then something has happened. When you see a man beating himself, that is beating his wife, then he has become mad. The understanding of the word of God, what God has set as standard, will help a person. The culture may say you can beat your wife, but God never recommended that. No one beats himself. Everyone will take care of his body, care for it and cherish it. So the body of a man is his wife. Ephesians 5 vs 23/29 says, 'No man hates his own flesh, but he nourisheth and cherisheth it even as the Lord the Church.' The Bible says the two of them shall become one flesh. If a man is one flesh with his wife and then he beats his wife, then he has become mad.

OM: If a member of your church reports to you that her husband has been beating her, or that a neighbour, also a member of your Church, raped her daughter, what would you advise her to do apart from praying for her.

MCL: You need to counsel them. Because taking a legal step – going to court – will not solve the problem. It will not undo what has been done. Except the spirit that is behind the behaviour is dealt with, the person cannot be free. Every misbehaviour has a spirit behind it. There is the spirit of rape/sexual abuse, adultery, fornication. That is why somebody who has raped will not stop at that one person. The spirit that is making him to do it will push him to do another one. It is the same thing with fornication.

OM: What if the man refuses to own up?

MCL: The Bible says in Proverbs 28 vs 13 that he that covers his sin shall not prosper, but he that confesses shall have mercy. If someone needs mercy, he has to accept and confess his sins, but if he covers it, the sin will uncover him in time. Because the spirit behind the sin will continue to push him and if he continues, it will get to a point that he will not be able to escape judgement, not even God's judgement alone, because he will be caught red-handed.

Female Christian Leader – Ibadan

Female Christian Leader: A man that beats his wife is a madman. If your wife is you, how can you be beating yourself and you would think you are normal? Many things contribute to battery of wives. The world is wicked and loaded with psychological problems. It starts from a broken home. That is, a boy sees the father beating his mother; he too will wake up one day and beat his wife. That is why marital counselling is very important. You do not just go into a relationship. A child that comes from a broken home, who is rejected, or who comes from an abusive and violent home will have difficulties loving people. Another factor is lack of respect for one another.

Olutoyin Mejiuni (OM): What do you say to women who have been battered by their husbands or a woman who says she has been sexually harassed by her boss?

FCL: This is not something to gloss over. A woman who has an abusive spouse would have seen the signs in courtship. Women marry for different reasons. Some do so to leave home because they have unhappy families. Some are looking for love so they make wrong decisions. These problems have to be tackled from the roots. That is why I have a special ministry for young women.

I advise women who have experienced rape or sexual harassment to forget the past. Don't cry over spilt milk; don't build a wall around yourself because of that. You don't have to be bitter to every man. I let them know that better days are still ahead.

Yoruba Traditional Religion – The Worship of Sango

Olutoyin Mejiuni (OM): Mama, have you heard about cases of rape …

Female Traditional Religious Leader (FTRL): If a man forces himself on a woman and Sango gets hold of him, Sango will seize his manhood and he will never be able to make use of it again. Sango cannot tolerate rape, he will not agree.

OM: You know these days some men rape women and children and then they beg for forgiveness. They even make the case that after all, when we ask God for forgiveness he forgives us, why then would a human being refuse to forgive?

FTRL: Sango wouldn't forgive! He will pull him out and deal with him in the open for all to see, so that the entire community can jeer at him. Also a man who tries to rape a woman who has traditional incisions or a Sango worshipper/supporter will not succeed. His semen will become water and ineffective.

OM: What should a woman who has been raped or a woman who had her breast or buttocks suddenly grabbed by a man do?

FTRL: Women who are not interested should slap and beat up such men thoroughly (*ko koko ko igbati boo, ko nan daadaa*), such that everybody will know he has done a wrong. Of course, those who are interested will sheepishly ask: so when should I see you tonight and how much would you give me? A rape victim should go to Sango and ask for help. Sango will come to her aid. If the victim is not sure of the identity of the assailant, and a parade of close to a hundred men is held, Sango will single out the assailant for punishment.

God should give Nigeria and Nigerian women peace and progress. Some women do not want to pick up concubines and get into prostitution, but because they are hungry and cannot feed their children, they prostitute so they can feed their children. This is the reason women prostitute and get into all kinds of things.

Discussions

From these interviews, one can say that all religious leaders oppose violence against women, although elsewhere, most had taken submission of wives to their husbands as a given. The Muslim female leader in Ibadan added a slant to this position, when she said a problem arises when women acquire Western education and become haughty to their husbands. A woman who is haughty is the one who is not submissive if we go by the responses of this religious leader. In the context where religious leaders preach submission of women to men, and most adherents believe it is the right thing to do, the haughty woman would most probably also be considered a stubborn woman. It is therefore not surprising that some illiterate/semi-literate women said some women are battered because they are stubborn.

One issue that the female and male Muslim leaders and the female traditional religious leader raised strongly is the connection between violence against women and poverty, and the role that the government should play. They were apparently raising the matter of the political economy of violence. The religious leaders were weighing in on the side of justice and morality (Keynes 1955) when they called on government to address the problem of poverty (the feminization of poverty and who benefits from poverty alleviation programmes), which religious leaders believe is implicated in battery and sexual abuse of women and children (Weissman 2007).

The female Muslim and male Christian leaders in Lokoja also thought that culture, 'our culture', is responsible for violence against women. The question is: which culture do they have in mind here? The cultures represented in Christianity and Islam? Nigerian cultures, our culture, before these two religions took over the cultural space? Or the culture that has emerged from the fusion of the new religions with traditional cultural practices when they have the same goal? There is a need to raise these questions because these religious leaders appear to be providing an understanding of violence against women as a phenomenon that is a result of belief systems, values and ideologies that are outside their own religions. They do not reckon with the fact that culture is dynamic; it changes voluntarily (in order to adapt) or by coercion as it happened to us Africans after the arrival of Islam, Christianity and colonialism. So for some people, 'our culture' reflects the Judeo-Christian and Islamic traditions; for others, 'our culture' are those traditional behavioural norms and values that were central to our lives before the new religions and colonialism; whereas for yet others, it is the culture that has emerged from the fusion of traditional norms and values with the norms and values of the new religions.

A good example is the Ogori Ovia Osese festival. Ovia Osese is the festival of the maidens, held by Ogori people of Kogi State. It is the initiation of grown-up girls, who are virgins, into womanhood. 'It is the period in which grown-up girls are taught how and what it takes to become women' (Boro 1992:8). Boro indicated that Christians, Muslims and Traditional religionists have embraced and assimilated the festival into the practice of their respective religions. These days, thanksgiving services are held in the worship places of all religions by the maidens and their families after an Ovia Osese. In addition, girls who want to marry in churches and mosques in Ogoriland have to first present their Ovia Osese certificates. The reason for the fusion of the tradition of Ovia Osese with the new religions may be traced to the fact that both are concerned with purity of young women before marriage.

According to this tradition, all young girls who are indigenes of Ogoriland, no matter where they are resident, have to go through the Ovia Osese before marriage. Those who cannot go through Ovia Osese are those who had lost their virginity before they were due for the rite of passage. Surely, by insisting that young girls who wish to marry in churches, mosques and traditional institutions in Ogoriland should present the certificate that was given to them at the grand finale of the Ovia Osese festival, the Ogori community is showing and teaching young girls why they should stay away from pre-marital sex. The certificate is a reward for staying away from pre-marital sex, while a lack of it is punishment for engaging in pre-marital sex. So the young girls learn this lesson through explicit informal learning. However, after my unofficial interaction[4] in Lokoja with the three elderly Ogori women who had themselves gone through the Ovia Osese, and who provided information about the Ovia Osese festival, one thought has refused to leave my mind. I have been wondering about what would become of Ogori girls if they would be unfortunate to become victims of child sexual abuse or rape before they were due to go through this rite of passage. I did not ask the three Ogori women who told me about the festival this question. My concern here is not about the merits and demerits of the instructions they are given (or non-formal education process that they go through) as part of their initiation into womanhood; this should be the subject matter for another work. My worry is about the requirement for participation in this rite of passage, being a virgin, especially in the context of rampart child sexual abuse, most of which goes unreported; and the requirement that they present their certificate of initiation to religious institutions before marriage.

Notes

1. This translates to: it is because of her character that we don't like.

2. There are lessons that women can learn from the mother's movement (*madres de plaza de mayo*) in Argentina. The women demanded that their children who had 'disappeared' under the military dictatorship in Argentina between 1976 and 1983 be brought back alive. See Hernendez (1997).

3. Like this male Christian leader, many Nigerians (although I suspect more men than women) have heard about the fattening rooms that turn Calabar women into good wives. However, this religious leader forgot about, or failed to equate a similar rite of passage in his constituency in Kogi State, the Ogori Ovia Osese festival with the Calabar fattening rooms. Ovia Osese is the festival of the maidens, held by Ogori people of Kogi State. It is the initiation of grown up girls who are virgins into womanhood.

4. My interaction with the three elderly Ogori women in Lokoja, although recorded on tape, was unofficial because I did not go to Ogoriland; I did not ask for, neither did I receive official permission from the traditional hierarchy in Ogoriland to hold interviews with the three women. I also need to add that the women tactfully refused to provide detailed information about the training for the girls preparatory to the final ceremony.

6

Women's Identities and Power

In the opening part of this chapter, I explore the meaning of power (but would not lay claim to undertaking an exhaustive exploration of the meaning of the subject), and make a case for why women need to attain or gain power, reorder unequal relationships of power, and resist repressive power in all spheres of life. In the two sections that follow, I link the identities of women that have emerged in the preceding chapters with women's abilities to attain political power, their experience of violence, and their abilities to resist violence.

Power

Nesbit and Wilson (2005) observed that definitions of power 'range from a view of power as brute force, through debates about individual versus structural capacities, to power as a complex social force that exists in, and produces, imbricated networks of shifting and contested relationships' (p. 496). On his part, Blackburn (1996) was of the view that 'the power of an individual or institution is the ability to achieve something, whether by right or by control or influence'. He further stated that power is 'the ability to mobilize economic, social or political forces in order to achieve a result' (pp. 295–296).

One assumes that the power resources which Marshall (1998) identified as wealth and control over jobs; numerical support; competence; expert knowledge; control of information; organizational capacity; control of instruments of force; occupation of certain social positions, etc., are among the economic, social or political forces that individuals, groups and institutions can mobilize to achieve a result. I would add that participation in decision-making processes as equals, not on assumption of equality, should be regarded as a power resource because of the possibilities that it represents. Nesbit and Wilson (2005) pointed out another approach to understanding power, and that is the view that 'power operates unseen and unacknowledged "behind the actor's back" to influence people and their activities. For example, social forces such as class, race and gender largely determine people's actions and thoughts'.

As we had indicated in Chapter Five, Foucault (1980) alerted us to the fact that we see power in terms of the apparatus of state; think power outside economic considerations unimportant; and believe that we do not exercise power, 'others' do. Foucault contended that in spite of the omnipotence of state apparatus, the state cannot take over the entire field of actual power relations, and so, it has to depend on, and work through existing power relations. He believed that power is 'present in the smallest, apparently most inconsequential human interaction' (Brookfield 2001:7), and is exercised through the body, sexuality, family, kinship, knowledge, technology, and so on. From Foucault's position, we can deduce that power is present in all spheres and institutions of life; in both the private sphere (home or domestic) and the public sphere (community, government).

Foucault (1980) believed that power is manifested in the modes of surveillance, regulation or discipline that adapt human beings to the surrounding social structure. And, the power of society is not limited to its ability to prevent people from doing bad things, but it includes the control of self-definition and the preferred way of living of its members (Foucault cited in Blackburn 1996). Foucault's thoughts around power manifesting as modes of surveillance, regulation, or discipline posit a positive and negative view of the power of society, and it is important because it focuses attention on the uses to which power and power resources can be deployed. When power resources are mobilized or utilized to enhance the capabilities of persons, groups and institutions, they become enablers and are viewed positively. However, when they inhibit capabilities, they are viewed as disablers, dead hands and repressive. Foucault then rightly cautioned that it is erroneous to think of power as inhibiting, controlling and repressive alone. He believed that resistance to power is found right at the point where power relations are exercised. Power, then, can represent both repression and resistance, with the implication that there can be no single locus and mode of power, because different individuals and groups can exercise different modes of power, at different times, and in such are to be found the possibilities of different kinds of resistances.

Surely, resistance to power can be forged by accessing and mobilizing the same power resources that can be used to inhibit and control, and by acts of individual will or active agency. The implication of these is that how we define power, how we relate to, and use power and power resources will be dependent on our value orientation, belief system and frames of reference.

But what do these mean for Nigerian women? Our relationship with power, or more specifically, our lack of access to power resources, contributes significantly to our low social status. Apart from numerical strength, on aggregate, when compared with men, women do not have those power resources that

Marshall identified (wealth and control over jobs; competence; expert knowledge; control of information; organizational capacity; control of instruments of force; and occupation of certain social positions), so they cannot mobilize what they do not have to influence decisions, policies, and behaviours and attitudes that will enhance the capabilities of women.

Interestingly, it is through education (formal, non-formal and informal) that persons and groups can acquire some of the power resources that Marshall identified. We recall that education is one of the key elements in the analyses and understanding of the processes that construct women's identities, and how the resultant identities empower or disempower women in this book. Through education, persons and groups acquire competence and expert knowledge; are able to gain control of information and strengthen organizational capacity; and are able to create wealth and control jobs; and also participate, seemingly as equals, in decision-making processes. This means that education, broadly conceived, ought to help women gain access to some of those power resources that they presently lack. Ordinarily, this would mean that highly literate women, that is women with higher education, already possess some power resources, and so they should be able to utilize and mobilize them to enhance their own and other women's capabilities.

The catch here, however, is that women who have gone through higher education, and who have had at least fourteen years of formal schooling, have also been influenced by that power that Nesbit and Wilson described as operating 'unseen and unacknowledged behind the actor's back to influence people and their activities'. Within the teaching-learning context, this power operates through the hidden curriculum. Outside classrooms, within and outside institutions of learning, the power operates through the processes of informal learning and socialization.

Unfortunately, when this power, the 'hidden power', tries unsuccessfully to inhibit women, especially highly literate women, from developing their capabilities, other tactics are employed. The more overt power resources are deployed, especially by men, who possess some other types of power resources that women do not have access to, even by virtue of the acquisition of formal education. We shall return to this point later in this chapter.

So, why do women need power? First, women need to attain or gain power in at least three different arenas because many women do not have the power resources already identified and because they need to resist hidden power. The first arena in which they need to gain power is that of the state. They need to become state actors. State power goes a long way in determining what rights and privileges a group can have; whether or not a group will have access to key resources and facilities; and whether a group can resist those characteristics that have been socially and institutionally applied to the group, and individuals within the group, which define their rights and duties, and affect the quality of their lives (Wiley 1994).

Of course, it is not just by being state actors that women can access power resources. Women can also access power resources such as competence, expert knowledge, control of information, and organizational capacity, through civil society movements. Armed with these power resources and their numerical strength, through civil society movements, women can influence and challenge state policies, as well as institutional and individual actions that inhibit women's capabilities. Being able to participate in civil society activities and mobilizing resources provided by civil society groups, to enhance the capabilities of women and other disadvantaged groups represent a positive exercise of power.

Another arena where women in Nigeria need to resist hidden power and gain power is the cultural sphere. An important power resource through which women can gain power in the cultural sphere is participation, as equals with men, in the decision-making processes in that sphere. Represented in the cultural sphere are institutions (religious and traditional institutions, the media, the educational system, and the home) where norms and values are determined, where knowledge is created and disseminated, and where moral standards (especially the moral defaults of the powerful {Alvin Gouldner, cited in Marshall 1998}) and beliefs are conventionalized and held up as sacrosanct.

The second reason women need power is because as human beings, women have the right to be(come) whatever they want to be, and they should not be denied that right. Finally, there are women who share values with men about how to enhance the capabilities of the majority of Nigerians. So, there is strength (in quantitative and qualitative terms) in having these groups of women pushing/ encouraging those viewpoints/positions, policies, attitudes and behaviour as participants with men in the process of governance and also as members of civil society.

While quite a number of Nigerian women already have some power resources, the ones that higher education grants them, many semi-literate and illiterate Nigerian women do not possess many power resources. However, both categories of women, literate women in particular, are as yet struggling to become state actors, struggling to build or be part of the women's movement; they are still unable to participate as equals with men in the decision-making processes in the cultural sphere, and they still have to consciously or unconsciously contend with hidden power which works against them. In the circumstances, the social status of Nigerian women is still low.

So, the question for the rest of this chapter is: would the identities of women that have emerged thus far in this book, especially in Chapter Four, assist women to gain productive power and resist repressive power?

Women's Identities and Women's Abilities to Attain Political Power

On aggregate, the responses that women gave to questions in respect of women's civic-political participation; the roles of women in the private and public spheres; what women consider to be their identities, and men's perception of women's identities, have implications for whether or not women can gain power, or transform power relationships. The task here is to determine how empowering and disempowering women's identities can be.

The following are the identities of women that have emerged from this study: first, is the individual character of women that influences and is influenced by their relationships with other people, their work ethic and performance at work. Second, is claiming and valuing those qualities and ascriptions that make men the male gender – some of their characters and their roles as breadwinners. Third, is the acceptance of the socially constructed female, one that is subordinate to and inferior to men. The last is the acceptance of what is deemed feminine – care, feeling, nurturing – but which has the potential for being put to productive use.

Men who think women should aspire to any political office do not appear to constitute a real problem to women attaining political power because their position is already positive. Many of them have implicitly and, at times, explicitly acknowledged two of the four identities of women that we have identified in this study as representing the potential that will help women perform well if they attain political leadership. The identities are: women's character (meticulous, trustworthy, firm, honest, not partial) and how it influences their relationship with others; their work ethic and performance; and, the positive view of women's femininity (care, feeling, nurturing) and its potential for productive use if women attain political power. Fortunately, men who support women and women (both literate and semi-literate) who affirm women are united in this respect.

However, and unfortunately too, most of the men who support women and women who affirm women also accept, mainly implicitly, women's subordination to men in private, especially given the assumption that women can better handle care-giving than men. Although they may not accept it, they are in agreement with the people who insist that women should be submissive to men and should therefore take subordinate positions to men in the public sphere. They reinforce women's identities as subordinate to men. The point here is not that women are subordinate to men because they cook or care for children/home/ husband. The point is that the women in this study all work outside the home, and so they are co-breadwinners. None works full-time inside the home as a care-giver. We recall that only a handful of all the categories of respondents who would support women in their aspiration to attain political power considered women's and men's roles at home as the same, complementary or about partnering.

Partnership is about fair distribution of rights, responsibilities and privileges. When a wife who is a co-breadwinner returns home after work to do care-giving and the husband does not partake in care-giving, the husband is being accorded, or is insisting on a privilege which patriarchy confers on him, and which his wife does not enjoy. When a husband who is a co-breadwinner insists on taking final decisions on matters concerning the family, he is insisting on a right and privilege that he is not granting his wife. When he then implicitly (through all kinds of backhanded tactics) insists that his wife picks the bills equally with him, he is clearly not sharing responsibilities commensurate with the rights and privileges that he enjoys in the home. In this case then, the woman is subordinate to the husband. Clearly, the subordination of a wife to the husband is implied in the response of one of the male respondents who said a woman should contest elections to public office, provided she has her husband's permission. The stress here is on permission. Only subordinates take permission from their superiors; partners or persons who are equals hold discussions, to agree or reach some compromise or disagree.

In addition, when many women and men believe that women should play the role of care-giver at home, and also aspire to political leadership if they wish, they fail to realize that women who spend much of their time shuttling between cooking, caring for the children/home/husband and breadwinning will not have much time left to partake in civic-political affairs. That is to say they will not have much time left to take part in the decision-making processes that have consequences for whether or not they can feed their children well; they can continue to work (in both the formal and informal sectors), and they will be drawn into conflicts, the sources of which they do not know and understand, and conflicts for which they are going to reap little and lose much. Clearly, also, they will not be able to take part in decision-making processes that can stem or heighten violence on their gender, and those that can pauperize women the more, and so increase their powerlessness and vulnerability.

The point that is being made here is that women and men who believe that women should aspire to any political office, and who also accept as given, the view/position that women are the sole care-givers, reinforce the view that women are subordinate to men, and they are the same with persons who think women should not aspire to certain positions because they are flexible and the home will suffer, and so they push women farther off from political power.

The obvious hindrance to women attaining political power in this study are the men and women who do not believe that women should lead men (because of all kinds of reasons, including the views that women are flexible, the home will suffer, religion forbids it, etc.) and some of those who will support women provided they meet conditions such as: 'will not misbehave when she gets there' or 'can balance domestic work with public duties'. The women in this group are those women who have accepted and internalized the view that men are superior to women, and they somewhat feel comfortable with it. Some play along with the view that men are superior because they think or know that there are immediate benefits to be reaped from playing along or conceding superiority to men. Many of the men in this category view women negatively, and they are also the types of men that have attempted to make women feel, or who have actually made women feel inferior at home/family, in educational institutions, the workplace and in the public.

These men say women ought to be flexible and that they are flexible. When they say women are flexible, they devalue flexibility, which accords with femininity, and so they say women cannot lead because they are flexible. They also say women ought to be flexible – meaning they should be pliable, indecisive, and not masculine. That is, they should not be bold, courageous, aggressive and firm. Given men's earlier position about flexibility, this means women should not begin to think of taking up leadership roles, since those are the characteristics of a leader. What this means is that they would rather have women remain flexible, and confirm they are flexible, so that they would have good grounds to continue to deny women leadership roles in the private and public spheres.

They also insist that women are care-givers, while men are breadwinners. They say women are best suited to the private sphere, where they will take subordinate position to men and then add the emotional blackmail – which is that the children will suffer if women give up their role of care-giving for political leadership. They refuse to acknowledge that women are breadwinners, because to do so will be to challenge their leadership roles, both in the public and private spheres.

They choose to ignore the fact that they know that a lot of women possess the characteristics that men lay claim to (courage, boldness, aggression) because if they acknowledge these characteristics in women, there will really be no grounds for them to continue to claim superiority over women, except on the basis of their male organs, patriarchy and religion, and these are shaky grounds. We recall that one semi-literate woman had said there is no special role for the male organ in leadership positions. Today, patriarchy is male privilege, whereas female and male respondents in this study have said men and women are created by God, and are equal before God.

Men who would not support women's aspiration to political positions, and so proffered a whole range of explanations for the position they have taken, are obviously putting up resistance to women attaining political power.

The Greed/Lust for Power and the Preservative Nature of Power

The resistance to women gaining political power is not because there is overwhelming evidence to show that women are incapable of holding the positions. The resistance appears to be what the male Christian leader in Lokoja referred to as the greed/lust for power by men. It appears that men cannot just think of loosening their grip on power. The female Christian leader in Ibadan who is also an academic, one of the women that the Anglican Church in Nigeria had refused to ordain as priests, agreed with the male Christian leader in Lokoja when she said it appears that men are afraid of loosening their grip on power. In her view, the ordained ministry should not be about power but service because, after all, 'minister' means 'servant'. This is equally true of participation in secular politics. Persons who attain political power do not see themselves as holding the positions in trust for the people that they supposedly represent. Rather, they are excited about wielding oppressive power. We take two scenarios. If women are truly caring, loving, or nurturing and have truly internalized the positive aspects of the socially constructed notions of femininity, and many of them begin to occupy top political offices (or the topmost jobs in churches and mosques), it may just be, as many women hope, that they will perform better than their male counterparts who have monopolized governance, both secular and religious, and so, they may put the men to shame. There will be limited violent conflicts, economic and social deprivations, and corruption. In other words, women may humanize the public sphere and performance. Now, men do not want to experiment, since they do not know how it would turn out. So, they will continue to devalue their own notions of the feminine, the traits that they would rather women have. By devaluing what they insist is feminine, they will ensure that women do not aspire to, and get to the top political and religious positions.

On the other hand, if some women are indeed like the men who presently wield political power, as some women have indicated, and men know it, men will forever block such women from gaining power because the women may, as one man indicated, oppress men. If this group of women gets into power, men's 'presidential role in macro society' will probably become insecure. Given this, men then block this group of women with all manner of tactics – divide and rule (women won't vote for women); lies (they are mentally and emotionally unstable); and emotional blackmail (the children will suffer).

Clearly, the identity of women that men would rather women favour, which is being feminine and subordinate to men, is not empowering. The identities that most women explicitly favour – their character; some of the characteristics ascribed to men, breadwinning – and positive views of the feminine – care, feeling and nurturing – have great potential for empowering women, but we should briefly focus on character, for it would seem that the rest of the identities of women can, and do take a cue from it.

Before we examine women's character, we need to remind ourselves that the women in this study have challenged sexism mainly through their internal resistance to oppression. They have also challenged men's domination in public by pointing out the beauty of their own character and the positive aspects of their femininity that make them potentially better materials than men for public service, especially political leadership. They have deconstructed male superiority by claiming and valuing their roles at home as breadwinners and co-breadwinners, and the fact that they possess some characteristics that are ascribed to men – courage, boldness, aggression, etc. However, the women concede to patriarchy, especially in the private sphere, thereby diminishing their abilities to transform relations of power, both at home and in the public sphere. By conceding to patriarchy, women inadvertently place limits on their abilities to: gain power, including the power to resist oppression; improve their economic well-being and reduce violence on women.

The Character of Women

We had observed that the traditional or indigenous education system in Nigeria covered, amongst others, the development of character. Fafunwa (1974) observed that 'indigenous African education places considerable emphasis on character training', adding that 'J.A. Majasan in his study of Yoruba education identified character training and religious education as the two main objectives of Yoruba education, and showed that other objectives were pursued through the latter.' Fafunwa also indicated that parents in traditional Nigerian society were concerned that their children should be upright, honest, kind and helpful to others and would go a long way to ensure that their children imbibed these values. He also stated that 'each child or youth is also expected to know about hospitality, etiquette and other social graces' (p. 21). Fafunwa further said that traditional education in the area of character training was severe, and that while persons would tolerate the absence of other aspects of education, the absence of 'good character' was thought to be a shameful thing, not just on the individual, but also on his immediate and extended family. Thus, among the Yoruba of Nigeria, when a person displays uprightness, kindness, etiquette, hospitality, and so on, it is said that: *Oni iwa* –meaning that s/he has character, but more appropriately, s/he has beauty of character. Today, there is a tendency to believe that a person who is cultured, that is, the one who has imbibed the norms and values of her community, whether negative or positive, is the one with beauty of character.

A point to note here is that throughout the section of his book that deals with the development of character, Fafunwa refers to the moulding of the character of 'each child', 'youth' and the 'individual' by the community. One does not therefore get the impression that the Yoruba, for example, expected particular character traits of their female children, as distinct from their male children. In other sections of the book, in dealing with respect for elders and peers for example, he is specific about how men and women were expected to greet elders.

Given the identities of women that have emerged from this study, we can conclude that the traditional belief about beauty of character still subsists among women, many of whom defined themselves through their character. We can take a quick look at the character of the female respondents in this study in

Appendix II. Of course, we can take the position that because women have been socialized to think first in terms of their character, one should not be surprised that they defined themselves more through their character.

Given the responses in the different sections of this book, it does not appear that men hold true to the ideals of good character. This is because women and men accused men of being corrupt, callous, dishonest and deceitful while some male respondents stated that women are light-hearted as regards corruption and 'women do not have much courage to mismanage money'. This means that to steal public funds requires courage, or amounts to being courageous, and women do not have the courage, because men have also said they are more courageous than women.

One important point that needs to be raised is that the Nigerian society of today is not exactly the same as the traditional society that Fafunwa described. He referred, for example, to the introduction of Islam, and the provision of additional instruction in character development by the Qur'anic schools (Fafunwa 1974). The same happened with the introduction of Christianity, especially with the work of the missionaries through the mission schools. The Islamic and Christian religions that were introduced to the country had no doubt been fused with the norms and values of the societies of the persons who brought the religions to Nigeria, and who also wrote the values and norms of the religions into our hearts and laws. The point that is being made is that the Europeans who brought Christianity to Nigeria, and the colonial administrators who were Christians, considered that sharp differences existed between the roles of men and women in the public and private spheres of life. They transferred this to our hearts and laws, and this worked to alter the status of Nigerian Women (Afonja and Aina 1995). Concomitantly, women were and are being evaluated, not in terms of the traditional beauty of character that Fafunwa described, but in terms of whether they are cultured – that is, according to the extent to which they have imbibed the norms and values prescribed by the new religions, or more appropriately, by the leaders/preachers of the new religions who are mostly men.

Now, unfortunately, a woman who is cultured is equated with a woman with beauty of character. The central plank of the difference between men and women by European values, 'when' the first set of missionaries came to Nigeria and according to the interpretations of the Bible that many religious leaders propagated then and do now, is that women are subject to men, and so they should be submissive to men. In this study, we have observed that a large percentage of our respondents are religious and they partake actively in the activities of their religious groups more than they partake in the activities of other groups. We have noted among most literate and semi-literate women that subordination to men is implicitly taken as given. We have also observed that Muslim and Christian religious leaders, especially female religious leaders, send conflicting signals to women and inadvertently reinforce male superiority. The point that is being made is that women and their characters are being judged, in the main, by how submissive, how flexible and pliable they are in their relationship with men.

We take the Yoruba proverb that says, '*Iyawo so iwa nu, o ni oun ko ni ori oko*', which translates to: a woman who loses her character complains of being unlucky with marriage. This statement implies that a woman's character is responsible for her marital woes (Yusuf 1995). It is not usually said that the man has no character because as Fashina (2001) had observed, 'It is expected that it is a woman who should possess the character that would be attractive to a man, and that will bring out the best in him' (p. 99).

Now we cannot turn back the hand of the clock, so we do not know how far back this proverb dates, and whether indeed Yoruba women were expected to bear the burden of good character way back before colonialism and before the advent of the missionaries. However, Fafunwa, as we have earlier noted, said children, youths and individuals were expected to be of good character. Definitely, there is a motive for or a benefit that will accrue to persons who insist that women bear the burden of good character in 'consensual' relationships.

Fortunately, there is another Yoruba proverb that makes it clear that women were not expected to bear the burden of good character in traditional Yoruba thought system. The proverb says: '*Iwa ni ewa omo eniyan, toju iwa re.*' This means 'character is beauty, watch/mind/nurture your character'. It is never said that, '*Iwa ni ewa obinrin*' or '*Iwa ni ewa okunrin*' – that is, 'character is the beauty of a woman' or 'character is the beauty of a man'. With respect to the earlier proverb which is oft-quoted, the woman who is cultured in a marriage is the one who is thought to possess beauty of character. If the cultured woman is the one that is deemed to have character, then character in this case is disempowering, except if we believe that being subordinate to men will improve the economic well-being of Nigerian women, end violence on Nigerian women, and help Nigerian women change relations of power, build a strong women's movement and occupy top political offices.

Given the aggregate of women's description of their character in this study, it does not appear that they think of themselves as cultured. Rather, it appears they think they possess beauty of character, and this is potentially empowering, as many women and men have pointed out when they supported women aspiring to political leadership, and this represents a possibility. The challenge, however, is that women concede to patriarchy. We cannot therefore assume that those women who described themselves as 'good', 'well behaved' and 'not troublesome' have not done so from the point of view of how cultured they think they are. If this is the case, their 'character' is potentially disempowering.

The point is that the Christian and Islamic religions that many of the women in this study subscribe to have been shown (especially by female religious leaders) to prescribe the subordination of women to men. When women accept this and mould their character to suit the injunction, they cannot then, by any logic, desire to lead any group comprising male and female members. They cannot be imams, they cannot be ordained priests of the Anglican Church in Nigeria, they cannot contest for political positions, and then, the thought of becoming a State Governor or the President of the country would be heresy. Even if they were not interested in political offices, they would not also care to build parallel, powerful women's organizations (the women's movement), through which they can actively pursue and struggle for their strategic gender interests, because they would not even see any need to build such organizations or movements.

Clearly, also, a religion that preaches the subordination of one human being to another cannot but be disempowering, given the greed/lust for power among human beings, especially among men, as it then becomes the basis for all manner of oppression: gender, race, class, generational, etc.

The Identities of Women (the Character of Women), Women's Experience of Violence and Ability to Resist Violence

In this section, we proceed to link the discourse on the character of women (we recall that many women had identified their character as defining who they are and what they believe) with the dominant discourse on why women experience violence. We should not forget that the reason why women and men believe women experience violence is implicit in the type of advice that they had given, or would give to victims and potential victims of violence respectively.

In the preceding paragraphs, we tried to show that in pre-Islamic, pre-Christian and pre-colonial Yoruba thought system, character was gender neutral, but that today, given the influences of the new religions and colonialism, women are expected to bear the burden of good character and beauty of character. It was also observed that women who defined who they were and what they believed in terms of the beauty of character in the traditional Yoruba sense, for example, had an identity that was empowering; whereas, those who believed that they had good character traits because they were submissive/subordinate to men, in line with what the new religions (Christianity and Islam) and the culture of those who colonized our country prescribed, had an identity that would not empower them.

The results of the analyses of data in Chapter Five, which is the chapter that dealt with women's experience of violence, make our position about *iwa* – good character/beauty of character – very clear. We should not forget that the same religions in which some women and men rooted their beliefs about what women's character ought to be (that of women being subordinate/submissive to men), have been shown by both the literate men and many religious leaders in this study as being intolerant of violence on women. However, in the following paragraphs, we make the point that an insistence that women be subordinate to men, as prescribed by Christianity and Islam, and the seeming intolerance of the two religions for violence against women throw up a basic contradiction, given, especially, the preservative nature of power. The point is that if a religion prescribes the subordination of women to men, and religious leaders preach this at every available opportunity, and followers believe it, violence, whether rape or battery, then becomes the means to ensure that women abide by the injunction. We should remember that it is the dominant voice in our society, the voice that concedes many privileges to men that determines what it means for women to be submissive to men.

In this work, we found that men perceived women as: weaker vessels; fragile; not courageous; not bold; care-givers; not mentally and emotionally stable; and they thought women are flexible and ought to be flexible. Given this view of who women are, it is expected, as the sacred texts have prescribed, that women be subject to men who are: breadwinners; bold; courageous; aggressive; etc. When women question men's views and actions, and taken-for-granted positions; when they confront men who attempt to treat them like mules; when they show themselves as courageous; and when they show that they are inflexible and are not sexual objects, they are deemed to be stubborn and not submissive. According to this thinking, a good woman, that is a woman with 'character', is the one who is meek, and flexible, and the bad woman is the one who is inflexible, perhaps outspoken and defends her interest vigorously. And so, some of the women and men in this study believed that battery is a 'natural' consequence of stubbornness and non-submissiveness. We recall that a respondent said he could hit a woman to establish the presidential role of a man in the house and to check the woman's excesses. Another said he could hit a woman if extremely provoked, to teach her to avoid confrontation.

We also recall that Aanwo, a literate female respondent who had articulated the role of women in the private sphere of life in terms of equality with men, was a victim of battery. She had also indicated that people thought it was normal for a man to hit a stubborn woman. The truth in Nigeria today is that, amidst plenty of religiosity, women who articulate views that reflect fairness and equality with men in marriage are deemed not to be submissive, and hence stubborn. We must not also forget that about half of the semi-literate women, and at least one literate woman, said women who had been hit by their husbands were stubborn, they were not submissive, and they had bad character. This is rather unfortunate, for what this means is that women believe that a person in 'authority' or position of power has the right to use force to maintain that authority (hooks 1984).

The point is that the insistence that women should be submissive to men sets the stage for men to heap violence on women, and it results in violence against women. Just the same way that an insistence that children obey parents unquestioningly, for example, results in both women (who are the main victims of all kinds of violence) and men, heaping violence on children.

Paradoxically, a woman or a girl who has 'character', that is a girl who is meek, gentle, and respects elders and persons in positions of 'authority' is an easy prey for (habitual) sexual abusers. When these totally corrupt and unkind men have abused girls and women whom society had taught to be meek, gentle, respectful and attractive, the same society, especially women who have made themselves gatekeepers for the views, norms and values that privilege men, then blame the victims for: being badly behaved; dressing badly and wildly; for walking around at night; not comporting themselves well; and, not praying hard enough. The truth is that women who have been taught to be meek and gentle and 'good' cannot defend themselves vigorously against rape and sexual harassment while the abuses are on, and after the experience, they are unable to talk about it because of the fear that they will be condemned as bad.

Conversely, women who have shown that they are inflexible, courageous, not sexual objects and not subordinate to men, have been victims of rape and sexual harassment because men (who are habitual sexual abusers; who lack discipline; who are aware of the pervasive culture of impunity, and the negative attitude towards rape victims and women who are not submissive in our society), want to show the women 'their place'. In cases like these, persons who would usually blame women for everything would say the rape victim had a bad attitude towards men and was haughty; otherwise she would have been able to handle the situation better.

By the traditional Yoruba view of character, and the type of character education that Fafunwa had indicated that a child, a youth and an individual was given in traditional Nigerian communities, men who visit violence of any kind on women lack character – 'iwà'.

We have to acknowledge that the opposition of religious leaders (both the traditional and new religions) to violence against women and the fact that some of the literate men opposed violence on women on the basis of their religious beliefs gives hope, and represents a possibility. The task would be to get the religious leaders to privilege the transformative aspects of their religions. We note, for instance, that contrary to the Qur'anic injunction that places the burden of maintaining chastity on both Muslim men and women, as it requires that men and women lower their gaze, adherents of the religion (and Christians as well) make a big issue of women's 'bad' and 'wild' dressing. They then emphasize the injunction that says women should cover up their bodies. Also, instead of emphasizing the biblical injunction that urges men to love their wives as Christ loves the Church, Christians emphasize the injunction that urges women to submit to their husbands.

7

Is Formal Education Empowering?

We had earlier observed that the consensus among opinion moulders and discussants in non-formal education settings is that access to formal education and literacy training for girls and women will ensure more active involvement of women in politics (Shvedova 1998), although Longwe (2000) had challenged the claim. We also observed that there is no value-free education, because how a person learns, whether or not s/he is able to learn, who teaches what and to whom, matters. In the light of the identities of women that have emerged from this study, and their implications for the ability of women to exercise power with other women to end domination, gain political power and resist violence directed at their gender, the task here is to find out whether formal education, which should ordinarily be a guarantor of access to power resources, has empowered or disempowered those who have acquired it. This question is pertinent, given the low social status of literate Nigerian women, the omnipresence of religion within and outside classrooms and institutions of learning, different forms of informal teaching and learning within and outside teaching-learning contexts, and the structure of the formal school in Nigeria.

But first, we take the views of religious leaders on women's education.

Religious Leaders on Women's Education

Islam

Male Muslim Leader – Lokoja

Male Muslim Leader (MML): The prophet said, speaking of knowledge is compulsory, it is a must on every man and every woman, therefore there is no differentiation, and there is no discrimination in the course of seeking knowledge as far as Islam is concerned. Fundamentally, a woman is a school. The prophet is saying, the first school of a child is the mother's laps. Again, the prophet is saying: educate a man you educate an individual, educate a woman and you educate a nation. That adage is from the prophet.

Female Muslim Leader – Lokoja

FM: Most people tend to believe that Islam forbids women from acquiring Western education. It is believed that it is only Islamic education that women should acquire. I want to say, that is not true. Islam says if knowledge is in China, go out and get it. Qur'an says read and acquire knowledge. By virtue of women's gender, they are expected to be the first teacher of children. As mothers, we have the role of bringing up children in the way of Islam. We teach them to be models for others to emulate and be good representatives of our communities. As much as possible, we try to give them both Islamic and Western education, so the women can compete favourably with others. If you train a woman, you are training a nation; and so, it is important that the girl-child is given education. FOMWAN mounts enlightenment programmes on the religion that we believe in, and that is Islam. It organizes workshops and seminars.

OM: What images of women come to you when you see literate and illiterate women? Do literate women show more self-confidence?

FM: The difference is about Western education. You discover that some illiterate women are even more vocal. They are bold in pursuing their concerns. At times, they even tell you: 'Is it because I don't have Western education, I know what I am doing.' Upbringing is important here. If you were brought up in an environment where you are not allowed to talk, you're going to be timid.

OM: Schools add to women's timidity then, such that by the time literate women are out of school, they become more timid than their illiterate counterparts

FM: It is not true, it is not true. Education added to socialization, yes.

OM: Our illiterate sisters appear more vocal, clearer about what they would and would not take but literate women are being careful …

FM: Women with Western education are taught protocol - manners of doing things. Unlike illiterate women who say it raw, you want to be polite and cultured in the way you present your case. That is why illiterate women are more vocal and forceful. Sometimes, it helps to be polite and at times, it helps to be bold and raw. When you do it politely and you are not getting there, you need to be more forceful. That is what I think we need, to get affirmative action implemented by the government. We have been taking it slow with them. We take it easy, we dialogue, to get them to implement 30 per cent affirmative action, and we are still not getting it. Suggestion is for more action. We should tell them what we want and how it should be done and should not continue softly softly, such that they get there and they just give a position to one woman, and say to one another: 'That should be okay for the women.'

Female Muslim Leader (FML) Ibadan: Seek knowledge from cradle to grave. Be knowledgeable in all aspects of life. It is important to have education, whether you are a man or woman. Muslim women are given both the secular and Islamic education. FOMWAN organizes adult education classes for illiterate women. At any rate, it is when you know what is in the Qur'an that you know how to worship God. Women have always had rights in the Qur'an. Western education is not in conflict with rights of women under the Qur'an because the rights have always been there.

Olutoyin Mejiuni (OM): What differences have you observed in the reactions of literate and illiterate women to issues?

FML: With both Western and Islamic education, a woman is in a better position to weigh and balance issues. Ideally, however, the Qur'anic injunction is more authentic because it is from the Almighty Allah. Difference is more pronounced when an illiterate in the Western sense does not have Islamic education. You see, Islam teaches everything. Qur'an talks about astronomy, biology, the computer, and the reproductive stages. In FOMWAN, we teach the Qur'an, beginning from the very first chapter. What Muslims do now is the Islamization of knowledge. You relate whatever you are learning to what the Qur'an has said about the subject.

OM: Are you saying there is no conflict between what women preach these days as women's human rights and Islam?

FML: Islam has given all the rights. It is probably because only the Muslims know and others are unaware, that is why they demand for the rights. The rights have always been given, but they have probably not been implemented. The Almighty Allah has given you, so you do not need to ask from human beings again.

Christianity

Male Christian Leader – Ibadan

Olutoyin Mejiuni (OM): Have you observed differences in the way highly literate and the not so literate women react to and handle issues?

Male Christian Leader (MCL): Anyone that has the spirit of God will be humble. There should be no differences in the way of doing things. If an educated person wants to live intellectually, definitely, the Bible says knowledge which is not Godly knowledge puffs up. Intellectual knowledge can make a person proud, but spiritual knowledge will make a person humble. A woman that is educated and does not mix spiritual knowledge with intellectual knowledge will be proud. A person who is not educated but has spiritual knowledge will behave normally, and that is where character development comes in. We teach people about God's character. If you imbibe God's character, you will behave in godly ways. When you are godly, you cannot be proud. God is the universal landlord and he is not proud. Persons that imbibe the nature and character of God will behave normally. To humble herself will become natural. She will not look down on other women because they did not go to school. After all, many of our parents did not go to school and we do not look down on them because they are illiterates.

When you talk of knowledge, it is not until you go to the four walls of the school or university. There is knowledge that you acquire through experience and there is knowledge that you acquire by age. What you get in class is a fraction of what you need. When you go out, you begin to get the real practical, applicable knowledge. What you get in school is theoretical knowledge, it is when you begin to go to work, that you would have real knowledge. No education is complete without the knowledge of God.

Female Christian Leader - Ibadan

Olutoyin Mejiuni (OM): What differences have you observed between literate and illiterate/semi-literate women?

Female Christian Leader (FCL): Women should celebrate themselves. The reason you're a lecturer in the university for example is because you had opportunities. Your parents were there to tell you to sit down and do your homework. You are who you are because you were privileged. You should therefore make every woman around you feel important. Look at the way some female bosses behave. Some male bosses are better than female bosses.

How Formal, Non-formal and Informal Education (and Learning) Construct Women's Identities

The position of religious leaders on the provision of formal education for women can be summarized as follows: First, that women (like men and children) should be given opportunities to acquire formal education, but that the knowledge of God's words and God's words as written in the sacred texts should be their main guiding principle, and second, that women who have acquired formal education should be humble.

Given the position of religious leaders on all the issues that have been raised in this study, it is possible to interpret what the religious leaders said in respect of women's acquisition of formal education in two ways. The first interpretation could be that women (men and children) should look more to their religion and religious leaders than elsewhere for the acquisition of knowledge. The position that women should be humble in spite of their acquisition of formal education could be interpreted to mean, as the female Muslim and Christian leaders in Ibadan said, that women should be submissive to their husbands (and persons in positions of authority, including religious leaders) in spite of their academic achievements.

It is not surprising that the religious leaders are so strident in their position that women should be humble in spite of their education. When we asked women to talk about the benefits of formal education, it was clear that many of the religious leaders could not be comfortable with some of the benefits that women had gained or hope to gain from education. The main benefit of education that women in formal work identified was connecting with other people. They said they were better persons as a result of education because they were able to relate to, interact with, and live with people from different backgrounds, religious persuasions, culture, race and tribes, and they were more understanding of the ways of other people. Next to connection to others, they identified autonomy as a benefit of education. They spoke of how education had enhanced their self-confidence, empowered them, and made them independent. Some said it had increased their knowledge and reasoning capacity, and yet others said it had opened up opportunities and given them prestige. One woman said it had helped her in bringing up children.

Female students believe that formal education will help them to improve their competence for their desired careers and also make them breadwinners; and help them to earn the respect of others and resist dominance and abuse by men. Some others said it would enhance their thinking capacity and knowledge, so they would be able to impart knowledge to others and deal with their responsibilities in the private and public spheres of life. Hear a few of them: 'I don't want to be a full-time house wife whose duty is to raise children and cook. I don't want to be maltreated by any man'; 'Higher education is important to me than early marriage. If I am opportuned to have my PhD, I will be a lady of substance, a breadwinner for the family, an independent woman'; 'It will help me gain higher and deeper knowledge to face my responsibilities in the society, my family and the Church...'; 'Education is the best asset a woman can have that cannot be stolen away, even by her husband, and it will help her fend for herself and the family in future'.

At this point, we recall Berggren and Berggren's (1975) view about education. They said: 'education was, and still is, a badge of superior status; literacy and schooling served and still serves the powerful classes; it is a symbol and justification of privilege and a safeguard for authority and self-interest' (p. 6). Ordinarily, humility is a desirable character trait. However, in the context of patriarchy, and given the fact that many religious leaders have taken the position that women have to be submissive to men, when religious leaders urge women to be humble when they have acquired Western education, one cannot but interpret this as an attempt to rein in educated women. That is to say, the call that women should be humble is an attempt to rein them in, so they do not begin to wear the badge of superior social status and so they do not begin to feel powerful like men, and by extension, challenge men's authority and superior position in all spheres of life.

We recall that we had earlier observed that the practice of religion is one of the processes of socialization, and religions are cultural systems, they are therefore powerful educational agents. Religious beliefs and practices are taught and learned through the processes of informal and non-formal education, and whether or not they appear in the curricula of formal educational provisions, they are almost always present as hidden curriculum.

To the question of who teaches what, and how; teachers (through the disempowering and empowering lessons that they teach students), fellow students (mostly through negative lessons) and religious leaders (through their negative and confusing messages), teach women whom it is valuable to be, and this is achieved through a system of rewards and punishment. This way, the processes of schooling and participation in religious activities construct and reconstruct women's identities. What one is saying in essence is that women and men who have formal school training, and who are themselves products of many influences (including norms and values that are held sacrosanct in different religions), many of which convey, reflect and perpetuate unequal relations of power, believe themselves to be capable of bestowing knowledge on those they consider to know nothing (Freire 1993; Bassey 1999). In addition, the hierarchical structure of relationships in formal schools ensures that particular subject matters are taught in particular ways, and some are not taught at all. In addition, students are unable to challenge the views and beliefs that lecturers pass across in class because of the fear in our environment that they may be deemed rude, for challenging an older person, or someone in a position of authority.

A number of men too, who consider that women are senseless and or know close to nothing, teach women implicitly and explicitly to know their place. They cite: 'careful observation of, and interaction with married women over time', their age, the fact that they are married; religion and the media as sources of knowledge. Women who have explicitly accepted that they are subordinate to men (mainly among female students, women in informal work and female apprentices) cite 'the way things are' and how God made things as sources of knowledge, and they communicate this to other women – friends, neighbours and their children.

Concerning access to education, that is whether or not women are able to learn, we note that literate women in formal work and in higher learning have had access to education (and many educative influences) in formal school settings, in religious settings, in their homes, and through day-to-day experiences. Semi-literate women and their apprentices, given unequal relations of power in society, have had: minimal access to education in formal schools, and access to non-formal and informal education in non-formal settings; in religious settings and during some other day-to-day interactions. There is another source from which all women in this study, whether literate or semi-literate, could probably access education, both as learners and teachers. These are the informal and non-formal, structured and semi-structured women's organizations, networks, friendships and associations that are either secular or religious that constitute the women's movement (Obilade and Mejiuni 2006).

In this study, only one literate woman and a few female students gave clear indications that they are members of NGOs, one of the non-formal and informal sources of knowledge for women. Too many women are members of religious groups and, for obvious economic reasons, they are members of cooperative credit unions. At least two semi-literate women indicated that their husbands do not like them participating in activities of groups. One key reason for the low involvement of women in activities of groups other than religious groups is because too many men dread the educative influences of women's groups, social clubs, etc., on women; so, they discourage their spouses from becoming members of these groups (Obilade and Mejiuni 2006). Husbands and boyfriends, prefer that their spouses belong to religious groups, as they are sure these will ensure their spouses' continuing flexibility and subordination to them. What women are being taught is to be 'cultured', that is, to imbibe and behave according to the norms and values that benefit most men, and some women.

Let us look at the experiences of literate women that have been cited in this study. But first, we have to note that literate women have experienced sexism, discrimination and violence, not only in the formal school system or while in school, but also in other spheres of life such as family, given the experiences of Tiwa and Segun and, in public places, as represented by Rebecca's experience. We will find details of some of those experiences in Box 4.3. So, for women who have gone through formal education up to the tertiary level, the experiences of sexism in school represent a part of the whole range of experiences of sexism that they are likely to encounter in their lifetime.

We take Adedigba's experience in primary school. She observed that boys' names were listed before girls' names in the class register in her primary school – an experience which left Adedigba feeling inferior to men, at least three decades before she recalled her experience. This was coupled with the fact that Adedigba and other girls went to cook and perform domestic chores for their teachers when they were supposed to be in school. This is clearly one form of the abuse of power that Bakare-Yusuf (2003b) pointed out in the teacher-student relationship, in Nigeria. The teachers' source of power is seniority (age and position of authority), but they make the girls and not the boys do domestic work because of the assumption that girls and women ought to do domestic work, an assumption that has its roots in the patriarchal structure of our society, and which has been made worse by colonialism and the new religions. Unfortunately, the practice of listing boys' names before girls' still subsists till date, at least in primary schools in Ibadan, one of the two locations of this research. After I had gone through some of the questionnaires that I had retrieved from respondents, and that includes Adedigba's questionnaire, I had a discussion with a friend who runs a nursery/primary school, about some of the responses that I got from the field, and she confirmed Adedigba's observation. My then eight-year-old daughter, who had listened in on our conversation got excited and exasperated and she said: 'Yes mummy, it is true, they call the boys' names before our own even though girls are more than boys in my class.'

Women said their male counterparts tried to get them to believe that women's success in education does not matter, for it will end in the kitchen. Look at Teniola and Rolake's responses. Kehinde, Ajoke and Debo, reported their experiences of different types of intimidation by male students and lecturers in the classroom. Medupin, Chigozie, Temitope, Aramide, Tundun and Olaore reported discrimination relating to political and classroom leadership, and marginalization in carrying out academic assignments. Atolagbe and Esther's experiences bring out their male counterparts as being unable to cope with women's academic success (Horner 1971). Allied to this is Theresa's experience of men setting boundaries for women's achievement in school. Aanwo, Folarin and Ngozi's experiences appear quite painful because men who assume that women are objects of desire believe that women's academic achievements are suspect. The details of the experiences that these women shared are in Box 4. 3. The preceding were women's experiences in schools, as stated by women.

During interviews with two male lecturers, one each in Ibadan (Dr A) and Lokoja (Mr B), both gave indications that they had heard young women complain about sexual harassment. When Mrs. J, also a lecturer at the Kogi State Polytechnic was asked the same question, that is, female students' experience of sexual harassment, she said she was not aware of any such complaints except, according to her, about five years before the interview, when a dubious girl alleged she was about to be raped somewhere off campus. She displayed a lot of irritation, as she gave her response.

In an interview with Mr S, a lecturer at the Kogi State Polytechnic in Lokoja, he enthused about being a father to all students, and told us how he tries to be objective in his interactions with them. He said although he is a Muslim, he does not allow his personal values or religion to influence his teaching. He also said he draws examples from both the Bible and the Qua'ran while teaching in class. When he was asked whether the examples that he gives in class favour the experiences of men alone or those of women alone, or both, he said they favour both. He told us about how, while teaching the structure of formal organizations which is hierarchical, he would usually use the class as a good example. According to him:

I say that class is an organization at that point in time, and I see myself at the top of that hierarchy. Next to me, we have the class representative. Okay. Down the line we have the men before the women. Now religion has come to play. Because in Islam, Islam has it that a woman should be subordinate to man. Here, I say if you have to go by Islamic injunction, the ladies, you come after men. That is what I do sometimes but again, you see when I want to tell students to learn to tolerate ....I cite Jesus.....

He then added that he encourages students by telling all of them that irrespective of sex, they all have the capacity to acquire knowledge. Notwithstanding his other example about Jesus and how he encourages all to acquire knowledge, Mr S's example of hierarchy to his class is a good example of how the hidden curriculum works.

In our observation of Mrs. H's English class at the Kogi State Polytechnic in Lokoja, we found out that no woman participated in the simulated argument that was held, because she taught Argumentative Essays (and other types of essays). There were nineteen male and seventeen female students in the class. Throughout the class that lasted one hour, the female students did not voluntarily reply to the lecturer's questions. In the interview that we held with Mrs. H after the class, we asked her about the obvious silence of the female students in her class. She said it was atypical of them not to talk in class, and that perhaps they were reacting to our presence in the class. We sat at the back seats and were not introduced to the class until after the lecture, so we asked Mrs H why it was the women who were responding to our presence and not the men?

Learning and Not-learning (Resisting and Rejecting) Empowering and Disempowering Lessons in Formal Education

What women know is that society considers them inferior to men and, what many men and some women would have women learn from their experiences is to be flexible – to be who society expects them to be. If learning is conceptualized as change in behaviour resulting from experiences, it is not so clear that most women have indeed learned to be who society expects them to be. While many have taken messages that disable and disempower them to heart, and have been thinking and behaving according to their precepts, some have resisted and rejected disabling messages and teachings.

Clearly, the experiences of women, as cited by women, the testimonies of the teachers, the silence of the female students in the English class and the implicit and explicit lessons that women were supposed to draw from their experiences, and that can, or may have resulted in negative or positive learning for the women are obvious. The formal school then, mirrors the larger society, as it denies women access to leadership at particular levels; as unequal relations of power get exhibited in teacher-student relationship and what is taught, and as women are told that success is foreign to women (who are sexual objects), and if they are successful, they will end up in the kitchen anyway.

We ought not to forget also that the literate women in this study also, in the main, participate in religious activities. This is more so for the young women who are still in school, and who, in comparison with literate women in formal work, spoke a lot about being submissive to men. Given the educational attainments of literate women, and their implicit and explicit belief that women be subject to men, one may be tempted to conclude that formal education has not empowered the women, given the barrage of influences which attempt to construct, and in some cases, have constructed their identity to one that is subordinate to men – an identity, which some of the women have internalized.

This is even more so when we recall the responses of literate women and men, and semi-literate women to questions around women's civic-political parti- cipation, the roles of women in the private and public spheres of life, women's identities, and women's experience of violence. There was no real difference in the responses of the two groups of women to questions around women's civic- political participation. In their responses to the roles of women in the private and public spheres, and women's identities, more semi-literate women than literate women made the point about being breadwinners or co-breadwinners, as a way of challenging male superiority. We also recall that while some of the literate women in formal work defined themselves through their husbands and children, semi-literate women had found psychological freedom in rejecting the notions of husbands and accepting the notion of 'Baba omo', that is, father of children. It appears that literate women want to be seen to be cultured and they also want to show that their academic successes have not gone into their heads. So, to avoid the scathing criticism that is explicit in being referred to as a member of 'Egbe Ki L'oko O Se', that is, a Yoruba expression that can translate either to: the 'ignore-your-husband group' or 'what-does-a-husband-have-to-offer group' (Obilade and Mejiuni 2006), they eulogise their relationships with their husbands and their love for their homes.

This is not to say, of course, that some women do not enjoy good relationships with their spouses, or imply that women have not found fulfilment in marriage. In addition, although it would appear that more semi-literate women than literate women had experienced violence or knew someone who had experienced vio- lence, literate women who had experienced violence did not react to their experience in a way that was significantly different from the way semi-literate women had reacted to their experience. We also recall that literate men gave more of the advice that was considered empowering on violence against women than did literate women, and although literate women gave more advice that was considered empowering than semi-literate women did, both literate and semi-literate women gave almost equal percentages of advice that was considered to hold the least possibility of empowering women. Interestingly, more women gave this type of advice (or advanced the easy arguments/comfortable positions) than men.

We also need to reckon with the fact that literate women in formal work showed discomfort with a wide variety of conditions and issues in tertiary education when, given their experiences of tertiary education, they were asked to indicate the changes they would like effected in tertiary education. The environment of teaching-learning was most mentioned as being unsatisfactory. Some of their responses can be found in Box 7.1. During one of our observations at the Kogi State Polytechnic, we noted that the large class where Mrs A's lecture was held was dirty, and could be better lit. The hall where Mr S's lecture was held was located on top of a hill. It was big, spacious and airy and the fans were working. However, the roads and footpaths that led to the hall were littered with faeces − an obvious indication that students have problems with toilet facilities. Apart from the teaching-learning environment which got the most flak and appeared to have overshadowed other concerns, the courses taught, and the ways the courses were taught were mentioned as areas where change is required. Only one respondent thought method of assessment needs to be changed. Morality, economic inequalities, and the attitudes of lecturers, especially in respect of abuse of power also got some mention. Sarah indicated that she wants a special law enacted to discourage lecturers from covetousness as they do not spare even housewives, and Hauwa would like to change the attitude of lecturers toward female students.[1]

Box 7.1: Changes that Women in Formal Work Would Like Effected in Tertiary Education

'I will like to effect changes in the kind of hostels that students live. Students' hostels were not usually conducive. I lived in a room of 6 legal occupants with each of us having one squatter. We were 12 in a room meant for 6' − Banke

'The environment of teaching should be less stressful and more comfortable. The education system is generally too stressful; fill the same forms each year etc' − Adeola

'There should be flexibility in the choices of courses taught and the mode of teaching. The environment should be made friendlier to intellectual property acquisition. I was a victim of rigid rules in my institution of higher learning. The designated lecture rooms were very inconvenient' − Inunkan

'Lecturers should be given more incentives to do their job, and if they do not, they should be penalized. Some of my lecturers at the university did not come for lectures but gave us topics to read just before exams and set questions on the untaught parts' − Adetutu

'Courses taught. There should be more practicals than theory' − Shade

'Changes in the courses taught; courses to be more practical, the environment should be more conducive for learning. Learning style should be modernized to meet trends of society. Teaching of morals is also very essential in order to make the individual a better person in the society. This is my view from my experience in the larger society after leaving the higher institution of learning' – Itunu

'Reduce the number of students that receive lecture per period. Lecture halls are always jam packed. Provide adequate chairs that will be convenient for all students. Learning cannot take place where too many students receive lectures together. A lot of them especially those at the back and outside (standing) won't gain anything'

– Idiat

'Change mode of dressing, effect changes in teaching/learning environment, change method of assessment. I want the individual to be educated in the real sense of the word' – Noimot

'Make education cheaper, let lecturers earn higher and the environment to be conducive for teaching. Because the institutions of higher learning must go through a change, a positive one' – Ihimoni

'Stop lecturers exploiting students financially. Male and female students exchanging visits in their hostels and entering rooms must stop' – Esther

'I would like to make lecturers teach better and also inculcate moral discipline. Most university students complain of lecturers' inability to be patient with them, they are rushed and lecturers hardly care for their moral lives' – Omolade

'I will stop lecturers from producing handouts. It is a way of exploiting the students and it does not make student attend class as they should do' – Kunbi

'Environment of learning and attitude of lecturers toward female students. There should be a conducive environment for learning. Provision of education should be free. Lecturers should stop harassing female students' – Hauwa

It is interesting, however, that apart from the two clear references to sexual harassment as an area where change is required, the women did not speak to the put down, their marginalization in politics/leadership and academic assignments, the humiliating remarks, and the intimidation that they experienced as female students, as areas in which change is required. The questions that came to mind then were: Can this be because the women assumed that those are issues that cannot be changed? Could it be that the women thought these are problems that women have to deal with at a personal level rather than collectively and institutionally? Or, are these literate women in formal work assuming (implicitly), like the young women in tertiary institutions and the semi-literate women did, that such is 'the way things are'?

Given the preceding observations, it is not surprising that the social status of Nigerian women who have gone through tertiary education is still low, when compared with that of men. This is because religion and socialization/informal learning within and outside classrooms and the school system interface with the hierarchical structure of relationships in formal education, especially tertiary education, to perpetuate unequal relations of power between men and women, construct (or further construct) the identities of women to one that is subordinate to men, thereby limiting the transformative potentials of formal education.

However, it also appears that the fact that women have had the experience of tertiary education, and the fact of the barrage of potentially disempowering experiences that the women have had in the institutions, have led them to attempting to resist and resisting oppression, especially in terms of questioning taken-for-granted positions, through reflection, which is an important component of Praxis (Freire 1993). Aanwo in Ibadan and Hauwa in Lokoja used education to deconstruct male superiority. Aanwo said:

> I believe that if a woman and a man can be judged equally academically, then they should be treated equally in other spheres of life too and a woman could be the head and guide in a community.

We should remember that Aanwo thought a woman's role at home is that of 'partner to the husband, mother to the children, co-breadwinner to the family'. Hauwa said:

> In the public sphere, women are always given the second position. It should not be so, since we attend the same school, pay the same fee and do a lot of things together. We ought to be given roles just like our male counterparts.

We also note the way Esther and Rolake handled men who could not cope with women's success. Esther, in spite of all the harassment, said she would smile, and she excelled always, except in the final year. Her smile is definitely a knowing smile, a smile that belies her determination and mocks her harassers. Rolake simply said, 'I never gave up'. The reactions of Esther and Rolake are forms of resistance, one in which they refuse to accept that they should be less successful than men. Another example of critical questioning and resistance is the one cited by Dr A of the University of Ibadan who told us that he once invited two of his male students who would usually put in extra work and assignments in his course to attend his postgraduate class. He said the next day in class, he called the two to talk to their course-mates about what they had learned from the postgraduate class, and they did. He said some of the young women in the class challenged him immediately, and asked why he had invited two men and no woman. He said he had to admit to the class that it was an oversight, and that it was the men who were on his mind then. He said he also had to let the class know that there was a woman who would also usually put extra efforts like the two men that he had invited to the postgraduate class, but she was not on his radar then. He then added that he thought the impact of the feminist movement was beginning to be felt, among female students. He said in about two or three departments in his Faculty, of the ten students who had Second Class Honours Upper Division, seven were women.

These resistances, that is, the critical questioning and the determination to further succeed, no doubt gave the women psychological freedom and, as such, they are confident individuals (Hooks 1984). This somewhat confirms Foucault's (1980) hypothesis that resistance to power is found right at the point where power relations are exercised (p. 142).

In the section where respondents were asked to comment freely on all the issues raised in the questionnaire that they had responded to, Aanwo said:

> Culture and religion are too deeply embedded in the African/Nigerian women for formal education to make much impact yet. The way women think 20 years ago on issues like marriage, dating, childrearing and even work has changed but a little, despite formal education. One would be surprised to note the little change that has occurred when educated women of these days are tasked on these issues.

In spite of Aanwo's cynicism, but more because of: the strengths and assets, and, dreams of the individual woman; the resistances that women have put up against oppression; and, the efforts of some women and a few men both within and outside tertiary institutions, there is hope that formal education and religion will serve women better.

The Challenges of Religion

We recollect that 68 per cent of highly literate women in formal work and 69.6 per cent of female students made obvious references to religion in the responses they gave in their questionnaires. Some of them (along with their semi-literate sisters), stated that religion has helped them to realize their assets/potential; their belief in the Almighty gives them peace and contentment, and is behind their willingness to lend a helping hand to others. The other benefits of religion that they identified were that it: guides their relationship with others; teaches dedication to duty, obedience, respect and faithfulness; teaches how to dress well; shapes character; keeps problems at bay, and is responsible for all achievements. Religion is therefore an important part of the lives of these women. The extent to which they have taken the teachings of their religions/religious leaders to heart is indicative of whether they think religion is the giver of meaning, and or rules. We do not want to devalue or diminish what religion (read spirituality) means to these women. To do so will be to ignore the importance of a holistic approach to the development of the human person (English 2005). However, our concern is that religion should enable, and not disable her adherents, especially female adherents.

The position of religious leaders on the issues raised in this research is therefore challenging. Many of the religious leaders identified culture as the problem. Culture was the whipping boy. The Christian and Muslim leaders appear unaware that their religions have become cultures (ways of life) in Nigeria of today. They also fail to realize that although certain aspects of their religions are empowering, the patriarchal values that are explicit and implicit in the religions fit and fuse with some of our indigenous culture to disempower women. These are: beliefs about women's nature; the belief that women cannot be overall leaders in the religions (and by implication and extension, the entire public sphere); the belief that women have to be submissive to men; and that, women are care-givers and not breadwinners.

However, in spite of the negative and confusing messages and signals from religious leaders, we acknowledge that they do convey positive messages too. The view that women need to take activist stance in respect of participation in civic-political matters and that they should watch out for the divide-and-rule tactics of men is a challenge to women to review their position/frameworks and strategies. Examples of the challenges can be found in the position of the female Muslim leader in Lokoja who thought that if a 'softly softly' approach to ensuring women's active involvement in politics is not working, a more activist stance may be necessary. The same goes for the male Christian leader in Lokoja who was very emphatic that Nigerian women today are no longer taking up activist stance as women in the past, like Mrs Funmilayo Ransome-Kuti did.[2]

Some religious leaders made the point that women ought to show love to men, their children and one another, and that men should love their wives. Female Muslim and Christian leaders in Lokoja and Ibadan, the female traditional religious leader in Ibadan, and the male Muslim leaders in Lokoja made the point about the need to improve the economic condition of women and the generality of the Nigerian people strongly. Some of the female religious leaders linked economic depression with the problem of violence against women.

Clearly also, most of the religious leaders considered that women (who have accepted their roles as caregivers and sole nurturers of children) should train children to be God-fearing so that they can affect the nation positively. And, the almost unanimous opposition of the religious leaders to violence against women is a window of opportunity for stemming the tide of violence against women. Finally, in spite of the confusing signals from the female Christian leader in Ibadan, she urges women to have confidence in themselves.

Hopes and Possibilities

Female students who were participants in a focus group discussion spoke about their strengths and assets, and some of the successes that they have achieved as members of groups as follows:

'I love to use my hands to make things. Because I love hats, I learned how to make hats, now I make hats and sell them, and I'm happy to see people wear them'.

'I love to sing and praise God, and there was no serious choir in my fellowship. So I mentioned it to my pastor who gave me the go-ahead to organize the choir. Also at home, I get people together to praise and worship'.

'I like to teach people. When it is time for exams, I gather my colleagues together and teach them'.

'I love choreography. When I was in secondary school and some visitors came to the school, I organized a performance. I also choreograph in the church, and I teach and guide people who want to choreograph'.

'I like advising people, especially girls. If their guys are maltreating them, that is, beating and cheating on them. There was a case where a guy promised to marry a girl and he later refused. The lady came to me and was crying. She didn't know what to do, maybe to go and beg the guy. I told her to be herself that she carries all the qualities and so there is no reason she should go and beg the guy. I also told her the guy will be the one to come and beg, for she has to make herself very expensive'.

'In my church, I noticed that the keyboardists were all men, so I took the challenge and I learned to play the piano. So now in my church, they miss my presence when I am not there to play the keyboard'.

'I like to pass on the talents that I have. In the class during lectures, I listen and I understand, so my classmates come to me after class so that I can put them through. Even before examination, people that are calling themselves 'head'[3] come to me to put them through. I look at my performance, it is better than theirs. As one is leaving, another will come, so I see myself as a teacher, the head'.

The same group of female students spoke of their dreams for themselves and for Nigerian women as follows:

'I want to be a leader in all ramifications – spiritually, financially, economically, even academically. Not only that, even in the country, I want to be leading men and dictating to them on what to do. I want Nigerian women to be courageous and to know that they are equals with men'.

'I want Nigerian women to involve themselves in politics and public administration. I want to become President of this country'.

'I want Nigerian women to be leaders. Since the time of independence, men have been ruling us during military rule and democracy. There are many things which they can't even do. They don't rule us well, but if women are given the chance, we will see many changes, and that is my dream. I am aiming to be a leader and I want every Nigerian woman to eradicate fear and thoughts such as: "I cannot do this one o since men are to be the head"'.

'I want Nigerian women to be equal to men. I want gender inequality and women's feeling of inferiority to stop, and women should see themselves as superior to men. I would like to be an adviser in all ramifications to both men and women'.

'Look at our country now, in all the businesses, the rich people are men. I want to be a business woman that is known all over the world. There should be more women, well known, in business. Women have the intelligence, they are creative, they do the thinking that make all the ideas that men use, and they will be using it as if they are the ones that own the ideas. I want to be very knowledgeable, and be the richest woman in this country'.

'I want Nigerian women to be spiritual in the sense that if you look at the spiritual aspect of it, women who are spiritual will be able to impact the fear of God. If you have the fear of God, you can tell people that God hates all the armed robbery, corruption, mismanagement and evil things. As a woman, I want to be a leader, for I want to bring women out of ignorance and diseases. I want women to know their rights because men are subjecting them to rigorous works, labouring, and they don't know their rights'.

From the foregoing, we can infer that those female students are not hopeless women. They know they have assets that they had appropriately channelled in the past, and they have dreams, they envision a better future for themselves and other Nigerian women, even though at times the dreams appear like dreams about dominating men who have hitherto been dominating women.

In the rest of the paragraphs in this chapter, we look at some of the efforts and the attitudes of female and male lecturers, and their potentials for empowering women, especially women in higher education.

Mrs J of the Kogi State Polytechnic in Lokoja, who will not encourage any student (male or female) in her department, a science-based department, to participate in students' union politics because they hardly have the time to do so, said she would rather that women excel first in a chosen career, before they marry. She draws from her own experience as an undergraduate who gave birth to, and reared children while still in the university. She said she drums this into the ears of her female students and her female children, and that two of her female children promised they would follow her counsel. One had already broken the promise.

Mrs H, also of the Kogi State Polytechnic in Lokoja believes that inequalities in the socialization of children are unjustifiable, and so she actively discourages sex-role socialization at home, and she has been labelled 'Thatcher' by her children. She indicated that although her view is incompatible with her religion, Islam, she still has peace with her creator. She believes that women should extend what they do at home - being mothers to children - outside. That is, being mothers in society. During our observation of her teaching, we found out that she practices her belief. In class, at least twice, she gave sharp rebukes when she thought the students needed it, but she was friendly. During the course of her lecture, a young woman who arrived late sneaked into a chair, and the men in the class, jokingly notified Mrs. H. that the girl, whose name they mentioned, had arrived. She ignored them.

During the interview, we asked her whether she ever took any interest in a student, and whether she has ever done a turn-around in the life of any student and she said yes. She told us that a good example was the young woman that came into the class, whom the men were trying to draw her attention to. She said after the young woman's first semester in school, she performed so woefully, she took active interest in her. She ensured that she attended classes, took interest in what she did out of class, gave her extra work and according to her, she was performing far better than when she came in and most people in school now saw the young woman as her adopted child. It appears that is what persons who demand that women do things differently from men want. Good enough, Mrs H's Head of Department had described her as diligent behind her back, when we were trying to book an appointment to watch her class and interview her. What this means then is that Mrs H imbues hard work and effective performance of her duty with care and nurturing. She also believes that women should participate actively in politics, because Aishat (the Prophet's wife) was a politician.

Mr B, the lecturer who said he led a few other lecturers to raise the matter of a case of sexual harassment at a departmental meeting, said he did not believe in sex-role socialization, because his own childhood was devoid of that. He said he grew up with his uncle in Lagos (the commercial capital of Nigeria) and had to do all household chores, which he now found beneficial. We pointed out that perhaps he just had to do those chores because of his position then. He answered in the affirmative, but added that it was now a part of him, and, he found it positive. He told us that his wife is an accountant, and she plays equal roles in the decision-making process in their home. He said that he had three daughters whom he loved, and he could not see why anyone would discriminate against them. He added that he was of the view that if women were given the chance to rule Nigeria, they would rule the country better than men, and cited the example of Deborah in the Bible, who was a housewife, a prophetess and a judge.

Professor W, whom we had met earlier, is a gender activist. She was a member of Women in Nigeria (WIN). In this work, one of her students (Folarin) had indicated that the professor had changed her own perspective of women's roles in public. Apart from Folarin's testimony, in informal conversations with some Faculty members at the University of Ibadan, they gave indications that Professor W carried out an overhaul of one of the departments in the university. In the interview that we held with the professor, she had indicated that when she assumed headship of her department, a science department, she decided to take immediate steps to rectify the gender imbalance in the chart depicting the presumed stages in human evolution. The chart, conspicuously displayed in the corridor of the department for several years, showed only male figures, indicating the evolution of the masculine gender (only male figures are traditionally represented in texts on human evolution). She said she promptly asked that one of the departmental graphic artists drew female figures beside the male ones, since both women and men are human and both evolved together! The artist, in his ingenuity, which was very much appreciated by Prof. W, depicted one of the female figures as pregnant. Till date, the exhibition hall of the department carries the diagram of the evolution of man and woman.[4]

The implications of Prof. W's action are numerous. An important one, among several, is that of making women visible in the academy, particularly in a department that deals with the source of all creation. Her action will no doubt contribute to the process of deconstructing the invisibility of women in the evolutionary process (Harding 2004) and the academia. The point about pregnancy is also extremely important, for persons in the academia have in the past shown some reticence about discussing pregnancy, a natural process, in the public sphere – the universities (Fashina 2000).

In conclusion, the barrage of discriminatory practices, abuse and violence against women notwithstanding, there is hope that education will become empowering for women. There is hope because: women have assets and strengths that they are aware of; they have been putting up resistance against oppression; and, there are female and male lecturers, and female (and one male) religious leaders who are challenging relations of power, and who are urging women to exercise their individual agency, and power, with other women to end domination.

Notes

1. See T. Fashina (2001) for some other instances of humiliation of women and lack of respect for the rights of women in tertiary institutions.
2. See N.E Mba (1982) for detailed analyses of women's political activities in Southern Nigeria between 1900 and 1965. This includes details of the political activities of Mrs Funmilayo Ransome-Kuti.
3. This is an apparent reference to men's claim to sole leadership in the public and private spheres.
4. One suspects that Sandra Harding, the feminist theorist, will feel satisfied with the point that Prof. W makes in depicting the evolution of men and women. Harding (2004) had raised issues about the social processes that made reasonable the belief that women made no contributions to human evolution.

Conclusion
and Recommendations

> I said in class one day that there were some people less entrapped than others by
> Plato's picture of the world. I said I thought we, after fifteen years of education,
> courtesy of the ruling class, might be more entrapped than others who had not
> received a start in life so close to the heart of the monster. My classmate, once a close
> friend, sister and colleague, has not spoken to me since then. I think the possibility
> that we were not the best spokespeople for all women made her fear for her self-
> worth and for her PhD (Reproduced in hooks 1984:13).

This is a paragraph from an open letter that one white female graduate student,
a former classmate of Bell Hooks (African American feminist scholar) in a
graduate class on feminist theory, wrote to Bell Hooks (Gloria Watkins). She
wrote the letter to acknowledge her anger (part of the collective anger that was
directed at Hooks in that class because of the kinds of issues that she raised),
and express regret for her attacks on Hooks.

In this work, we have attempted to show how religion, socialization/informal
learning/the hidden curriculum and tertiary education interface to construct
women's identity, and how the construction presents undemocratic and flawed
gender relations which lack rational justification. However, the potential for
challenging and reordering the status quo exists in the women who perceive
themselves as different from who men would rather they are.

Specifically, one of the conclusions reached in this book is that the identities
of women (that is, the character of women), or more precisely, the identities
that women favour, and or those that many men would rather women favour,
represent a major factor in determining whether women have political power
and whether women experience violence, and the actions that they are able to
take when they experience violence. This is irrespective of the educational
attainments of women. Allied to this, we also reached the conclusion that men
would rather women favour identities that disempower and disable them because
they have a need to preserve the power that dominates. Fortunately, from analysis
of data, there are indications that formal education (and religion) will serve

women better in future if we pay attention to certain issues. Those issues are set forth in the paragraphs that follow.

Democratizing the Domestic Sphere

First, we need to democratize the domestic sphere - the private sphere of life. We cannot take the submission of women to the will of men in the private sphere as a given, while we are advocating the equitable involvement of women in the public sphere, and seeking to eradicate violence against women in the private and public spheres. Men who have been socialized to see women as their subordinates in the private sphere cannot then move to the public sphere and see women as equals. Such men must believe that women who assert equality with them in the public sphere must be suffering from 'illusions of grandeur'. In the study reported in this book, very few men and women assumed the equality of men and women in the private and public spheres in the same breath.

While a handful of men who have gone through sex-role socialization of different shades cannot see any rational justification for the process, and so genuinely work for equitable gender relations in the private and public spheres, most men who see women as equals in the public do so grudgingly. They will themselves to do it, thus causing some of them to become split personalities, who preach equality of women with men, and 'accept' women as equals in public, but oppress their wives and children at home.

The point being made is that the concession that the female respondents in this book and women's rights activists, who wish to reorder gender relations to end violence against women, and for a democratic public sphere, presently, overtly and covertly, grant to patriarchy is untenable. To be stark, the argument is that we might be wasting too many resources mounting all those campaigns for women's political participation and for eliminating violence against women, when we concede that we should be submissive to men at home. I have often asked myself whether I walk this talk. I know that I have put up resistances, and there have been fallouts and pains as a result, but I am convinced that I have not failed woefully in the project.

Let me quickly add that for different reasons, many women do not see any problem with being submissive to their husbands, and not to all men, as many of the female respondents in this book took for granted and as the female Christian leader in Ibadan espoused. Some of the reasons women believed in the subjection of women to men in the private sphere include: the way things are; they do not just know any other way; religion prescribes it; the rewards and punishment for accepting and behaving according to norms are bountiful or grave.

The responses of female participants in this book to the roles of women in the private and public spheres are particularly instructive in this respect. While they take the submission of women to men in the private sphere as given, they affirm women's ability to lead in civic-political capacities, the public sphere, strongly. They cite women's humaneness, their integrity, their character, their firmness, etc., as attesting to their capacity to govern. They also cite equality of men and women before God. These groups of women belong to the category of people who argue that unlike the private sphere, the public sphere is public because it is a space for everybody, and so, it is the business of government to regulate activities in the public in a fair, equitable and just manner.

However, the truth is that, as yet, persons do not come to the public sphere as equals. In the public sphere, wealth is determined by the attitudes, values and behaviours of those who own and or pay for the means of production and, to a lesser extent, by those who offer their labour (however conceived) in exchange for pay. There are men and women whose roles, and expectations and the values linked to those roles are usually well defined in their context; there are babies, children, teenagers, young adults, adults and senior citizens, and persons with disabilities in those groups, who have their strengths and frailties. Now, when we expect that persons who govern will regulate the public sphere in a fair, just and equitable manner, we forget that they also enter the public sphere, not as equals with one another, and they were also socialized as men and women.

Reordering Gender Relations in Cultural Institutions

If women can break away from the belief that submission to a husband (and in-laws in some parts of Nigeria) is a given, then this next suggestion will strike a chord. There is a need to democratize the leadership of religious and traditional institutions with women and men who do not believe in the subjection of women to men. One was quite taken aback by the sharp and firm way the female Muslim leaders rejected the idea of a female Imam, and the appeal to due process and culture that the male Christian leaders used to camouflage resistance to women's ordination into priesthood. While this suggestion appears utopian, we can still take some practicable steps. We can encourage religious leaders to privilege the transformative aspects of their religion, given the multiple face of religion. And, there should be more involvement of gender activists (who do not concede to patriarchy at both the cognitive and practical aspects of their lives) in the activities of religious organizations, especially in tertiary institutions and in the discourse of religion and women in the larger society.

The positions of religious leaders on the issues that were explored in this book are pointers that feminist educators and other women's rights activists should search for and keep up-to-date information about religion, both the oppressive and the liberatory aspects, as it is currently preached and practiced in their communities.

Women in higher education institutions should, as a matter of urgency, encourage more female-oriented community-based organizations and non-governmental organizations to become very active in higher institutions. This should take the wind off the activities of religious organizations in the institutions. If they approach their activities from potentially empowering frameworks, they can assist the young and older women in those institutions in a transformational learning process which may result in the transformation of their identities. Female students who become active participants in the activities of such organizations, or active participants in the organizations that they initiate, are likely to become leaders in the women's movement which can exercise the power to end the domination of women in Nigeria. There are women's organizations in Nigeria that are active in this respect. Some of them are: Women Against Rape, Sexual Harassment and Sexual Exploitation (WARSHE), headquartered in Ile-Ife; Female Leadership Forum (FLF), headquartered in Lagos; and BAOBAB for Women's Human Rights, also headquartered in Lagos. The challenge is to have more of these organizations work with students all over the country, and to have the existing students and the ones that are yet to come on board constantly checking their frameworks and strategies.

One recommendation that is easy to implement is that the names of pupils in class registers in primary schools should be arranged in alphabetical order, and this should be done speedily. The argument that boys' names are listed before girls' names because organs of government want disaggregated data falls flat, smirks of laziness, and is a camouflage for discrimination. There is need for a general overhaul of the educational system, especially tertiary education in Nigeria. Tertiary institutions need to become centres of excellence for the production of knowledge and for setting the agenda to change the country, the continent and the black race through innovative and creative processes that honour the humanity of participants in the system. There is also an urgent need for tertiary institutions to set in motion the process of formulating and adopting anti-discrimination/anti-sexist and sexual harassment policies and procedures. As yet, only cases of harassment (usually badly handled) are resolved at the whims of the leadership of most institutions, at times using the institutions' codes of conduct, when they are available.

Socialization, informal learning and hidden power (exerted through cultural institutions and emotional relationships) matter. Feminist educators and other scholars/activists in Nigeria need to pay more attention to how cultural instruments and institutions, and other educative influences and agencies, impact the lives of women.

Monitoring the Character (*Iwa*) of Persons Who Shape Lives

In addition, as one of the lecturers that we interviewed at the University of Ibadan suggested, the character of those who shape lives and mould other peoples' characters (lecturers, religious leaders and leadership of higher institutions) should be brought under constant scrutiny.

We noticed the interface of patriarchy and poverty. One would hope that persons who resolve economic dilemmas would use fair and just yardsticks instead of patriarchal norms. This is what is befitting of individuals, especially public officers who have '*Iwa*'.

Finally, I hope that other scholars and activists will work to expand and deepen some of the issues that have emanated from my interrogation of the process of the construction of women's identities and the role of formal, non-formal and informal education and religion in the process. For instance, how can we work to deconstruct, demystify, and neutralize (the sources of) power and also power resources that dominate, and then preserve itself, using seemingly rational arguments and the obviously irrational ones; emotional blackmail; physical coercion; the devaluation and valuing of qualities which others have that make the 'powerful' feel less powerful or very powerful; non-recognition of values that persons hold dear; and the appeal to God; so that such power becomes unattractive to women and other oppressed groups?

References

Afonja, S. and Aina, B., eds., 1995, 'Introduction', in *Nigerian Women in Social Change*, Ile-Ife: The Programme in Women's Studies, pp. 1–46.

Aina, B.,1995, 'Nigeria Women in the Urban Labour Force: Trends and Issues', in S. Afonja and B. Aina, eds., *Nigerian Women in Social Change*, Ile-Ife: The Programme in Women's Studies, pp. 90–115.

Akiyode-Afolabi, A. and Arogundade, L., eds., 2003, 'Gender Audit: 2003 Election and Issues in Women's Political Participation in Nigeria', Lagos: WARDC.

American Bar Association Central and European Law Initiative, 2002, *The CEDAW Assessment Tool: An Assessment Tool based on the Convention to Eliminate All Forms Discrimination Against Women (CEDAW)*. Washington, DC: ABA-CEELI.

Bakare-Yusuf, B., 2003, 'Beyond Determinism: The Phenomenology of African Female Existence', in *Feminist Africa*, Issue 2, (http://www.feministafrica.org) 4 January 2004.

Bakare-Yusuf, B., 2003, 'Yorubas Don't Do Gender: A Critical Review of Oyeronke Oyewumi's "The Invention of Women: Making an African Sense of Western Gender Discourses"', *(http://www.codesria.org/links/conferences/gender/BAKARE/20%oyusuf.pdf,)* 18 March 2004.

Bassey, M.O., 1999, *Western Education and Political Domination in Africa: A Study in Critical and Dialogical Pedagogy*, Westport CT: Bergin & Garvey. Available at (www.questia.com)

Berggren, C. and Berggren, L., 1975, *The Literacy Process – A Practice in Domestication and Liberation? London,* Writers and Readers Publishers Cooperative.

Blackburn, S., 1996, *Oxford Dictionary of Philosophy*, Oxford: Oxford University Press.

Boro, E.B., 1992, 'Brief on Ogori Ovia Osese', in *Ogori Ovia Osese Festival, 1992 Official Souvenir/Programme.*

Brookfield, S., 2001, 'Unmasking Power: Foucault and Adult Learning', *Canadian Journal for the Study of Adult Education, 15, 1, pp.1–23.*

Calhoun, C., 1994, 'Social Theory and the Politics of Identity', in C. Calhoun, ed., *Social Theory and the Politics of Identity,* Oxford: Blackwell, pp. 9–36.

Clark, M.C., and Wilson, A.L., 1991, 'Context and Rationality in Mezirow's Theory of Transformational Learning', *Adult Education Quarterly*, 41, 2, pp.75–91.

Cranton, P., 1994, *Understanding and Promoting Transformative Learning*, San Francisco: Jossey-Bass.

Dipo-Salami, O.M., 2002, Stooping to Conquer? Women Bargaining with Religion and Patriarchy in Ile-Ife, Nigeria, The Hague: Institute of Social Studies, Research Paper submitted in partial fulfillment of the requirements for obtaining the degree of Master of Arts in Development Studies.

English, L.M., 2002, 'Learning How They Learn: International Adult Educators in the Global Sphere', *Journal of Studies in International Education*, Vol. 6, No.3 (http:// jsi.sagepub.com) 22 April 2009, pp. 230–248.

English, L.M., 2005, 'Spirituality', in L.M. English, ed., *International Encyclopedia of Adult Education*, New York: Palgrave Macmillan, pp. 603–605.

Evans, N., 2003, Making Sense of Lifelong Learning and Respecting the Needs of All, (www.questia.com), 10 May 2009.

Fafunwa, A.B., 1974, *History of Education in Nigeria*, London: George Allen and UNWIN.

Fashina, O., 1998, 'Some Reflections on Human Nature and Sexual Oppression', Paper presented at the WARSHE Training Workshop titled: Help for Victims of Rape, Sexual Harassment and Sexual Exploitation, Ile – Ife, Nigeria.

Fashina, O.M., 2000, 'Academic Freedom and Female Academics in Nigeria', in E.Sall, ed., *Women in Academia: Gender and Academic Freedom in Africa*, Dakar: Council for the Development of Social Science Research in Africa, pp. 121–127.

Fashina, T., 2001, 'Women's Rights: Teaching and Learning Process in Nigerian Tertiary Institutions', in S. Jegede, et. al., eds., *Nigeria's Tertiary Institutions and Human Rights*, Lagos: Committee for the Defence of Human Rights (CDHR), pp. 90–115.

Fasokun, T.O. and Mejiuni, C.O., 1991, 'Politics in Adult Education', in E.T. Ehiametalor, and A.B. Oduaran, eds., in *Fundamentals of Adult Education*, Benin-City: NERA Publishers, pp.101–107.

Federal Government of Nigeria, 1997, *Statistical Information on Nigerian Universities*, Abuja: National Universities Commission.

Federal Government of Nigeria, 1999, 'The Constitution of the Federal Republic of Nigeria', in *Official Gazette*, No. 27, Vol. 86, Lagos: Federal Government Press.

Ferrero, D.J., 2005, 'Does "Research Based" mean "Value-Neutral"?', in *Phi Delta Kappan*, Vol. 86, No.6.

Findsen, B. 2006, 'Social Institutions as Sites of Learning for Older Adults', *Journal of Transformative Education*, Vol.4, No.1, (http://jtd.sagepub.com) 22 April 2009, pp. 65 – 81.

Foucault, M., 1980, *Power/Knowledge: Selected Interviews and Other Writings 1972-1977*, New York, Pantheon Books.

Freeman, J. ed., 1975, *Women: A Feminist Perspective*, Palo Alto CA: Mayfield Publishing Company.

Freire, P., 1993, Reprinted 2002, *Pedagogy of the Oppressed*, New York: Continuum Publishing Company.

Freire, P., 1973, Reprinted 2002, *Education for Critical Consciousness*, New York: Continuum Publishing Company.

Garret, S., 1987, *Gender*, London: Tavistock Publication.

Harding, S., 2004, 'Introduction: Standpoint Theory as a Site of Political, Philosophic, and Scientific Debate', in S. Harding, ed., *The Feminist Standpoint Theory/Reader – Intellectual and Political Controversies,* New York: Routledge, pp. 1 – 16.

Hernendez, A., 1997, *Pedagogy, Democracy and Feminism – Rethinking the Public Sphere,* New York: State University of New York.

Hooks, B., 1984, *Feminist Theory from Margin to Center,* Boston: South end press.

Hooks, B., 1989, *Talking Back, Thinking Feminist, Thinking Black,* Boston: South End Press.

Hooks, B., 1998, 'Feminism: A Transformational Politic', in M. F. Rogers, ed., *Contemporary Feminist Theory – A Text/Reader,* New York: McGraw Hill, pp. 457–462.

Horner, M.S., 1971, 'Feminity and Successful Achievement: A Basic Inconsistency', in M.H. Garskof, ed., *Roles Women Play: Readings Toward Women's Liberation,* Belmont CA: Brooks/Cole Publishing Company, pp. 97–122.

Hrimech, M., 2005, 'Informal Learning', in L.M. English, ed., *International Encyclopedia of Adult Education,* New York: Palgrave Macmillan, pp. 310–312.

Hunt, C., 2005, 'Adult', in L.M. English, ed., *International Encyclopedia of Adult Education,* New York: Palgrave Macmillan, pp. 33–36.

Hunt, C., 2005, 'Meaning-Making', in L.M. English, ed., *International Encyclopedia of Adult Education,* New York: Palgrave Macmillan, pp. 391–395.

Ibrahim, J., 2004, 'Introduction', in Ibrahim, J. and A.Salihu, eds., *Women, Marginalisation and Politics in Nigeria,* – OSIWA, Global Rights, and CDD, pp. 1–12.

Ibrahim, J. and Salihu, A. eds., 2004, *Women, Marginalisation and Politics in Nigeria,* OSIWA, Global Rights, and CDD.

Idowu, E.B., 1962, *Olodumare – God in Yoruba Belief,* Ikeja: Longman Nigeria Ltd.

International Institute for Democracy and Electoral Assistance, 2000a, *Democracy in Nigeria: Continuing Dialogues for Nation - Building,* Stockholm: International - Institute for Democracy and Electoral Assistance (International-IDEA).

International Institute for Democracy and Electoral Assistance, 2000b, *Supporting Democratic Development in Nigeria,* Sweden: I-IDEA.

Irinoye, O. and Idika-Ogunye, C., eds., 2003, *Silent Voices – Research Study on the Leadership Roles of Female Students in Nigerian Tertiary Institutions,* Lagos: FLF.

Jarvis, P., 1995, *Adult and Continuing Education –Theory and Practice,* London: Routledge.

Keynes, J.N., 1955, *The Scope and Method of Political Economy,* New York: Kelley & Millman. Available in (www.questia.com).

Lander, D., 2003, 'Activist Women as Action Learners: A Visual Genealogy of Community Organising for lifelong Learning', in *Proceedings of International Conference on Researching Learning Outside the Academy,* Glasgow: Centre for Research in Lifelong Learning, pp. 246 – 253.

Larsson, S., 1997, 'The Meaning of Life-long Learning', in S. Walters, ed., *Globalization, Adult Education and Training – Impacts and Issues,* London: Zed Books Ltd, pp. 250–261.

Longwe, S.H., 2000, 'Towards Realistic Strategies for Women's Political Empowerment in Africa', *Gender and Development*, Vol. 8, No. 3, (https:libproxy.stfx.ca:9433/login) 4 February 2005, pp. 24–30.

Luttrel, W., 1997, *Schoolsmart and Motherwise: Working Class Women's Identity and Schooling*, London: Routledge.

Macpherson, C.B., 1979, *The Life and Times of Liberal Democracy*, Oxford: Oxford University Press.

Mama, A., 1996, *Women's Studies and Studies of Women in Africa During the 1990s,* Dakar: CODESRIA.

Mama, A., 1997, 'Feminism or Femocracy? State Feminism and Democratization', in J. Ibrahim, ed., *Expanding Democratic Space in Nigeria,* Dakar: CODESRIA, pp. 77–98.

Mba, N.E., 1982, *Nigerian Women Mobilized – Women's Political Activity in Southern Nigeria, 1900-1965,* Berkley: University of California.

McDonald, B., Cervero, R.M. and Courtenay, B.C., 1999, 'An Ecological Perspective of Power in Transformational Learning: A Case Study of Ethical Vegans', *Adult Education Quarterly*, 50.

Maduka, C., 1991, 'Distance Learning', in Ehiametalor, E.T and Oduaran, A.B., eds., *Fundamentals of Adult Education,* Benin-City: NERA Publishers. pp. 134–146.

Marshall, G., 1998, *Oxford Dictionary of Sociology*, Oxford: Oxford University Press.

Marsick, V.J. and Volpe, M., 1999, 'The Nature and Need for Informal Learning', in *Advances in Developing Human Resource*, 1:1 *(http://*adh.sagepub.com) 22 April 2009, pp. 1–9.

Marsick, V.J.,Volpe, M. and Watkins, K.E., 1999, 'Theory and Practice of Informal Learning in the Knowledge Era', in *Advances in Developing Human Resource*, (http://adh.sagepub.com) 22 April 2009, pp. 80–95.

Mejiuni, O., 2005, 'Identity', in L.M. English, ed., *International Encyclopedia of Adult Education,* New York: Palgrave Macmillan, pp. 295–299.

Mejiuni, O. and Obilade, O.O., 2004, 'No Pains, No Gains – Exploring the Dimensions of Power in Poverty Reduction, through Transformational Learning', in J. Preece, ed., *Adult Education and Poverty Reduction: A Global Priority*, Gaborone: Department of Adult Education, University of Botswana, pp. 240–245.

Mejiuni, O. and Obilade, O., 2006, 'The Dialectics of Poverty, Educational Opportunities and ICTs' in A. Oduaran and H. Bhola, eds., *Widening Access to Education as Social Justice,* Dordrecht: the UNESCO Institute for Education and Springer, pp. 139–148.

Mennell, S., 1994, 'The Formation of We-Images: A Process Theory', in C. Calhoun, ed., *Social Theory and the Politics of Identity,* Oxford: Blackwell, pp. 175–197.

Merriam, S.B. and Cafarella, R.,1999, *Learning in Adulthood,* San Francisco: Jossey Bass Inc.

Merriam, S.B., Mott, V.W. and Lee, M., 1996, 'Learning that Comes from the Negative Interpretation of Life Experience', *Studies in Continuing Education*, Vol.18, No.1, pp. 1–23.

Nesbit, T., and Wilson, A.L., 2005, 'Power', in L.M. English, ed., *International Encyclopedia of Adult Education*, New York: Palgrave Macmillan, pp. 496–499.

Obanya, P., 2004, *The Dilemma of Education in Africa*, Ibadan: Heinemann Educational Books (Nig) Plc.

Obilade, O., and Mejiuni, O., 2006, 'The Women's Movement and Access to Education', *Adult Education in Nigeria*, Vol. 12, pp. 1–14.

Odah, A.A., ed., 2001, *FEF/WIW Beijing + 5 Impact Assessment (1995-2000)*, Lagos: Friedrich Ebert Stiftung.

Ogunrin, A., 2004, 'University Education and Waged Employment as Predictors for Women Empowerment in Osun State, Ile–Ife', Thesis submitted to the Obafemi Awolowo University, in partial fulfillment of the requirements for the award of the Master of Arts degree in Adult Education.

Oloruntimehin, O., 1998, 'The Sociological Perspective of Sexual Abuse and Violence', Paper Presented at the WARSHE Training Workshop titled: Help for Victims of Rape, Sexual Harassment and Sexual Exploitation, Ile–Ife, Nigeria.

Parrinder, G., 1969, *West African Religion*, London: Epworth Press.

Pateman, C., 1983, 'Feminism and Democracy', in G. Duncan, ed., *Democratic Theory and Practice*, Cambridge: Cambridge University Press.

Pereira, C., 2005, 'Domesticating Women? Gender, Religion and the State in Nigeria under Colonial and Military Rule', in *African Identities*, Vol. 3, No.1, pp. 69–94.

Quigley, B. A., 2005, 'Literacy', in L. M. English, ed., *International Encyclopedia of Adult Education*, New York: Palgrave Macmillan, pp. 381–387.

Rogers, M.,1998, *Conterporary Feminist Theory*, New York: McGraw-Hill.

Schrewsbury, C.M., 1998, 'What is Feminist Pedagogy?', in M. Rogers, *Contemporary Feminist Theory*, New York: McGraw-Hill, pp. 167–172.

Shvedova, N., 1998, 'Obstacles to Women's Participation in Parliament', in A. Karam, ed., *Women in Parliament: Beyond Numbers*, Stockholm: International IDEA, pp. 19–54.

Smith, M.F., *Baba of KARO - A Woman of the Muslim Hausa*, London: Faber and Faber Ltd.

Stacey, J., 1998, 'Disloyal to the Disciplines: A Feminist Trajectory in the Borderlands', in M. Rogers, *Contemporary Feminist Theory*, New York: McGraw-Hill, pp. 490–504.

United Nations Development Programme, 2002, *Human Development Report 2002*, New York: Oxford University Press.

United Nations Development Programme, 2004, *Human Development Report 2004 – Cultural Liberty in Today's Diverse World*, New York: UNDP.

UNHCHR, 1996, UN General Assembly – World Conference on Human Rights, Vienna, A/CONF.157/23(http://unhchr.ch/huridocda/huridoca.nsf/(symbol)a.conf.157.23.en).

WARSHE, 2004,'Communique', Issued at the end of the Women Against Rape, Sexual Harassment and Sexual Exploitation Workshop/Round Table titled: The Survivors of Rape and Other Sexual Assaults: The Search for Justice, 1 June 2004, Ibadan, Nigeria.

Wiley, N., 1994, 'The Politics of Identity in American History', in C. Calhoun, ed., *Social Theory and the Politics of Identity*, Oxford: Blackwell, pp. 131–149.

WIN, 1985, *Women in Nigeria Today*, London: Zed Books.

Weissman, D. M., 2007, 'The Personal is Political and Economic: Rethinking Domestic Violence', *Brigham Young University Law Review*, Issue: 2, Available at (www.questia.com)

Yusuf, Y.K., 1995, 'Contradictory Yoruba Proverbs About Women: Their Significance for Social Change', in S. Afonja and B. Aina, eds., *Nigerian Women in Social Change*, Ile-Ife: The Programme in Women's Studies, pp. 206–215.

Appendices

Appendix I

Assessment of Women's Potential for Participating in Civic-Political Matters, and their Performance in the Public Sphere

Positive View (the positive views were typical)	Negative View (the negative views were atypical)
Literate women said Women • are firm and stick to their guns; • are home builders; • are competent; • are tender-hearted, can manage resources and are focused; • are meticulous, mild, God- fearing and account for whatever they spend well; • are hardworking, honest, intelligent, straightforward and lovely; • are more sincere and honest in the offices than men; • are transparent and prudent; • are capable and dependable, and have no heart to steal; • are better managers and leaders; • have conscience and are sensitive to the feelings of the family and society; • are better managers of resources than men, I believe so much in women; • are honest in their commitment; • are even more capable than men; • at the helm of affairs scorn corruption and bribery; • Would not tolerate non-challant attitudes to duties and will not condone indiscipline; • Are more reliable than men, are not corrupt like men; • Will not overlook acts of indiscipline as leaders.	**Literate women said** Women • are always humiliated in the society, may be sabotaged; • are too harsh; • since she is a woman, other members may not want to cooperate with her.

Semi-literate women said

Women

- will listen to us. They are gentle and nice;
- have feelings;
- can do better than men;
- will not allow other women suffer;
- can do things better than men;
- have feelings as mothers, their breasts will react to grumblings;
- can do things better than men;
- are not callous and dictatorial, they possess milk of kindness
- are not arrogant and dictatorial;
- are wonderful, they use their God-given brain to ensure normalcy;
- will know how to manage the country better than men;
- will feel the suffering of the nation;
- who is a mother will understand how to run this nation;
- are aware of other women's problems and will sort them out;
- can do better;
- will listen to advice;
- know how to manage things;
- have the milk of kindness;
- stand by their words, their No is No;
- are not stingy like men;
- are trustworthy;
- will understand other women and help us;
- will bring peace;
- are sympathetic, they think deeply, they will listen;
- will effect changes in the economy;
- will perform better than men
- have milk of kindness and they are mothers;
- are very good;
- will take care of the women folk;
- can make a change because they are mothers, they know where the shoe is pinching the women folk;
- will help her counterparts who are suffering.

Semi-literate women said

Women

- should not contest elections;
- will go against the will of God, for God has made man the head;
- can't supervise people, she will be wicked;
- will not be able to do what a man can do as governor or president;
- will not be taken seriously.

Literate men said Women	Literate men said Women
• are better managers of resources and good listeners; • are human beings like men; • are more prudent in management than men; • are equal to men in intellectual capability, more suited to discharging official functions than men; • are more dedicated to their jobs than men, not easily influenced to perpetuate evil, they are mothers, have love for all; • are considerate; • have the fear of God, they don't have love of money like men; • will not be partial in taking decisions; • have the ability to lead, and some times, are better than men; • are trustworthy; • are considerate and play motherly role; • do better than men for they are meticulous; • can manage resources better than men; • can organize people better than men, for they are soft and outspoken; • are more responsive and attentive to issues than men; • know how to handle financial transactions and social activities than men; • tend to be more accountable and transparent than men; • make good managers as they can be very meticulous; • are more trustworthy; • can manage money, they are caring; • have legible handwriting, hate cheating; • are lighthearted as regards stealing and corruption; • are good in financial management; • are good custodian of funds, not much courage to mismanage money.	• are not mentally and emotionally stable; • do not posses physical ability that official functions of a governor or president requires; • are better as treasurers for they are trustworthy and fearful; • can hardly undergo the rigours associated with certain offices and the dangers there in, and are often unable to harmonize certain key/very demanding offices with private/domestic responsibilities; • should not handle tedious roles because of their fragile nature; • can easily be influenced by the management; • are too tender, their decisions will be influenced by men, they are too uncertain. Can easily change her decision with little pressure; • are tools to support men, if they win elections, they will whip the arse of men and oppress men and their fellow women; • will have difficulties controlling diverse people, dealing with cultism and general insecurity; • are influential in this country; • have the ability to check the excesses of the male counterpart who are favoured culturally to be the head of the group; • are not good in keeping secret, too tender to hold executive positions; • can be used to source money from rich men; • are not as agile and bold as men; • may not be able to cope with the attendant problem of being a president.

Appendix II

Women's Character

Literate Women in Formal Economy	Female Students
• Hate cheating; • Relate well with people; • Intelligent; • Upwardly mobile; • Flexible; • Love myself; • Believe in modesty; • Pursue course that I believe in; • Impulsive; • Can boldly challenge any man; • Tolerant; • Pleasant; • Contented; • Disciplined; • Modest; • Goal-getter; • Aggressive; • Balanced; • Self-sufficient; • Ambitious; • Don't like cheating; • Well behaved; • Ambitious; • Caring and close to tears when angry; • Try to provide for, and protect the children; • Care for others; • Not proud; • Generous; • Upright; • Sociable; • Resilient; • Loving; • Caring; • Hardworking; • Visionary; • Hold on to my convictions; • Gentle; • Hate lies; • Focused; • Cannot be intimidated; • Humane personality; • Determined; • Dedicated to my beliefs; • Trustworthy; • Loving and caring mother; • A woman of principle; • Easy-going person.	• Sensitive to other's feelings; • Good person; • Dislike being cheated; • Highly rational and smart; • Easy-going; • Can be very determined; • Hospitable and jovial; • A helper and builder of destiny; • Trustworthy; • Simple; • Love honesty and hard work, never intimidated; • Believe in hard work and honesty; • Don't tolerate nonsense from men and women; • Humble , humorous and unique; • Can stand on my own without the assistance of a man; • Sympathize with people; • Slow to anger, patient and enduring; • Have single male lover; • Loving and caring person; • Have a positive self-concept. I have respect and dignity for myself; • Love making friends; • Kind and care for others ; • Love to make people around me happy; • Self-willed and strong-willed • Charming, confident, intelligent goal-getter; • Not inferior to anybody; • Of high integrity and independent; • Don't under-rate people; • Disciplined and well behaved; • Love good things; • Peaceful and helpful; • Lovely, caring and contented; • Gentle, easy going, humble and hardworking.

Semi-literate Women in the Informal Economy	Female Apprentices
• A good woman; • A breadwinner; • I'm good; • I'm up and doing; • I am the breadwinner; • Hardworking; • I'm hardworking and peace-loving; • I'm hardworking and trustworthy; • I hate lies and gossips; • I'm gentle, I'm not quarrelsome, I'm hardworking; • Can't hide my feelings, don't like hurting people; • Stand my ground about my likes and dislikes; • Hate cursing, and I hate that people go hungry; • I'm a simple, gentle and caring girl; • I hate cheating and I'm hot-tempered; • I am concerned about people. I feel for others; • I am jovial, not troublesome; • I work hard, even while pregnant; • I am hardworking, peace-loving, always in position of leadership, though illiterate; • I avoid trouble; • I care for people; • I'm a good woman.	• Hardworking; • Easy-going, don't like trouble, but hate cheating; • A good person, peace-loving; • I am patient, I can endure; • I'm helpful, always help my parents; • I am generous, good and neat; • I am humble; • Quiet, well behaved, hardworking like cooking, mind my business; • I don't take what is not mine; • Quiet, I don't look for trouble; • I'm a positive person, I don't like negative things; • I'm jovial, I like to make friends; • I'm obedient; • I have good character.

Appendix III

Similarities between Women and Men

Literate Women Said:	Female Students Said:
• I aspire to be successful and to be an • achiever; • I am aggressive; • I am earning a living; • I am independent-minded; • I am courageous; • I don't jump to conclusions; • I discharge my duties; • I am diligent; • I face the challenges men face; • I like to have my way; • I do what men do; • I have the same education that men have • I can do what men can do and achieve the same result; • I worked hard at school; • I have the same qualification; • I am useful to the society; • I work hard; • I am pushy; • I am daring; • All are created in the image and • likeness of God; • I am tolerant; • I fend for the family; • I am bold; • I've got thinking faculty; • We were created by the same creator; • We are all human beings; • I have determination.	• I am strong-willed; • I can bear burdens; • I can do what men can do better; • I wish to be acknowledged, recognized and appreciated by others; • I want to be relevant and contribute to development; • We can both think, read and reflex • We both work hard and have courage; • We both aspire to greatness; • We both have leadership abilities; • I am disciplined and focused; • I can do what men can do; • Aggressive and independent; • I am strong-hearted • I do the jobs they do, study the course they study and contest positions like they do; • I am human like men; • Same in academics and politics; • We are the same in education and competing to occupy leadership positions; • We are the same academically; • I look like my father, have some masculine features; • We have the same education; • I am energetic; • I pursue and try to realize my goals and dreams; • I am brave and have a target; • I am intelligent, industrious, an evangelist and educated just like some men; • I am human, educated, can see, feel, reason and courageous; • I work hard and I am steel-minded; • I never quit and I am effective.

Semi-literate Women in the Informal Economy Said:	Semi-literate Female Apprentices Said:
• I support/feed the family; • They work, I work; • I shoulder some of the responsibilities they shoulder; • I am a breadwinner too, as I support the family; • I am up and doing; • I support like the head of the family; • I have been breadwinner for 9 years since my husband passed on; • I am hardworking; • I support the family too; • I can do what men can do; • I go to the stadium to watch football and male-oriented sports; • I support the family too; • I am hardworking; • I support the family as my husband does; • I am strict like men • They work, I work; • They shoulder responsibility; I do, and even perform better; • I can do what they can do; • We all are human beings; • We are all living beings; • I also provide something for the family; • They drive, we drive; • I provide for my family and send the children to school; • I support the home; • I am bold like men; • What men can do, women can do; • I provide for the household like my husband; • I support the home.	• I work like a man and also repair electronics in my house; • I can work hard like men; • I support my family and pay my child's school fees when necessary; • I can work as much as a man can do; • We are human beings and breathe same air; • We are all human beings; • I do the work that men do.

Appendix IV

Differences between Women and Men

Literate Women in Formal Work Said:	Literate Men Said:
• Women are not egoistical; • Women and men are physically and psychological different; • Men and women have been ordained by God for different things; • Men and women have different desires; • I exhibit the normal hormone of caring that every woman has; • Women differ from men in the area of leadership at home; • I'm not strong-hearted; • Women are not as powerful as men; • I am a mother, I am feminine; • I am emotional; • God made me a woman; • Physical features; • I'm a mother and wife; • I am caring and God fearing. **Female Students** Said: • Can get pregnant; • Physical features; • Can't take sole responsibility for family; • God created a woman; • Our individuality, not maleness or femaleness; • Sexuality, physical strength and emotional aggression; • Have breast and can carry pregnancy; • Biologically and physically; • They have XY chromosomes, I have XX chromosomes; • I don't underrate people; • Mode of dressing; • I do domestic work, they don't; • Some of men's choices; • Have a womb and motherly affection; • They behave stupidly, going out with two or more ladies; • Voice, and men can only transfer sperm; • The experiences women have.	• Men are emotionally stable; • Men have the ability to withstand pressure more than women; • Men are mentally stable; • Men are better leaders than women; • Men assigned the presidential role of micro family and macro society; • Men are different from women physically; • Women are a little bit weak; • Women are a bit patient; • Women are more sensitive than men; • Men are naturally bossy; • Men want to achieve aim forcefully; women are peaceful in doing same; • Women give birth to children and care for them; • Women carry pregnancy; they are vulnerable to humiliation, discrimination and attacks; • Men claim superiority over women; • Men take final decisions at home on any issue; • Men don't nag like women; • Men think more logically; • Men are bolder; • Men are dubious, women are not; • Both sexes dress differently, although women copy men; • Women are careful; • Men and women differ in terms of traditional, religious and constitutional obligations; • Men are naturally stronger; • Men are more aggressive; • We are assertive; • Men are more articulate; • Women are subservient; • Craze for current fashion is prominent among women than men; • Men are less flexible than women; • Men are determined and cannot be easily; convinced/influence by management, unlike women; • Men are stricter; • Men are courageous; • Man provides, woman is a caretaker; • Men are not submissive to women; • Men are given greater opportunities; • Men are hard, authoritarian and rush to decisions; • Men are more adulterous.

Semi-literate women in the Informal Economy
Said:
- Features;
- They will be able to get up and talk in some places, and I will not be able to;
- Not just similar to men at all;
- Nothing;
- I am a woman;
- I manage the home, they don't. I give birth, he can't;
- Women's brain smaller than men's;
- Not just like men;
- 'I no go like to maltreat women if I be man';
- I'm just a woman;
- Men are seen as the head of family.

Female Apprentices
Said:
- I do domestic work, they don't;
- Men are more intelligent; more wicked, richer than women, people respect them;
- Women give birth to children;
- I'm more reasonable than men;
- They stand while urinating, women bend down.

www.ingramcontent.com/pod-product-compliance
Lightning Source LLC
Chambersburg PA
CBHW032133020426
42334CB00016B/1143